ARMS AND POLITICS IN LATIN AMERICA

ARMS AND POLITICS IN LATIN AMERICA

REVISED EDITION

By *EDWIN LIEUWEN*

Published for the
COUNCIL ON FOREIGN RELATIONS
by
FREDERICK A. PRAEGER, *Publishers*
New York • *Washington* • *London*

Frederick A. Praeger, Publishers
111 Fourth Avenue, New York 3, N.Y., U.S.A.
77-79 Charlotte Street, London W. 1, England
Published in the United States of America in 1961
by Frederick A. Praeger, Inc., Publishers

Second printing, 1965

This is a revised edition of the book first published
by Frederick A. Praeger, Inc., in 1960, for the
COUNCIL ON FOREIGN RELATIONS

The Council on Foreign Relations is a non-profit institution devoted to study of the international aspects of American political, economic and strategic problems. It takes no stand, expressed or implied, on American policy.

The authors of books published under the auspices of the Council are responsible for their statements of fact and expressions of opinion. The Council is responsible only for determining that they should be presented to the public.

Library of Congress catalog card number: LC 61-18248

Manufactured in the United States of America

American Book–Stratford Press, Inc., New York

PREFACE

In its relations with Latin America, despite their many common interests, the United States has always had to contend with problems arising from disparity in power, differences in historic background and culture, and some conflicts of economic interest. Over the past decade the difficulties flowing from these traditional differences have been compounded by the coincidence of rapid economic change and popular expectations on the Latin American side with the requirements of world-wide responsibilities and the exigencies of the cold war on the side of the United States. Beneath the surface of the inter-American solidarity of official statements and institutions real questions have arisen concerning the security needs of the hemisphere and how to fill them, the reconciliation of immediate with long-range considerations, and conflicts of priority between military and other aspects of policy. The United States government has found great difficulty in developing policies which would enjoy broad official and public support both in the United States and in Latin America. At times it has appeared as though the disagreements over objectives and over methods were irreconcilable.

The displays of hostility and violence that marked the tour of Vice-President Richard M. Nixon through South America in 1958 bluntly demonstrated that all was not well in relations with the other American republics. As a consequence, United States policy in Latin America is currently undergoing a thorough reappraisal. To bear fruit such a reappraisal cannot be confined to pointing out "mistakes" to be rectified or "misunderstandings" to be cleared up. It must explore the sources of political conduct in Latin America: both those elements which are the legacy of its turbulent history and those which are the product of its current economic and social revolution. A key element in the picture is the role of the armed forces. How has it affected the policies of Latin American governments and the attitudes of their peoples? And how has it influenced the interests and the policies of the United States?

In 1957 the Council on Foreign Relations, convinced that a thorough analysis of these questions would throw light on problems of great importance to the security of the hemisphere which have been especially troublesome in our relations with Latin America, decided to embark on a study of the role of the military in Latin America and its implications for United States policy. In April of that year I was awarded a Carnegie Research Fellowship to undertake the study and to write this book.

It was soon apparent that the most diligent research in libraries and documentary collections would leave many questions unanswered. For example, no one had previously attempted to study the social and political role of Latin America's armed forces. Historians have shown great interest in individual military men in connection with the phenomenon of personalism in politics, but their emphasis was upon the ephemeral *caudillo* rather than on the environment from which he emerged. Political scientists have focused attention on laws, constitutions, and political parties, but have paid little heed to the armed forces as an institution and a vital factor in the complex of political power. The armed forces themselves have been understandably silent on their extramilitary role. In their journals and official statements they continually reaffirm their nonpolitical, purely professional functions. Yet in practice it is their political activities that assume paramount importance. Similarly, in regard to the military aspects of United States foreign policy, though a good deal of published material is available, serious deficiences in information and a general lack of interpretation understandably remained.

Fortunately, I have been able to draw upon the knowledge and experience of members of the Council on Foreign Relations to fill many of the gaps in information and to untangle numerous puzzles of interpretation. The study group organized to advise and work with me on the project was composed of men uniquely qualified to discuss contemporary Latin America and the problems of United States foreign policy. It included military experts, former diplomats, businessmen, journalists and scholars. Occasional guests, official and unofficial, with special knowledge of current problems and conditions were invited to lead the discussion or to attend meetings of the group.

Between June 1957 and April 1958 the study group held a number of meetings, at which discussion was focused upon working papers prepared by me with the purpose of raising the principal issues of the proposed study. The discussions, which were spirited, shed much light on matters which would otherwise have remained obscure. Only rarely did the group reach agreed conclusions, hardly a surprising result in view of the controversial nature of the questions under discussion, particularly those involving past and present American policies. Accordingly, the analysis, interpretation, and recommendations in this book do not necessarily represent a consensus of the members of the study group. Although I drew heavily upon their knowledge and experience, I am solely responsible for the facts and opinions presented.

To the study group I am deeply indebted for ideas, suggestions, admonition, and encouragement. In addition, I wish to express my special appreciation to Philip E. Mosely, Director of Studies at the Council, for suggesting the study and guiding it toward completion; to Henry M. Wriston, Chairman, and other members of the Committee on Studies; to Percy W. Bidwell for a critical reading of the manuscript; and to John C. Campbell for his patient and sympathetic superintending of the entire work. For their unflagging help in research and typing chores I wish to thank my research assistant, Leslie Robinson, and my secretary, Mrs. Olive Knox.

EDWIN LIEUWEN

PREFACE TO THE SECOND EDITION

In the two years since the first edition appeared, the extraordinarily rapid march of events in Cuba has had serious repercussions upon the problem of hemisphere security. The unexpected ease with which a Communist beachhead was firmly established in Cuba and the widespread appeal that Castro's violent social revolution evoked among Latin America's depressed masses precipitated a sweeping reappraisal of the United States' policies in Latin America. For the first time since the second World War the area took on a high priority status in Washington. The most obvious evidence of the change in climate was the agreement of the Eisenhower administration in mid-1960, reversing long-established policy, to major U.S. economic support for Latin American social welfare projects designed to raise the living standards of the masses and to head off additional Castro-type revolutions.

The Cuban problem also put the inter-American security system to the test. From the standpoint of the United States, the organization was found wanting. Neither the Conference of Foreign Ministers at Santiago, Chile, in August 1959 nor the similar meeting held at San José, Costa Rica, one year later produced anything in the way of effective collective action toward preserving the security of the hemisphere.

As concern over a Communist-controlled Cuba mounted, the patience of the United States gave out and it decided to act alone. Carrying through preparations begun under the Eisenhower administration, the Kennedy administration attempted in April 1961 to carry out a policy which can only be described as unilateral, indirect intervention in Cuba.

The debacle of the invasion attempt of anti-Castro forces supported by the United States not only weakened the United States' moral position but has also strengthened Castro. Thus, at mid-1961, the threat to the security of the hemisphere posed by Cuba remained, and there appeared to be no acceptable immediate solution to the problem.

The new chapter (Chapter 11) which has been added to this edition analyzes the Cuban revolution and the new problems which it has posed, in the light of the general theme of the book: the need for broadly conceived and effective policies on the part of the United States to meet simultaneously the real threats to the security of the hemisphere and the consequences of militarism in Latin America.

E. L.

CONTENTS

Part Two

MILITARY ASPECTS OF THE LATIN AMERICAN POLICY OF THE UNITED STATES

INTRODUCTION

THE IMPORTANCE OF Latin America to the United States is obvious, whether the standpoint be political, economic or military. On the political side, if we consider only the role of the twenty republics in international organizations, it is sufficient to note that they control one-fourth of the total vote in the General Assembly of the United Nations, and all save one vote—that of the United States—in the Organization of American States. Understandably, when issues between the Soviet bloc and the free world or vital matters of more strictly hemispheric concern are at stake, especially if they come before international bodies, it is vitally important for the United States to have support from Latin America. The main political objective of United States policy, accordingly, has been to keep the Latin American governments and peoples firmly associated with the United States and the Western world, and to counteract any tendency on their part to drift toward the neutralist or Communist camps.

The objective has been clear enough to both Democratic and Republican administrations in Washington since World War II. Yet the impression that Latin America has been neglected, that it has become a low-priority area in the eyes of our policy-makers, has been widespread in Latin America and exists also in this country. Perhaps this was unavoidable. In the troublous contemporary world the area of great decisions is the Eastern Hemisphere. As a consequence the energies of our leading statesmen, diplomats, and soldiers have been primarily absorbed in dealing with the problems posed there by the threat of communism and the demands of the cold war, and by the political and social upheavals attendant upon the upsurge of nationalism in Asia and Africa.

In all these developments Latin America appeared to be involved in only a marginal way. It had been almost completely isolated from the fighting during World War II. The expansionist Soviet policies of the postwar period, though they threatened the entire Old World, posed no more than a remote challenge to Latin America. Finally, Latin America's own social and political problems seemed to lack the drama, the importance, and the sense of urgency that prevailed in areas more immediately threatened by Communist imperialism.

Consequently, it was natural that United States policy should aim primarily at political stability, at the maintenance of peace and order, at securing Latin American political support in the United Nations—all this without assuming too heavy burdens at a time when so many were being taken on elsewhere, on the more active fronts of the cold war. To ensure stability and to promote calm along borders between American nations, the United States worked with the Latin American governments to set up machinery under the Organization of American States, which, in effect, outlawed wars within the hemisphere. In this search for stability, it was natural that Washington should cooperate with incumbent governments, regardless of their political coloration. In so doing, the United States, still smarting from the adverse Latin American reactions to previous interventionist policies, hewed strictly to the principle of nonintervention in the internal affairs of the other republics.

These political objectives and policies were "correct," even if they were open to criticism, both in the United States and in Latin America, as being too limited, too negative, too lacking in imagination. Some critics chided Washington for "neglecting" Latin America, for "taking it for granted." Others objected to the lack of concern for the growth of democratic institutions evident in so rigid an adherence to the nonintervention principle that no distinction was made, for example, in our dealings with the despotism existing in the Dominican Republic and with the democracy that prevailed in Uruguay. Criticism has found political expression, especially in Latin America, on no subject more than that of economic relations, a fact which warrants consideration of the economic interests of both the United States and Latin America, and of the prospects of reconciling them.

Economically, as well as politically, Latin America is obviously of the greatest importance to us. It accounts for a large portion of our foreign trade, larger than that of any other major region of the world. This is the main economic interest for both sides, with each providing an indispensable market and a source of needed goods for the other. In addition, United States citizens and corporations have invested in the Latin American area nearly $9 billion, also an amount greater than in any other region in the world. So far as the United States government is concerned, the vested interests of its citizens are inseparably intertwined with the security interests of the nation, for the bulk of the investments are in mining and petroleum enterprises, the products of which are indispensable to the American economy in peace and in war. Accordingly, it has been the policy of the United States government to promote trade and to encourage private investments, protecting them as best it can. These private investments, of course, also serve to develop Latin America, thus adding to its economic capacity, and, by making it more self-reliant, cutting down its needs for economic aid from the United States government. Such aid in recent years has been relatively modest, approximately $70 million annually in the form of loans (principally from the Export-Import Bank) and $35 million per year in emergency grants and technical assistance.

And yet, despite policies which Washington considered adequate and sound, and despite the undeniable benefits received from United States trade, investment, and public assistance, Latin American governments, supported by their public opinion, have been far from satisfied. Well aware of much larger assistance programs the United States is sponsoring in Europe and Asia, they resent treatment which looks like that reserved for a poor relation. As their own economic problems become more critical, the greater is the pressure they exert on the United States government to increase its assistance. In many cases this pressure represents a search for a scapegoat to blame for troubles of their own making.

It was natural that the United States government should be hesitant to provide large sums to governments which had not put their own economic houses in order. But the main danger has been political. Policies that were economically sound and that adequately served our economic interests could and did jeopardize our political interests because they aroused antagonism in Latin America. And Latin American governments have not been above looking for alternative means of support. If the United States, for example, should fail to meet minimum requests for public loans, it runs the risk not only that the U.S.S.R. will begin to supply such assistance, but also that the existing high level of U.S. private investment will be placed in jeopardy.

The third consideration, in addition to the political and the economic, is the military: Latin America's importance to the security of the United States. Its proximity alone makes it strategically vital. In addition, the importance of the area is further enhanced by its store of raw materials and by the location there of the Panama Canal, the United States naval base at Guantánamo Bay in Cuba, and other military bases which the United States might need in the event of another war.

Ever since the formulation of the Monroe Doctrine in 1823, the United States has considered it necessary for reasons of national security to keep outside powers from gaining footholds in the hemisphere. The present threat comes from the U.S.S.R. Therefore, the contemporary form of this historic principle is the prevention of any dangerous growth in Soviet influence, and the defense of Latin America against the Communist threat, both from without and from within.

The defense of Latin America is viewed by the United States, today as in 1823, primarily as a military problem. It is a job that the United States, as the leading power, assumed unilaterally until the time of World War II. Since then, however, the growth of inter-American cooperation in response to the totalitarian threats from Europe has given rise to a multilateral defense system. Wartime cooperation and planning led to the signing in 1947 of a military alliance, the Rio Pact, directed against any attack on an American state. Thus today, maintenance of the security of the hemisphere is considered a common responsibility.

In accordance with this concept, an elaborate collective-security system has been built up. The Inter-American Defense Board, made up of high-ranking military men from each of the American republics, meets regularly and plans for the mutual defense of the hemisphere. Under special bilateral agreements, the United States has made grants of military aid to twelve of the Latin American republics, and under the "reimbursable" provisions of the Mutual Security Act it supplies arms to all twenty. "Standardization" of military equipment is another important aspect of U.S. policy. Use of United States military equipment in Latin America is not exclusive, because of the competition of European armament manufacturers, but standardization of training, tactics, and methods is proceeding apace under the guidance of military missions, which have been a monopoly of the United States ever since World War II.

However impressive in outward appearance, the elaborate collective defense machinery must be judged in the light of the military realities in Latin America today and of the political objectives of the United States. A merely cursory attempt at such a judgment raises certain questions: (1) whether the military defense of Latin America in the current stage of the cold war is in fact a pressing matter; (2) whether it is even a remote possibility that in the foreseeable future that area would be subject to invasion by forces of the Soviet bloc; and (3) whether Communist conquest through internal subversion is a significant present danger requiring military countermeasures, in view of the limited capabilities of the local Communists in all twenty republics. The broad assumption upon which United States military programs presumably rest, that Latin America "is threatened by Communist aggression both from within and without," is deserving of searching analysis.

On one side of the equation, of course, are the capabilities and intentions of the Soviet Union and of the local Communists. On the other side are the Latin Americans themselves, who seem little concerned with the threat of Soviet invasion or of Communist seizure of power from within. Despite the United States military programs, the armed forces of Latin America are too small and ill equipped to do much about resisting a major Soviet attack in the unlikely event that it did occur, but they may well be adequate, with or without United States aid, to cope with armed Communist subversion. Consequently, it is at least open to question what practical military application the multilateral defense concept may have.

Another legitimate question is whether United States military policies are really preparing Latin America's armed forces for a meaningful military role in the cold war. The programs themselves are small. Do the Latin American officers and men who are being trained by U.S. missions have a real prospect of engaging in military operations? Does the standardization program, even if modern weapons were supplied under it, have a realistic military objective? These matters need a clarification which they have not had in public print.

Beyond the question whether United States military programs make sense in terms of the realities in Latin America is that of their relevance to political objectives. Washington cannot and does not ignore the obvious fact that the armed forces play key political roles in most of the republics. Nor can it ignore their seemingly insatiable desire for arms. Thus military training and assistance are provided to secure—and to ensure—political cooperation. The arms supplied help to keep the armed forces friendly; the missions provide a means for cementing political as well as professional relationships. Political gains are expected to flow from the military programs: well-disposed governments, support for U.S. policies in international organizations, and assurance of access to military bases and strategic raw materials in Latin America. A further objective of the military programs is to promote political stability in this low-priority area so that our maximum energies can be devoted elsewhere. The simple reasoning is that the better the army in any Latin American republic, the less likely that internal order will be subverted.

Like the military objectives, these political goals require critical investigation, both as to whether they are in fact being attained, and whether the military programs may be giving rise to unintended side effects or political consequences that will affect our future relations with Latin America, for good or for ill, over the long run.

Even on issues of the cold war, by which the United States set such store, political cooperation from Latin America has been something less than wholehearted. Only one of the twenty republics contributed troops to the United Nations forces fighting in Korea. Although the Latin American governments belatedly agreed to outlaw communism at the tenth Inter-American Conference in Caracas in 1954, many have not effectively implemented this pledge. On the other side of the picture, dictatorial regimes, such as those in the Dominican Republic and Cuba (until 1959), have perverted the anti-Communist drive into a campaign to throttle all their opposition, most of it non-Communist. Moreover, friendly ties established with military dictatorships, as in Peru before 1956 and in Venezuela before 1958, left an aftermath of hostile reactions toward the United States when those regimes fell.

The tour of Vice-President Richard M. Nixon in 1958 brought this popular resentment into sharp relief.

There were signs that military assistance, though it failed to raise Latin America's capabilities as a partner in the free-world coalition, encouraged local arms races and exacerbated old rivalries and suspicions, as between Peru and Ecuador. Also, the coincidence between the military programs for Latin America, carried out by the United States under the impetus of the cold war, and the rise of militarism in that area in the late 1940's and early 1950's suggested that the United States' increasing ties with the armed forces had inclined the latter even more decidedly toward political domination. True, this development may have helped achieve the immediate objective of stability, but it was an open question whether stability based largely on the good will of military leaders often ruling by dictatorial methods would endure for long, and whether it was in line with the long-range interests of Latin America or of the United States. Although we obviously had no deliberate policy of encouraging militarism or coddling dictators, such results all too often occurred, and when they did, popular hostility toward the United States rose. Much of the available evidence seems to indicate that the military aspects of United States foreign policy have been appreciated and supported by scarcely anyone in Latin America save the armed forces, which, after all, make up but a small fraction of the total population. Surely this fact, if substantiated, has serious political implications for our long-term relations with Latin America.

Another danger has to be considered in any estimate of our current military programs: whether in concentrating on the anti-Communist theme and on stability we have taken sufficient account of Latin America's own problems and of the dynamic nature of its contemporary society. It is more than possible that policies aimed at essentially static security goals have been unresponsive and even contradictory to the normal social evolution of the people. So again the question arises: Has the United States, in the effort to gain the cooperation of armed forces, been losing the support of the rest of the population?

In order to get at the root of these problems, and to judge our present policies, it is necessary to subject to thorough analysis the institution (i.e., the armed forces) toward which United States military programs and policies have been directed, and especially to measure its political and social role. We must first look at the history of the military in Latin America, to find out something of their origins and their aims, and to try to discern patterns over the whole area despite the inevitable differences between countries. A detailed study of the domestic role of the armed forces is important both for a deeper understanding of Latin American politics and also because the course of internal development is intimately related to attitudes and decisions on foreign affairs.

The analysis of the role of the military, which follows in Part One of this book, shows how long and how deeply, in all but a few countries of Latin America, the activities of the armed forces have permeated the national life, dominating politics either directly or by assuming an Olympian role as arbiter among the civilian contestants. Into the class and group antagonisms of Latin American society the military have entered sometimes to provoke change and reform, sometimes to enforce social stability. In economic affairs and in foreign policy also their voice is likely to be decisive. Rare indeed—again with the exception of a few countries—have been the occasions when the armed forces assumed a detached position when important national or international issues were at stake.

The Latin American military's assumption of a broad range of extramilitary functions is no recent phenomenon, but a heritage of early nationhood. What is new is the nature and magnitude of the problems with which the armed forces are dealing. The relatively stable societies of the nineteenth century have suffered severe tensions and social cleavages. Static economies have undergone dynamic processes of growth and development. Meanwhile, modern communications and technology have broken down the area's former relative isolation from world affairs. That was already evident in World War II; now Latin America is inexorably caught up in the global struggle between the Western world and the Soviet bloc.

The armed forces' response to these revolutionary national and world developments has been generally unsure and inadequate, often based on nothing more than a desire to hold power. Whether trying to hold back the process of change or to ride the tides of social revolution, they have not been notably successful as statesmen. But the fact that they have held power, and in many countries still hold it, makes it all the more necessary to analyze what their role has been and is likely to be in the future.

In recent years the changing nature and growing complexity of internal problems has inevitably produced new difficulties, not only for Latin American governments but also for outside powers, and above all for the United States. Prior to the 1930's, before the social ferment reached serious proportions throughout Latin America, the policy problems were relatively simple, despite the antagonism engendered by the issue of "Yankee imperialism" and intervention. The consequences of political change were not unduly disturbing, for politics was the privilege of upper groups, and revolutions were generally of the palace variety. Sudden changes in government, save in the case of Mexico after 1910, were not apt to involve significant shifts in foreign policies.

With the adoption of the "good-neighbor" policy and the greater inter-American solidarity resulting from the deepening danger of war in Europe, relations between the United States and Latin America seemed easier and friendlier than ever before. This spirit was carried over into the war years—though notably absent from U.S.-Argentine relations—as the Latin American governments were generally agreed that the external menace to the hemisphere had to be met. Most of them provided cooperation and in turn received cooperation from the United States, including moderate financial assistance and lend-lease military aid. This wartime harmony, however, tended to obscure some of the changes taking place in Latin America, and with the coming of the cold war the achievement of U.S. objectives has become more difficult, principally because the aims of the United States and of the Latin American nations have seemed increasingly incompatible.

Even before World War II ended, many Latin American countries were undergoing rather sweeping political and social changes. Thereafter their "revolution of rising expectations" spread and gained momentum at the very time that the United States was fixing its attention almost exclusively on the cold war. Thus, while the United States increasingly insisted that the security of the hemisphere against the Communist threat must be the major consideration in a common foreign policy, Latin Americans were more concerned with their internal problems, and their governments looked to the United States less for leadership against communism than for assistance in shouldering their economic burdens.

Meanwhile in the United States, policy-makers plunged rapidly ahead to deal with what they defined as the hemisphere's immediate problem, security. Although the economic problems were not lost from view, the military aspects of policy suddenly assumed new importance. Through military missions, planning bodies for hemisphere defense, and military aid programs the United States was brought into broad and direct contact with Latin America's armed forces. More and more their role took on a special significance in the attainment of United States objectives, both military and political.

This divergence between the United States' immediate foreign-policy objectives and Latin America's basic aims suggests the approach of a major crisis. For the continuing process of social and political change now in progress in the other American republics cannot be contained by policies aimed only at stability, security, and opposition to communism. As this revolution proceeds, if it is not guided in ways which win mass support, opportunities for the Communists to make gains at the expense of the interests of both the United States and of Latin America are almost certain to expand. Thus, defense against a future, rather than an immediate, threat may well be the real security problem in Latin America. Is the United States sufficiently concerned about this future danger to the hemisphere? Are present policies properly designed to meet it? If not, what can and should be done about it?

An associated problem also arises. In terms of power in the world today, Latin America comes close to rating as a nonentity. Not only is it militarily weak; it is economically backward and politically unstable as well. Despite its 180 million people and its vast store of natural resources, it cannot now be a strong partner of the United States in the current struggle between the West and the Communist powers. That fact must color anything we try to do in the military field. But it also raises certain questions. Why are Latin America's capabilities so limited? Does the area possess a real power potential? If so, what can the United States do to help improve Latin America's capacity to contribute more substantially to the general strength of the free world?

The United States also confronts the serious problem of how to fit the military aspects of its foreign policy in Latin America into over-all policies. Is the emphasis upon immediate security perhaps out of line with our political objectives and long-term interests? Are conflicts between different components of our foreign policy undermining our position and prestige in Latin America? If so, what can be done to reconcile them?

The answers to these vitally important sets of foreign-policy problems are intimately connected with present and future relationships between the United States and Latin America's armed forces. Satisfactory resolution of problems involving the military aspects of policy, though only a segment of the total picture, can be of greatest importance.

This study has been undertaken in the hope that it may contribute to a clear analysis of them, and that it may shed some light on their implications for the future policies of the United States in its relations with Latin America.

Part One

LATIN AMERICA'S ARMED FORCES

Chapter 1

THE ARMED FORCES AND THE OLD ORDER, 1810-1914

THE COLLAPSE OF Spanish authority in Latin America ushered in an era of predatory militarism. The leaders of the revolutionary armies who secured independence and claimed the credit for creating and consolidating the new republics emerged as the new rulers. Within each nation undisciplined, ambitious local chieftains vied for supreme power. Politics became the plaything of the military. For more than a generation, nation after nation was subjected to the whims of army-officer politicians who ruled by the sword, perverted justice, and pillaged the treasury. Through the first half of the nineteenth century these *caudillos* and their followers lived, with all too few exceptions, as parasites upon the society they were supposed to protect

The nineteenth-century histories of the sixteen Spanish-American nations were essentially military.[1] Except in Chile and Costa Rica, the military dominated politics throughout most of the century. Only in Portuguese America (Brazil), where independence was achieved without prolonged fighting and where a new emperor, of royal Portuguese lineage, preserved the existing governmental structure, was the post-independence curse of predatory militarism avoided. French America (Haiti), after inde-

[1] Panama and Cuba did not become independent nations until the twentieth century.

pendence had been won, followed the same militaristic road as its Spanish-American neighbors.

Origins of Militarism

Though the independence movement itself was the circumstance which brought the military into politics, some unintended preparation for the army's new role had been made by the Spanish crown in the late colonial period. Charles III's reforms, undertaken in the 1760's for the purpose of maintaining the security of his new-world empire, included a build-up of the armed forces of Spanish America. He organized a colonial militia wherein the sons of creole (that is, white American) families were offered the opportunity for a career in arms. Upon successful completion of cadet training-courses they were commissioned lieutenants and accorded the same military *fueros* (privileges) as the Spanish regulars.

Since eligibility for a commission was restricted to the creole elite, the officers naturally tended to identify themselves with the upper classes from which they came. This aristocratic identification continued even after independence, when the officer corps began to be drawn more and more from the middle groups in the society. Also, the *fuero militar,* which exempted personnel of the armed forces from the jurisdiction of civil courts, tended to raise the army above the law, creating a privileged caste exempt from public liability and civil responsibility.[2] Here, then, was the origin of the military caste system and the praetorian tradition in Latin America.

The group of creoles trained in colonial militias and in the Spanish regular army was large enough, however, to form only the nucleus of an officer corps. The long, bloody wars for independence from Spain in the period between 1810 and 1825 brought into existence large revolutionary armies, of which both officers and men were largely civilian

[2] Lyle N. McAlister, *The "Fuero Militar" in New Spain* (Gainesville: University of Florida Press, 1957), p. 15.

amateurs rather than career soldiers. In each of the various areas where fighting took place, the armed forces were makeshift in their organization, with no institutional tradition and no real professional *esprit de corps*.

Independence once achieved, the leaders of the revolutionary armies moved easily and naturally into the political vacuum created by the disappearance of royal authority. Thus at the very beginning of nationhood the armed forces assumed extramilitary (that is, political) functions. And as their military mission, that of defending the new nations against reconquest from Europe, became less meaningful and real, the military rulers, determined to preserve their vested institutional interests, placed more and more emphasis upon politics.

Talented creole professionals, like Simón Bolívar and José de San Martín, usually trained in the Spanish army, had led the revolutionary forces to victory and independent nationhood, but they were unable to establish stable and lasting political systems. By 1830 they were no longer on the scene. Instead, undisciplined amateurs, schooled in the violence of the revolutionary struggles, seized control of the various regions, thereby destroying the grand designs for unity for which the liberators had planned and fought.

In general, those who emerged as the masters of the sixteen independent Spanish-American states were of a lower order—socially, intellectually and in their patriotism—than the leaders of the revolution. The wealthier creole officers tended to eschew political responsibility and to retire to their landed estates. Scions of the propertied elite, they had no taste for the hard life of the barracks. Neither did they relish risking their lives in the jungle of politics. Such tasks were left to the clever, ambitious sons of the unstable, amorphous middle groups.[3] For the latter, an army career provided the opportunity to break through the arbitrary restrictions of the old social order, to shoot one's way into

[3] Daniel Hidalgo, *El militarismo, sus causes y remedios* (Quito: R. Racines C., 1913), pp. 146-148, 158.

a share of the power, wealth, and social prestige enjoyed by the landed oligarchy and the church hierarchy. The officer corps possessed little or no concept of the military career as a profession, and the men in the ranks consisted mainly of undisciplined armed hordes of volunteers, whose allegiance went to the strongest officer-politician in their locality.

The plethora of ambitious, opportunistic military men made politics in nearly every country little more than an endless process of dissension, intrigue, and revolutionary turmoil. The struggle centered around the presidential office. Once in power, a military president would take advantage of the opportunity to feather his own nest, paying off his backers with the residue. A vicious cycle of revolution developed. The victorious revolutionary forces seldom had sufficient resources to distribute spoils to everyone, and so the disgruntled would sow the seeds of a new military conspiracy. A new revolution would break out, which could succeed only with sufficient support from the army, and a new *caudillo* would emerge. Then would come the inevitable redistribution of offices, honors, privileges, and spoils. A constituent assembly would then be convoked to frame a new political charter, which, of course, lasted only until the next successful revolt. Thus, in the first half-century of independence, nearly everywhere politics was little more than military convulsion and anarchy.

Latin American militarism was peculiar in that its horizon did not extend beyond the domestic scene. Not military glory, saber rattling, and foreign conquest, but civil war, the fight for political power and for the opportunity to exploit and oppress the civilian population were its characteristics. Power was in the hands of a predatory military caste led by army generals such as Juan Manuel de Rosas in Argentina, Antonio López de Santa Anna in Mexico, José Antonio Páez in Venezuela, Ramón Castilla in Peru, Juan José Flores in Ecuador, Andrés Santa Cruz in Bolivia, José Fructuoso Rivera in Uruguay, Francisco Solano López in Paraguay, Rafael Carrera in Guatemala,

Jean Pierre Boyer in Haiti. Military *caudillos* were not all predatory nor equally bad. A Castilla or a Páez might well be considered progressive when compared with a Rosas or a Santa Anna. In most Latin American republics, however, the general pattern of political rule until about 1860 was military, and more often than not the military rulers were interested only in power and in the spoils of political office.

Between independence and World War I the Spanish-American republics experienced 115 successful revolutions and many times that number of abortive revolts. A typical example of the latter was the captain's conspiracy against the regime of General Castilla in Peru in 1845. Restless young officers, frustrated in their demands for promotion and higher pay, disgusted by the bungling and the corruption of their superiors, gradually became imbued with a "regenerating" mission. Their secret lodge, seventy-nine officers strong, decided to establish a dictatorship of uncorrupted youth by dismissing all officers above the rank of commander. Plans for the coup, which included seizing the president and the main barracks in Lima, were carefully drawn up. But Castilla was warned in time. The conspirators were arrested, but few were cashiered. Most of these, sent abroad as military attachés or as students of European armament systems, or given innocuous desk assignments, lived to plot another day.[4]

This was the nineteenth-century pattern of revolution, one which is still familiar in the more backward Latin American countries today. Sometimes the contest was among ambitious senior officers for control of the presidency. Nearly always the rebels styled themselves reformers. Seldom, however, were revolutions in any sense fundamental; when successful, no genuine reform usually resulted, no remodeling or reorganization of the country's basic institutions.

The typical Latin American revolution, prior to World

4 Ricardo Palma, *Tradiciones peruanas* (Madrid: Espasa-Calpe, 1953), pp. 1109-1112.

War I, was not a mass movement. The combatants were limited to rival military chieftains and their adherents. Sometimes in the background interested members of the landed oligarchy or of the small group of educated civilian professional men would engage in political intrigue, but the overwhelming majority of the population was not affected. The so-called revolutions were merely palace revolts, fights for the spoils of office within the officer corps, in which members of the civilian elite would sometimes join. When a revolt succeeded, the top personnel in government would be supplanted by the victors, but for the masses all that occurred was a change of masters.

Thus did ambitious army officers set themselves up as a privileged caste in politics. Long after the original revolutionary leaders had passed from the scene, their professional descendants continued to insist that the nation which their forebears created and consolidated still needed the services of military leaders for its defense and its security and for this owed them public office, privileges, and rewards. To make their argument incontrovertible, a group in the armed forces simply took political charge of the country. Usually their top general became president. This was the culmination of advancement in the military profession.

Caudillismo

Praetorianism and *caudillismo* were inseparable political phenomena, because the *caudillos* were generally the products and representatives of the armed forces. A few clever civilians, a Dr. José Francía in Paraguay or a Gabriel García Moreno in Ecuador, played *caudillo* roles, but this was only possible with the backing of armed forces, to whose interests any *caudillo* was obliged to cater in order to remain in power.

"Caudillism," Jesús de Galíndez has written, "was a characteristic flower of the Hispanic American political plant. . . . It was not a political concept but a psychological type." [5] Nearly every *caudillo* tended to conform to that type. He was generally an army officer and a representative of the armed forces. He was necessarily a man possessing superior energy, courage, and self-confidence, and for this reason inspired a certain awe and respect in his followers. He believed in his inherent right and destiny to govern; he was a man with a mission.[6] But differences were often as striking as similarities. Some *caudillos* were cruel tyrants, others were benevolent despots. Some were well educated, others illiterate. Some were selfish plunderers, others were patriotic reformers sincerely devoted to public service and the national welfare. In general, the early years of nationhood produced the worst specimens. After the mid-nineteenth century, in the major countries at least, the primitive types were succeeded by a more sophisticated variety. Justo José Urquiza replaced Rosas in Argentina; Porfirio Díaz superseded Santa Anna in Mexico.

More often than not, the *caudillos* and their "praetorian guard" forced themselves upon the people as political masters. They were not reluctant heroes, answering the need to fill a political vacuum created by the disappearance of other authority. They were not the only force available for governing. The civilian creole elite (the land barons, the clergymen, and the middle groups of professional men), who had backed the revolution in their antagonism to the monopolistic control of high government offices by the hated Spanish officials, were more than willing to take over or share in the task of governing, and they occasionally did so. It is often assumed that these civilian groups voluntarily abdicated their political responsibility to military chieftains.[7] In fact, they had no choice. To have tried to

[5] Jesús de Galíndez, *Iberoamérica, su evolución política, socio-económica, cultural y internacional* (New York: Las Americas, 1954), p. 199.

[6] George I. Blanksten, *Constitutions and Caudillos* (Berkeley: University of California Press, 1951), pp. 34-37.

[7] For example, the recent textbook by Donald E. Worcester and Wendell G. Schaefer, *The Growth and Culture of Latin America* (New York: Oxford University Press, 1956), p. 538.

govern alone would have required fighting the army leaders first, and with the latter in control of the means of violence they could have had no hope of winning. In some countries, notably Peru and Argentina, the civilian elite did attempt to manage political processes but came out second best in their rivalry with the armed forces. Where the military were disciplined early, as in the unique case of Chile under Diego Portales, the civilian oligarchy was able to assume—and did assume—control of the nation's political machinery.

Praetorianism and *caudillismo* thrived in Latin America because the environment there was propitious. The precolonial period with its local *caciques* and its regional Indian chiefs, and the colonial period with its Spanish *conquistadores, adelantados,* captain-generals and viceroys, had built up a tradition of authoritarian, strong-man rule. In addition, the long struggle for independence gave exaggerated political importance to the leaders of the revolutionary armies. It was perhaps inevitable that people who had lived so long in the midst of armed conflict would suffer an aftermath of rule by the victors. And in the immediate postrevolutionary milieu, when in the various new nations effective political control could be achieved only by use of force, it was natural that power-seeking military chieftains would come into control.

Additional factors contributing to the phenomenon of *caudillismo* included the geographical features which made orderly government difficult, the racial composition of the population (the high percentage of Indians, Negroes, and mixed bloods), the poverty and ignorance of the masses, the "feudal" social structure (especially the absence of a large and responsible middle class), and, finally, the authoritarian attitudes of the military profession itself.

The Traditional Order

The rule of the military did little to disturb the dominant economic and social position of the rural propertied elite. As late as the first quarter of the twentieth century, even in the more advanced countries, the pattern of Latin America's predominantly rural-oriented society and economy was much like that of the colonial era. One author describes the Chilean situation, which was more or less comparable to that in the other Latin American countries, as follows:

> There was a land-holding aristocracy, well-educated, far-traveled, highly cultured, in full control of the national life; and, quite apart from them, a lower class . . . constituting the fixed tenantry of the rural estates. . . . A man's status has been determined by whether or not he owned a hacienda or, at least, by whether he belonged to a land-holding family. Position in life, occupation, opportunity depended mainly on this. . . . Here has existed a New World country with the social organization of Old Spain; a twentieth century people still preserving a feudal society; a republic based on the equality of man, yet with a blue-blood aristocracy and a servile class as distinctly separated as in any of the monarchies of the Old World.[8]

And, just as in the colonial period, the upper clergy were also included in the traditional social order; they too connived with the other two components of the oligarchic triarchy, landowners and army officers, to preserve the *status quo.*

With the great majority of the population inarticulate, poverty-stricken, and politically apathetic, the military were under no popular pressure to change the existing social system, nor did they show any inclination to do so. Throughout the nineteenth century they continued to identify themselves with the propertied elite, often making use of their political offices to amass fortunes and become landowners themselves. They accommodated themselves to the social and economic system they inherited. In this generally static society the military politicians themselves

[8] George M. McBride, *Chile: Land and Society* (New York: American Geographical Society, 1936), pp. 12-14.

were about the only group for which social mobility was possible.

Though the officers of the armed forces were the dominant group in politics, especially in the first half-century of independence, they did not have complete control. For within the tripartite aristocracy there prevailed a continuing struggle for power. Often, in the aftermath of the collapse of a military dictatorship, a lawyer-politician representing the landowners would set up a civilian constitutional regime. Such governments were usually of short duration, however, for their tenure depended upon the continued backing of the armed forces. In addition to their simple threat of force, the military leaders very early found they could cow the civilian elite by making demagogic appeals to the masses. This tactic was effectively used by Generals Rosas of Argentina and Santa Anna of Mexico.

In most countries, not long after independence, small bodies of middle-group professionals (lawyers, doctors, intellectuals, and some army officers) and merchants formed so-called liberal parties, ostensibly to mitigate the evils of the rule of the tripartite oligarchy. The latter, in the face of this challenge, generally formed conservative parties. The declared aims of the incipient liberal parties, whose leaders were influenced by the ideals and principles of the French and American revolutions, were federalism, anticlericalism and progress, as opposed to the centralism, clericalism, and unyielding dedication to the *status quo* which marked the conservative parties of the landowners and upper clergy.

One thing both parties had in common, at least until the latter half of the nineteenth century: they were directed by army generals. Typical of many Latin American republics was the evolution of mid-nineteenth century politics in Colombia. In the 1837 elections the Conservatives emerged victorious, but when civilian President José Ignacio Marquéz attempted to reduce the influence of the military element, the defeated Liberal candidate, General José María Obando, launched a revolt. The Conservatives preserved their hold on the government only by transferring the presidential power to General Pedro Alcántara Herrán, the commander of the loyal government forces. In 1845 another military strong-man, General Tomás Cipriano Mosquera, was selected to carry on the Conservative party tradition. To meet this kind of competition, the opposition Liberal party also found itself a man-in-uniform. General José Hilario López emerged victorious in 1849 as a result of a split in the Conservative party, and, for most of the next thirty years, the Liberals and their anticlerical and federalist principles held sway in Colombia. General Obando won the 1853 elections only to be overthrown the following year by a Conservative conspiracy backed by the army and headed by General José María Melo. A Liberal revolution led by General Mosquera (the former Conservative strong-man, now turned Liberal) ended this brief Conservative interlude. Mosquera took over the presidency himself a few years later, ruling as military despot from 1861 to 1864 and again from 1866 until 1867, when he was finally driven into exile by his own Liberal party. Uniformed politicians continued prominent in Colombia's late nineteenth-century political panorama.

Many authors have claimed to detect a tendency on the part of the military men to side with the conservative parties, and a tendency of the *doctores* (civilian politicians) to identify themselves with the liberals. Actually the ideological differences between the parties was not great, for political organization, for the most part, was a mere association of friends motivated by personal rivalries and ambitions. Both parties accepted the existing social order. The active politicians in both, that is, the *doctores* and the army officers, were nearly all members of the small, amorphous, middle class. Their overriding interest was power, regardless of party. The apparent tendency of the military toward the conservatives was due to the inherent conservatism of rank and age, but this was counterbalanced by the tendency of ambitious younger officers to advance through association with the liberal party.

A complicating political crosscurrent was regionalism, which had been a major factor in splitting Latin America into many independent states. Moreover, the post-independence regional and local allegiances help explain the intense factionalism and turbulence of Latin American politics. For example, in Argentina, under Rosas, the natives of Buenos Aires battled the provincial armies of the interior; in Ecuador the coastal armies fought those in the interior; and in Venezuela the *andinos* vied with the *llaneros* and the coastal city forces.

Decline of Militarism

The worst excesses of militarism began to die out in the major countries during the latter half of the nineteenth century, as governments became progressively more civilian in character. Francisco García Calderón, influenced by the theories of Herbert Spencer, interpreted this transition as an inevitable, evolutionary law of history. On the eve of World War I he wrote:

> . . . Invariably we find the sequence of two periods, one military and one industrial or civil. The Independence realized, the rule of militarism sets in throughout the republics. After a period of uncertain duration the military caste is hurled from power, or abdicates without violence, and economic interests become supreme. Politics is then ruled by "civilism." [9]

While this may be an oversimplified interpretation, a real change did take place. Militarism partly consumed itself through its own outrageous excesses; partly it was mitigated by rising new civilian forces. Much of Latin America began to enter a new epoch. The chaotic aftereffects of the long wars for independence began to subside. Political experience was accumulated, culture diffused, illiteracy reduced. Immigrants began to come in. A heavy influx of foreign capital financed construction of telegraph

[9] F. García Calderón, *Latin America: Its Rise and Progress* (London: Fisher Unwin, 1913), p. 86.

lines and railroads. And along with people, capital, and technology came modern European ideas.

A concomitant development was the decline of *caudillismo*—in Chile by the 1830's, in Argentina after 1860, in Uruguay in 1890, and in Colombia at the turn of the century. Even in those countries where militarism remained dominant, like Ecuador, Peru, and Venezuela, more responsible types tended to gain control. And in Mexico, Díaz crushed the military adventurers, disciplined—for the first time—the armed forces, brought about order at the expense of liberty, and paved the way for economic development. In Brazil, where the modernizing occidental impact helped bring about the collapse of the Empire in 1889, there occurred a five-year *caudillo*-praetorian interlude before a semblance of orderly republican government was established.

Economic development and growing political stability mainly affected the larger countries (Argentina, Brazil, Chile, and Mexico) and the small white countries (Uruguay and Costa Rica). Where immigrants and Western technology did not flow in, as in Central America and the Caribbean republics, and where large Indian populations continued to live in abject poverty exploited by a white elite, as in Paraguay, Bolivia, Peru, Ecuador, and Guatemala, the traditional order of society (landholder dominance) and politics (*caudillismo* and praetorianism) continued to prevail.

This is not to suggest that anywhere in Latin America the traditional order was seriously threatened. Nearly everywhere the tripartite elite of large landholders, high churchmen, and army officers remained dominant. With material progress, immigration, and urbanization, new economic and social forces were beginning to emerge, but these trends had not made sufficient headway by the time of World War I to disturb seriously the oligarchy that had traditionally ruled the Latin American nations.

One reason for the decline of the militaristic turmoil in

the major countries was the merging of the armed forces into unified national bodies. Less and less they represented rival political parties or regionalist factions. This "nationalizing" of the various armies in the more advanced countries was partly a response to public criticism of the chaos, waste, and destruction engendered by the soldiery in the past, but mainly it was due to the general modernizing and technological influence that came from Western Europe in the late nineteenth century.

For example, in imitation of the modern military establishments of Prussia and France, truly national, regular standing armies were created in Argentina and Mexico in the 1880's. This change more than anything else relegated to secondary importance the voluntary local militias of the various regions and, along with it, the regional *caudillos*. In this task of enforcing political stability by the unified armed might of the central governments both the civilian elite and the generals cooperated. As in the past, the ranks were filled from the lowest rungs of the social ladder, while the officer caste continued to come from the aspiring middle groups. Unification of the armed forces probably enhanced, rather than diminished, their potential political power, but they showed decreasing inclination toward political domination so long as acceptable civilian regimes looked out for their privileged position.

Another military factor contributing to political stability in the latter nineteenth century was technological. After 1860 the increasing complexity and expensiveness of imported European equipment, especially artillery, favored effective political centralization in that it rendered individual weapons like the rifle, the machete, and the bayonet less effective in combat. Consequently, it became progressively more difficult to launch rebellions without at least some support from the nation's regular armed forces. By the end of the century, the day of the volunteer, makeshift, armed rebellion was past nearly everywhere in Latin America.

The Beginnings of Professionalism

There also occurred toward the end of the nineteenth century a significant development in Latin America's armed forces which had a great deal to do with the trend toward increasing political stability. This was the rise of professionalism, which at least offered some prospect of curbing militarism. Professionalism meant, first, that the officer corps turned its energies to the exercise and development of its military function; second, that the armed forces tended to become the servants rather than the masters of the state; third, that their function became increasingly limited to the "legitimate" military duties of maintaining internal security and defending the country against external aggression. Professionalism was the antithesis of militarism, which connoted military influence in, or preponderance over, politics, dominance of the military caste over the society it was designed to protect, and overemphasis upon military considerations in national budgets and planning. During the first quarter of the twentieth century the degree of militarism or professionalism existent in the officer corps in a given country was closely related to what was happening in the society at large. In most cases the trends toward economic development, social progress, and political stability, retarded by militarism, were by contrast considerably enhanced by professionalism.

It was probably inevitable, as militarism declined, as governments became more stable, as economic development progressed, that Latin America's armed forces would become more professional bodies. However, an important impetus for this change came from Western Europe, as part of the general West European impact upon the area. At the end of the nineteenth century, French and German missions began introducing modern military methods. They also helped inculcate professional pride and *esprit*. In the early twentieth century United States marines were engaged in similar tasks in the Caribbean area.

In the vanguard of professionalism was the Chilean

army, which invited a German mission in 1885. When Prussian General Emil Koerner arrived, he found that the army which had just emerged victorious in the War of the Pacific against Bolivia and Peru was woefully lacking in technical knowledge and was equipped with obsolete weapons. Koerner began his renovation program with the reorganization, along modern European lines, of the Escuela Militar, where cadets were trained to become officers. The more promising young officers he dispatched to Europe for a tour of duty with the German army, and during the 1890's he set up a War Academy for the training of senior officers. He also created a general staff, of which he himself became the chief.

In January 1891, Koerner's already great influence over the Chilean armed forces increased still further when his defection from President José Balmaceda helped turn the tide of revolution in favor of the Constitutionalist forces. In the aftermath of victory, the Prussianization of the officer corps was extended to the ranks. In 1895, thirty-seven German officers were employed in the mission. By the end of the century, Chilean troops, trained, uniformed, and equipped along the most up-to-date European lines, were quite ready for the war that threatened with Argentina. It was Koerner also who provided the impetus for the enactment of the Chilean Congress of the first general conscription law in Latin America. The German professional influence in the Chilean army continued strong to the outbreak of World War I.[10]

Argentina soon followed in Chile's lead. A German mission, employed in 1899, promptly set about overhauling the Colegio Militar and setting up a War Academy. At this time Uruguay and Bolivia also brought in German instructors. An indirect German influence in other Latin American countries came via Chile, which in 1905 began sending military training missions to Colombia, Venezuela, Para-

[10] Fritz T. Epstein, *European Military Influences in Latin America* (manuscript in possession of author in Library of Congress, 1941), pp. 116-127.

guay, and El Salvador. These nations, plus Ecuador and Nicaragua, also sent some of their officers to the acknowledgedly superior Chilean military schools. In Brazil, Ecuador, Peru, and Guatemala, French military training missions and instructors were employed by the turn of the century.[11]

The United States trained and modernized the armed forces of the Caribbean republics and of two of the Central American republics. This American activity, however, was not in the same category as that of European missions. The United States professional military men were not invited. Rather, the United States government first intervened by force of arms, then reorganized the military forces of the occupied country in an effort to promote political stability and more responsible government.

Following the second military occupation of Cuba in 1906, United States army officers set to work establishing a responsible professional, nonpolitical army there. The nucleus of such a force was formally established in 1908. The United States marines undertook similar tasks in Haiti during the 1915-1934 occupation, in the Dominican Republic in 1916-1934, and in Nicaragua, 1926-1931. In addition, United States army officers directed the reorganization of the Panamanian police force in 1918-1919.[12]

A few foreign naval missions were active in Latin America after the turn of the century, notably the British in Chile and Argentina, and the United States in Brazil beginning in 1918.

Of course, the general caliber of the various armed forces differed widely. Obviously, factors such as political stability, economic advance, literacy, health, climate and the general character of the population served to produce a much better army in Uruguay, for example, than in Honduras. Nevertheless, evidences of the increasing professionalism were present in virtually all of Latin America's armed forces in the early twentieth century. Objective

11 Same, pp. 128-168.
12 See below, Chapter 7, pp. 183-184.

academic requirements for entry into the various military academies were revised steadily upward, and in most countries the military educational system itself underwent periodic improvement. Military staff systems, hitherto unknown in Latin America, were organized. In some countries, new laws and regulations requiring professional *expertise* and merit as criteria for promotion had signal effects in bringing the best professionals to the top. The same legislation also revealed determined efforts on the part of civilian *políticos* to convert the armed forces into nonpolitical professional bodies excluded from exercising any function aside from their two "legitimate" military duties: preserving internal order and defending the nation against external threats.

The gradual elevation of the career in arms into a respectable profession attracted to it more responsible and better-educated types of men. As in the past, the new cadets were drawn from the middle groups, but increasingly technical proficiency and devoted, patriotic service were rewarded rather than political opportunism. Increasingly, the military academies in the more advanced countries were filled with the serious, responsible sons of the growing urban professional and commercial groups.

Notable as this trend toward professionalism was, however, it had won only a partial victory. Many of its gains were not firmly established, some proved but temporary, for militarism was to recur with a vengeance in the second quarter of the twentieth century.

The growth of truly national, professional armies was undoubtedly an important factor in helping to produce international as well as domestic calm. In South America, for example, five wars were fought in the period 1825 to 1883, but after the latter date none occurred until the Chaco War broke out in 1932. Peace was at least partly a product of the decline in militarism and rise in professionalism. Ambitious regional military chieftains who had previously provoked boundary squabbles were now held at bay. Also, political refugees in exile in neighboring countries found it much more difficult to develop forces capable of challenging a government's regulars.

Outwardly, the new-found stability seemed to show that the traditional social order was firmly consolidating its position. Actually, as the succeeding chapter will show, relative peace made possible the broad material progress and the social changes which ultimately challenged the traditional order of society.

Chapter 2

THE CRUMBLING OF THE TRADITIONAL ORDER, 1914-1959

WITH THE COMING OF the twentieth century, the traditional order started to crumble. A landed aristocracy, a praetorian military caste, and a Catholic church hierarchy could no longer monopolize power, wealth, prestige and influence. Society and the economy began to undergo fundamental transformations which were soon reflected in politics. New social and institutional forms reshaped the environment.

The extent and intensity of change was uneven. Mexico struck out on the revolutionary path early in the century, while a country like Nicaragua still lives today in the nineteenth century. Despite their distinct identities, however, all the Latin American states felt the impact of fundamental changes in their own society and in the world environment.

World War I marked the beginning of the end of the old system under which Latin America's well-established economic and social organization was firmly tied to a stable old-world order. Fractures in the neat international system of trade and diplomacy precipitated by the 1914-1918 upheaval were compounded by such subsequent crises as the great depression, World War II, and the cold war. The ideological impact of socialism, fascism, and communism, and the influence of the New Deal all helped hasten the breakdown of the old order.

Part of what happened was a logical projection of currents already present in the nineteenth-century historical stream. Economic change, especially the tendency of the "colonial" economy to give way to industrialization and diversification, brought about modifications in the social structure as well. At the same time, the changing world environment introduced new explosive factors into Latin American affairs, which not only greatly accelerated existing trends but also gave rise to entirely new ones. The end of the process of change—even the precise direction of it—was not entirely clear. What was clear was the dynamic effect upon Latin American politics.

Economic Transformation

It was in the last quarter of the nineteenth century that Latin America began to feel intensively the impact of the industrial revolution.[1] Technological advances that had already transformed manufacturing, agriculture, transportation and communications in Western Europe and the United States were transferred to Latin America by foreign investors and traders and by European immigrants. In the process, the natural resources of the region were developed to produce the minerals and food exports that contributed to a threefold increase in the area's international trade between 1875 and 1914. Concurrently, the population, which had remained relatively stable since independence, increased rapidly—from 30 million in 1875 to 60 million by 1900, and to 80 million at the outbreak of World War I.

These were the years when Argentina became the world's leading exporter of wheat and beef, when Brazil began to supply the world with most of its coffee, when Chile became the world's largest nitrate producer, when Bolivia became a major factor in the international tin market, when Mexico's silver output skyrocketed, and

[1] The reader should be forewarned of the general unreliability of statistics on Latin America, and particularly of statistics emanating from Latin American sources. As the purpose here, however, is to trace the economic transformation only in its broad lines, the element of unreliability in statistics does not affect the general picture that is drawn.

when the Caribbean republics (including Central America and Colombia) became exporters in large volume of sugar, coffee, and bananas. It was also the time when the communications systems of these countries were built up by foreign capital to serve export agriculture and extractive industry.[2]

This economic transformation did little, however, to alleviate the lot of the mass of the people. The corporate manager was as stern a taskmaster as the *hacendado*. Latin America's economy remained essentially colonial. It provided minerals and foodstuffs to the industrial countries, upon which it depended for manufactured goods. The investment of foreign capital in mining and transportation enterprises reinforced the social and economic position of the rural oligarchy, for the latter, as producers of export crops, also benefited from the stimulus to foreign trade. However, the increased trade and productivity were not reflected in rising living standards for all classes in Latin America, as they had been generally in the industrialized nations.

The disturbances and dislocations caused by the first World War dealt a severe blow to this smoothly working international economic system. As the late Miron Burgin so ably expressed it:

> . . . World War I . . . marked the beginning of the end of much of the environment that had been so carefully and often brilliantly constructed in the preceding century, and as the efforts of the postwar years toward reconstruction appeared doomed to failure Latin America felt increasingly the impact of the upheaval beyond the seas. In a very real sense Latin America had lost its moorings. It could no longer count upon Europe to maintain intact the order in which Latin America had grown and prospered, and had felt secure. In the aftermath of World War I, Latin America was forced to mobilize all its moral and material resources in order to adjust itself to a new, tortuously emerging world environment. It had to dis-

[2] Sanford A. Mosk, "Latin America and the World Economy, 1850-1914," *Inter-American Economic Affairs*, Winter 1948, pp. 61-68.

card some of the axioms and tenets which in the light of the new reality and experience appeared to have lost their usefulness and validity. And it had to find new values and formulations that conformed more closely to the urgent needs of the moment. . . .[3]

The most urgent need, which grew out of the experience of being cut off from the supply of manufactured goods, was greater economic independence. To this end there began a determined drive for industrialization, in order to bring an end to exaggerated dependence upon overseas markets, with their unstable prices and uncertain demand, and to raise living standards. The urge to industrialize was stimulated by the failure of attempts in the 1920's to rebuild the international economy, by its collapse in the 1930's, and by experiences of the early 1940's which again demonstrated the hardship suffered by colonial economies during wartime.

Industrialization proceeded most rapidly in the larger countries which had such minimum essentials as capital, a limited technological "know-how," and a developing internal market. In Brazil and Argentina, it was estimated that the value of industrial production exceeded agricultural output by the beginning of World War II. Chile, Mexico and Uruguay were not far behind. Other Latin American countries also tried industrialization, though with considerably less success, as a way out of their colonial economic status. Particularly in the little republics of the Caribbean and Central America, primitive subsistence agriculture remained the basis of livelihood for most of the population.

Considering Latin America as a whole, however, an economy that had been almost exclusively agricultural was transformed between 1914 and 1959 into one that was both industrial and agricultural. Though nearly three-fifths of the working population were still employed in the rural sector of the economy, they produced less than those in

[3] "New Fields of Research in Latin American Studies," in Angel del Río, ed., *Responsible Freedom in the Americas* (Garden City, N. Y.: Doubleday, 1955), p. 189.

industry. Already by 1947 it was estimated that manufactures surpassed agricultural output in value.[4] In the major countries industrialization was a steady, continuing trend, one that was making them decreasingly dependent upon foreign suppliers.

Under the combined stimulus of industrialization, urbanization and immigration, Latin America's population more than doubled (from 80 million in 1914 to 180 million in 1959), but since output of goods and services expanded at an even more rapid rate, the standard of living rose. In the quarter-century between 1933 and 1958, for example, while population increased by one-half, production more than doubled. Although Latin America's per capita income was still low even in the most prosperous countries and growing at a slower rate than that of the United States, a notable advance had taken place. For example, between 1938 and 1949, Mexico's annual per capita income doubled (from $60 to $121) and Brazil's more than tripled (from $33 to $112).

The surge in income was particularly rapid in the period immediately following World War II. Between 1945 and 1951 the average per capita increase is estimated to have been 4.7 per cent annually.[5] During this period industry grew more rapidly than agriculture. For example, while total production rose 43 per cent, manufactures increased by 70 per cent (from $6.8 billion to $11.4 billion).[6]

After 1952 the rate of economic growth slackened considerably. During the five-year 1952-1956 period the average annual increase in per capita income was barely over 1 per cent, before picking up somewhat in 1957.[7] Factors

[4] Edward G. Cale, "Economic Bases of United States-Latin American Relations," U. S. Department of State, *Bulletin,* July 19, 1954, pp. 79-80; Gary McFain, "Latin America Industrializes," *Commonweal,* April 16, 1954, pp. 31-32.

[5] United Nations, Economic Commission for Latin America, *Economic Survey of Latin America, 1955* (New York, 1956), p. 3.

[6] Cale, cited, pp. 79-80. These figures are for 1945 and for 1952.

[7] *Economic Survey of Latin America, 1955,* cited, p. 3; same, *1956,* p. 3; same, *1957,* p. 83.

contributing to the decline included the exhaustion of international balances accumulated during World War II, price declines in foodstuffs and minerals, shrinkage in export markets, and the easing-off of new investment. In this situation, the insistence of most Latin American governments upon maintaining high levels of consumption discouraged badly needed investments in basic power and transportation enterprises as well as in agriculture and industry. In addition, the adverse shift in the terms of trade after 1952 created serious balance-of-payments problems for most of the South American countries, and their economic woes were compounded by chronic inflation, particularly in Argentina, Brazil, Chile, and Bolivia. Favorable developments over the next few years will hinge upon improvements in the economic conditions of other industrial countries (principally the United States and Western Europe) and upon strengthening of international financial cooperation.

A high degree of economic nationalism characterized the drive for economic independence. To protect and encourage industry Latin American states resorted to import controls, exchange restrictions, tariffs, and government subsidies. In addition, they challenged ownership of their industries by foreigners. Argentina purchased its British-owned railroads and public-utility enterprises; Uruguay and Argentina set up meat-packing plants to compete with those owned by American corporations; Brazil and Argentina insisted upon domestic control of their oil resources; and Chile extended its controls over foreign-owned copper-mining corporations. Nearly every country passed legislation requiring foreign corporations to grant labor special advantages. The most spectacular attacks on foreign companies were made by Mexico in 1938 when it expropriated the holdings of British and American oil companies, by Bolivia in 1952 when it nationalized the tin mines, and by Guatemala in 1953 when it confiscated part of the United Fruit Company's lands. Because the growth of economic nationalism coincided with the increasingly prominent position of United States capital (by the end of 1958 United States private investment in Latin America totaled over $8.8 billion),[8] United States investors bore the brunt of the attack.

After 1955 economic nationalism seemed to be less sharply directed against foreign interests. Growing receptivity to foreign investment, particularly in petroleum and mining enterprises, was evident in all the major countries, and in Bolivia and Guatemala; there were no confiscations or expropriations after 1953. In one aspect of economic nationalism, however, in the tendency of the state to play an ever-increasing role in the process of economic development, there was no apparent let-up. From the time of World War I, the absorbing force of government enterprise steadily took over public utilities, transportation, power development, and even a large fraction of domestic manufacturing. In addition to moving into large areas previously left to private enterprise, the state also assumed an increasing responsibility for the welfare of the working population. To that end it often deliberately adopted inflationary wage and credit policies. The dominant role of the state in economic life, of course, gave all the more importance to the question of who controlled the state apparatus.

Social Change

The economic changes which followed the crisis of World War I were major causes, and also partial effects, of profound social change. In every Latin American country the traditional order of society which had held virtually unquestioned supremacy in the first century of independence was challenged in some degree; in the larger ones it was overthrown. In Argentina, Brazil, Chile, Uruguay, and Mexico (countries which included over two-thirds of Latin America's population and land area) "the power

[8] Raymond F. Mikesell, *Foreign Investments in Latin America,* Economic Research Series (Washington: Pan American Union, 1955), mimeographed, pp. 2, 10, 14; *New York Times,* December 7, 1958, sec. 3, p. 1.

which a well-entrenched and unbending conservative elite formerly derived from mere ownership of vast landed estates . . . passed to the newly emerging laboring, industrial, and middle-class groups in thriving urban centers." [9] In Bolivia and Costa Rica, and very recently in Venezuela and in Cuba, similar shifts occurred in the locus of social power. Serious, but unsuccessful, challenges were thrown up to the old order in Guatemala, Colombia, Ecuador, Peru, Paraguay, El Salvador, and Panama. The only republics which did not feel deeply the modern pressures of economic change and social upheaval were Haiti, the Dominican Republic, Honduras, and Nicaragua, representing but 5 per cent of Latin America's total population.

Even in Peru, a country generally thought of as backward with the old order firmly entrenched, the change was striking. José Luís Bustamante, a former president (1945-1948), described it as follows:

New means of communication have brought us closer to the rest of the world, encouraged interchange and contacts with the exterior. . . . Public education, deficient but undeniable, has elevated in our people the degree of civic consciousness. . . . The multiplication of official services, with the consequent increase in the bureaucracy, and the organization of commercial enterprise on a modern basis, has created in our cities an improvising and numerous middle class. The industrial era has begun, and with it the visible phenomenon of displacement in the activities of work. The artisan is declining; the *campesino* is becoming a laborer . . . the urban factories gather in the elements which desire to better their standard of living, they organize themselves into syndicates and form a new class of manual laborers. . . . Likewise the Indians of the highlands migrate to labor on the coasts . . . and this is serving to break up the feudal system in the highland region.[10]

[9] John Johnson, "The New Latin America and the United States," *The Pacific Spectator*, Summer 1955, p. 245.

[10] *Tres años de lucha por la democracía en el Perú* (Buenos Aires: Bartolomé U. Chiesino, 1949), pp. 14-15.

The transformation of an almost exclusively rural and agricultural economy to one that was also urban and industrial was the fundamental cause of the social upheaval. The absorbing force of manufacturing activity in cities like Buenos Aires, São Paulo, Santiago, Rio de Janeiro, Montevideo, and Mexico City sucked in labor from the countryside, swallowed up the bulk of the post-World War I immigrants, and created conditions and opportunities which stimulated the growth of an ever-larger middle class. All of this led to huge concentrations of population in metropolitan areas. For example, 4 per cent of the Chilean population lived in Santiago in 1913, 17 per cent in 1957. In the latter year, 13 per cent of Mexico's people resided in the capital city, compared to only 4 per cent in 1913.[11]

In Argentina, 70 per cent of the population was living in rural areas in 1870, but by 1938 70 per cent lived in cities. Chile also, by that time, was no longer a semifeudal agrarian society; true, the old order persisted in the countryside, but the basis of the socio-economic structure had become urban and industrial; the city now dominated. In Mexico a frontal assault had been made upon the power, the wealth, and the social position of the landed oligarchy in the violent social upheaval that began in 1910. The revolution itself hastened the shift in the nation's center of gravity from rural agriculture to urban industry.

By 1940 southern South America was one of the most heavily urbanized areas in the world. Forty per cent of the Argentine and Uruguayan populations and 34 per cent of the Chilean lived in cities of 25,000 or more. The comparable figures were 40 per cent in the United States, 33 per cent in Canada, 30 per cent in France, and 8 per cent in India. Latin America's twentieth-century urbanization involved more than simple migration from farm to city, for, although half the urban increase was due to rural migrants, they represented less than a quarter of the natural

[11] Figures from *World Almanac and Book of Facts* (1913 and 1958).

increase in farm population.[12] In other words, Latin America's entire population was expanding at the extraordinarily rapid rate of 2.5 per cent annually, faster than any other area in the world.

The industrialization-urbanization trend gave rise to new social groups and classes. No longer did society consist only of an elite of large landholders, an insignificant professional and commercial middle class, and a great mass of illiterate agricultural workers. Now there were also industrial entrepreneurs and small capitalists, large professional groups and masses of literate city wage earners. It was these new urban-oriented groups that brought pressure to bear for fundamental changes in the traditional order of society.

The elite of Latin America's urban civilization were the industrialists. The industrial entrepreneur after World War I was the leader, director, and controller of economic change. He challenged the monopolistic control of the government, of the economy, of the whole society enjoyed during the previous century by the landholders in alliance with the ecclesiastical and military hierarchies. "Energetic and self-confident he has been impatient with social and economic conditions that hampered his freedom of action. He has acquired prestige by virtue of his contribution to the economy, and he has demanded and received political recognition commensurate with his economic power." [13] Often, in the more advanced countries, he had to overcome the resistance of foreign corporations already in control of the nation's raw-material output, and everywhere he sought tariff protection in order to survive the competition from West European and United States manufacturers.

In Brazil, the industrialists came to the fore in the 1930 revolt against the heretofore dominant coffee barons. Their influence in government, the army, and society has grown progressively ever since. The most spectacular example was

[12] Kingsley Davis, "Latin America's Multiplying Peoples," in Asher Christensen, ed., *The Evolution of Latin American Government* (New York: Holt, 1951), pp. 138-140.

[13] Burgin, cited, p. 190.

"Count" Francisco Matarazzo, an imaginative Italian immigrant who took advantage of the broad-range business opportunities that accompanied the surge of industrialization during World War I. By the time he died, in 1937, he had established a huge national network of banks, factories, trading organizations and transportation companies which made him the wealthiest man in Latin America. His successors and their industrial and banking colleagues carried on and accelerated the remaking of Brazilian society.

Similar stories can be told elsewhere. In Argentina a rising industrialist group, already important in Argentine society, became politically powerful under Juan Perón. Its members either operated independently, with liberal favors and support from the government, or participated as partners in government-sponsored enterprises. In Chile, by the turn of the century, the industrialists were the power behind the newly formed Radical party, which, in the depression following World War I, successfully challenged the rural interests represented by both the traditionalist Conservative and Liberal parties. What President Arturo Alessandri, a Radical, could not accomplish legally in his initial years of office, sympathetic young army officers achieved by force in the revolution of 1925. The strangle hold of the old oligarchy having been broken, Chile ultimately became one of the most highly industrialized countries in Latin America. In Mexico, generals of the revolution became captains of industry as well as presidents of the republic. Apostles of the new order, they attacked the old feudal agrarian structure. They became substantial businessmen—"millionaire socialists," as one author called them. Among them were President-Generals Alvaro Obregón, Plutarco Elías Calles, Abelardo Rodríguez, Emilio Portes Gil, and Manuel Avila Camacho.[14] More recently, particularly since World War II, rising industrialists have

[14] Carleton Beals, *Lands of the Dawning Tomorrow* (Toronto: McClelland, 1948), pp. 240-242.

become politically important in Colombia, Venezuela, Guatemala, Uruguay, and Peru.

The industrialists represented only a minority, the upper segment of the amorphous middle class. Desirous of consolidating their new position, they often invested in land, hoping to gain thereby some of the social prestige still enjoyed by the rural oligarchy. Between them and the urban workers were various other middle-class groups—small and medium entrepreneurs, clerks, shopkeepers, professional workers, technical specialists, and government officials. Nearly the entire middle class was urban, for rural Latin America, excepting southern Chile and southern Brazil, was practically devoid of independent farmers with medium-sized holdings.

In Argentina, Brazil, Chile, and Uruguay, this urban middle class consisted of immigrant stock; in the predominantly Indian countries, like Mexico, Peru, and Guatemala, it was made up of *mestizos* (mixed bloods). People in the middle range of incomes—white-collar workers—made up about half the population of countries like Argentina, Chile, and Uruguay. The proportion was somewhat less in countries with large rural populations like Brazil and Mexico.[15] The power of the middle class, a heterogeneous conglomeration of unrelated occupational groups, was weakened, however, by a notable lack of common purposes and ideals.

Organized labor was considerably more cohesive, and soon more powerful. It was made up principally of urban workers; rural labor, generally, remained disorganized, illiterate, and under the control of the *hacendados*. A by-product of industrialization, the labor movement did not really get started until World War I, although in Argentina, Chile and Cuba attempts were made to organize the workers in the last decade of the nineteenth century. Organized labor became strongest in the most industrialized countries (Chile, Brazil, Argentina, Uruguay) and in those

15 Sir Ronald Fraser, *Latin America: A Personal Survey* (London: Hutchinson, 1953), pp. 226-227.

where the disintegration of the old order was most complete (Mexico and Bolivia). But in nearly all countries the political might of urban labor was reflected in protective labor codes and social-insurance legislation. Even in those where the agrarian oligarchy was still dominant, it found an accommodation with the urban workers politically expedient. This was evident, for example, in the pro-labor clauses of the constitutions of Peru (1933), Colombia (1936), Venezuela (1936), Ecuador (1938), Bolivia (1938), and Nicaragua (1939). More often honored more in the breach than in the observance, the labor laws nevertheless paid deference to a potentially important new force in Latin American society.

Governments depending on the support of labor came to power in many countries, the most notable examples being those of Lázaro Cárdenas in Mexico, Juan Perón in Argentina, and Jacobo Arbenz of Guatemala. In most countries, trade-unions displayed little real independence; rather, they were generally under the thumb of labor *caudillos*. Paternalistic governments often took charge of the labor movement and of the social welfare of the workers. In Chile, Cuba, Mexico, and Argentina, however, organized labor began to emerge as a truly independent force.

Relations among the emerging new classes were generally unstable. Initially, in the early stages of economic nationalism, domestic capital and labor joined forces against foreign enterprise and the traditional order. Especially in the Indian countries, the middle groups led the illiterate, rural, poverty-stricken masses toward accommodation with and assimilation into modern, urban culture and civilization. After World War II, however, class warfare between the domestic industrialists and organized labor was more characteristic than cooperation. Faced by labor's increasing independence and its bid for a dominant role in some countries, middle-class ardor for cooperation with the workers has cooled considerably.

Political Upheaval

It was inevitable that the broad economic and social changes taking place in Latin America would ultimately produce serious political disturbances. The industrialization-urbanization process and the accompanying growth of new classes precipitated new political movements, nearly all of them more broadly based than in the past, many of them demanding sweeping reforms. Political processes became more complex. No longer so meaningful were personal feuds, federalist-centralist bickering and church-state battles. Politics was no longer an exclusive game played according to established rules. And it was a game further complicated by foreign example, and even participation, when Fascist, Nazi, Communist and other ideologies appeared upon the Latin American political scene.

The creation of new sources of wealth, the spread of new ideas, and the awakening of the urban masses produced far-reaching dislocations. The church began to lose its grip over the minds of the populace, the *hacendado* became powerless to prevent his peons from trying to find in the city's factories escape from their miseries, and the *caudillo* could no longer win and hold power by sheer force, or even by the display of courage and character. New economic and social conditions demanded a new balance of political forces. The old feudal loyalties to the general, the landlord, and the bishop were progressively replaced by impersonal ties with the business firm, the labor organization, or the governmental machine. Personal rivalries gave way to party rivalries. The strong-man in politics became less of an arbitrary ruler, more of a representative of well-organized and institutionalized pressure groups.

The new political leaders came from the middle groups in society, as did their predecessors. But there was a real difference. A budding politician's rise to power no longer depended upon the favors and backing of the old oligarchy; rather it depended upon his influence over the urban population. This usually required that he sponsor programs of national renovation and social reform. Men like Colonel Juan Perón in Argentina demonstrated that political success might be won by demagogic appeals to the aspirations of urban masses.

The post-1930 era, particularly, was a time of rapid change, one that promised political reward to the shrewd and energetic who best knew how to exploit the new conditions. Such a man was Getulio Vargas, who came to power in the 1930 revolution in Brazil.

> If the early utterances of Vargas are carefully studied, it will be seen that, while he is in a way the typical Latin American "strong-man" looking for a "revolution" to bring him to power, at the same time he exhibits certain attitudes which are distinctly of his era, the era which followed the first World War and which saw the rise of fascism in Europe. What those who would make him out to be an "old-fashioned dictator" fail to realize is that the character of his regime is not a matter of personal temperament or choice with the dictator, but is determined for him by the socio-economic and political forces of his age.[16]

The new roads to power followed no consistent pattern. The top rungs of the political ladder could be reached by an economics professor such as Victor Paz Estenssoro in Bolivia (1952), a lawyer-politician like Arturo Frondizi in Argentina (1958), a bureaucrat such as Adolfo Ruíz Cortines in Mexico (1952), a novelist such as Rómulo Gallegos in Venezuela (1947), or a young army officer such as Major Arbenz in Guatemala (1950). But all of them had this in common: they claimed to represent the people and they treated social and economic problems as fundamental.

Sometimes the new leaders unleashed forces they could not control. The leaders of revolutionary Mexico, for example, had a most difficult time keeping unruly labor and military elements in line for a quarter-century after the 1910 revolution. And in Bolivia in 1952, immediate na-

[16] Samuel Putnam, "The Vargas Dictatorship in Brazil," *School and Society*, Spring 1941, p. 115.

tionalization of the tin mines was contrary to the original program of MNR leaders; they were forced to capitulate to popular pressures.

The significant new political fact was that the people were demanding a voice in government, and after 1930 they were getting it, as the result of a series of revolts and subsequent parliamentary advances. With this new voice, they demanded economic independence and progress, social justice, and political sovereignty. Government, they insisted, had to serve the humble as well as the great. The old oligarchies, quite naturally, resisted these demands and yielded only to overwhelming pressure.

The chief political vehicle for Latin America's awakening masses in the period from World War I to 1930 were middle-class parties, such as the Radicals of Argentina and Chile, the Colorados of Uruguay, and, to some extent, the Liberals of Colombia. After the great depression, however, labor-oriented parties rapidly became the chief challengers to the traditional political system in most Latin American countries. Following World War II, such parties held power, at least for a time, in Argentina, Bolivia, Brazil, Cuba, Costa Rica, Guatemala, Mexico, Uruguay, and Venezuela.

The labor-oriented parties were reform parties, and as such they had a certain appeal to the middle groups. To a large degree they and the middle-class parties had common programs.[17] Both were exponents of political democracy; they called for universal suffrage, secret ballots, free elections, an end to army intervention in politics, and genuine representative governments. Political practice, however, was not always in accord with party programs. Democratic ideals were often perverted into despotism by such labor-supported leaders as Presidents Calles in Mexico, Perón in Argentina and Arbenz in Guatemala, who proved to be as authoritarian as the old oligarchy.

Industrialization was the panacea of labor-oriented

[17] Robert J. Alexander, "Latin American Aprista Parties," *Political Science Quarterly*, July 1949, pp. 236-237.

parties, the only means of attaining economic independence, social equality, and a higher standard of living. Consequently, such governments went into the business of economic planning on a grand scale. In most countries they set up national development corporations to speed and direct the transformation of feudal agricultural societies into modern industrial states. Inevitably, the characteristic economic policies of these labor parties were nationalism, in dealing with foreign interests and asserting economic independence, and state socialism in subsidizing and building up domestic industry.

For the rural sector of the economy they demanded agrarian reform, the break-up of the latifundia system and distribution of land to the peons. Land reform, however, made little progress in the face of determined landlord resistance. Partial success was achieved only where violent social upheavals took place, as in Mexico and Bolivia. More often than not, efforts to launch agrarian reforms as in Venezuela in 1948 and Guatemala in 1954, led to revolution and the ouster of the reform government. Pro-labor governments found it much safer, after paying lip service to the need for land redistribution, to proceed with agricultural reform gradually through encouragement of diversification and the introduction of modern methods and machinery.

Claiming to represent the people, labor-oriented governments took it upon themselves to look after their charges. They sponsored broad programs of social security, and set aside increasing percentages of the national budget for public health and welfare. They introduced the concept of universal education, and, in vigorous efforts to reduce illiteracy, expanded school systems, especially in rural areas.

In the field of international relations, the labor-oriented parties, in contrast to the traditional parties, adopted vigorous policies. They demanded a larger role in international councils. Their anti-imperialism, a consequence of economic nationalism, struck hardest at Western Europe and the United States. Yet Latin American labor's opposition to totalitarian regimes demanded at least ideological identification with the foreign policies of the Western powers.

Foreign Ideologies

Although Latin America's new labor parties often showed a certain kinship with European revolutionary movements and ideologies, in essence they remained indigenous. Fascists and Communists, however, made determined efforts to use these popular and potentially strong groups as a means of gaining power for themselves.

What revolutionary foreign ideology Latin American leaders identified themselves with depended upon the times; they had to be flexible enough to make necessary changes. For example, in the early 1940's Paz Estenssoro and his comrades of the National Revolutionary Movement (MNR) in Bolivia were closely associated with fascism, but when they came to power a decade later, after the destruction of the Hitler and Mussolini regimes in World War II, their old European totalitarian associations had been conveniently discarded. Similarly, President Gabriel González Videla of Chile accepted the Communists' support in the 1946 elections, then turned against them in 1948 in order to cooperate with the United States and to receive United States aid.

Fascism enjoyed its Latin American heyday during the 1930's, when Hitler and Mussolini were flowering in Europe and when the great depression was building up pressure for reform everywhere. Significant Fascist movements appeared in Brazil (the Integralistas), Mexico (the Sinarquistas), Chile (the National Socialist party) and Uruguay (the Herreristas). During the early 1940's, the influence of Spanish fascism (General Francisco Franco's *Hispanidad* movement) was apparent in Argentina and Colombia. On the eve of World War II many strong-men such as Vargas of Brazil, Jorge Ubico of Guatemala, and Oscar Benavides of Peru displayed sympathetic affinity with the Axis powers; during the war the Peronist movement in Argentina and the Villaroel regime in Bolivia showed similar tendencies. With the defeat of the Axis powers in 1945, however, the Fascist threat as such vanished, although Perón and other dictators continued to make use of much they had learned from European fascism.

The Communist challenge was of longer duration than the Fascist, although it was never as serious. Communist parties began their activities in Latin America a few years after the Russian revolution of 1917. During the 1920's, they gained toe holds in several countries, usually in the embryonic labor movements. Their strength became significant in Chile, Brazil, and Uruguay during the 1930's. In the immediate postwar period, following wartime quiescence in line with Moscow's interests and instructions, the Communist drive took on new vigor. The Communists won 600,000 votes in the 1945 elections in Brazil and were a decisive factor in the elections of 1946 in Chile. In Cuba, in 1947, they nearly got control of the labor movement, and in Guatemala in the early 1950's they came close to taking over the government.

Except in Guatemala, however, the Communists never attained sufficient strength to make a serious bid for power. As of 1958, only in the major countries (Argentina, Brazil, Chile, and Mexico) and in Cuba were there sizable Communist parties, and in no country did they represent as much as 2 per cent of the voting population. Communist influence, however, was undoubtedly stronger than party membership would suggest.[18]

The Communists' chief strength was inside the labor movement, but they also developed a significant following

[18] In 1957, Communist party membership was estimated as follows: Argentina—50,000, Bolivia—3,000, Brazil—50,000, Chile—40,000, Colombia—5,000, Costa Rica—1,000, Cuba—30,000, Dominican Republic—negligible, Ecuador—5,000, El Salvador—1,000, Guatemala—1,000, Haiti—negligible, Honduras—500, Mexico—5,000, Nicaragua—500, Panama—500, Paraguay—2,000, Peru—5,000, Uruguay—5,000, and Venezuela—10,000. Source: U.S. House Committee on Foreign Affairs, *Mutual Security Act of 1957*, Hearings, 85th Cong., 1st sess., pt. 5 (Washington: GPO, 1957), p. 941.

among certain professional groups, particularly the intellectuals. Their strategy was to undermine the pre-eminent position of the United States in Latin America by backing nationalistic economic policies, encouraging anti-Yankee prejudices, and identifying the United States as the supporter of the traditional order of society and of predatory militarism. Meantime, posing as champions of the people they intrigued endlessly in order to capitalize on the political and social revolution that was in process throughout Latin America. Though by 1955 their party was outlawed in sixteen of the twenty countries, and though the Soviet diplomatic, cultural, and trade offensive was not notably successful, the Communists' drive for influence and power continued unflaggingly. The Latin American milieu still appeared propitious for the continued conduct and expansion of their subversive operations.

Significance of Revolutionary Change

Latin American pundits had long taught that broader-based governments and more evenly balanced political forces would bring stability. In fact, however, the emergence of new popular forces after 1930 brought greater instability. Argentina, Brazil, and Chile, for example, all relatively peaceful in the first quarter of the twentieth century, were unusually turbulent in the quarter-century following the great depression. To look at the most recent period, since 1954 successful revolutions toppled incumbent regimes in Guatemala (1954), Brazil (1954), Argentina (1955), Colombia (1956), Haiti (1956), Honduras (1956), Venezuela (1958) and Cuba (1959); during the same period presidents were assassinated in Panama (1955), Nicaragua (1956), and Guatemala (1957).

Such turmoil led some observers to remark that the more Latin America's politics changed the more it remained the same. How erroneous such an observation was became readily apparent when one penetrated beneath the political surface. After 1930, political instability in the Latin

American republics was far more fundamental than in the first century of their independence. True, personalistic politics and border disputes still contributed to political turmoil in the small republics of Central America and the Caribbean. They constituted, however, only a small minority of Latin America's total area and population. In most countries, palace-type rebellions were being superseded by broadly based revolutions, class conflicts that altered fundamentally the relations among the various groups in the society. The revolutions that occurred in Mexico in 1910, in Chile in 1925, in Argentina and Brazil in 1930, in Cuba in 1933, in Guatemala in 1944, in Venezuela in 1945, in Bolivia in 1952, and in Cuba in 1959 were reflections of radical economic change and deep social tensions. They signaled the crumbling of the traditional order.

Those who expected a sudden swing to democratic government to result from the emergence of these new popular political forces, however, were soon disappointed. Once in power, the new groups often felt it necessary to be most undemocratic, in order to maintain themselves in power against the intransigent opposition of the oligarchy and to carry out basic reforms. Perhaps it was impossible for genuine democracy to take root until the gulf between rich and poor had narrowed, until education had overcome illiteracy and made the masses of the people conscious of their political rights, duties, and responsibilities, until the various groups struggling for political control had compromised their differences and worked out a mutually acceptable concept of national aims and aspirations. Perhaps, as Cecil Jane wrote over a generation ago, despotism was temporarily a *sine qua non* in Latin America for reform and progress, and political liberty, prematurely achieved, was an invitation to economic stagnation, social disintegration, and political chaos.[19]

[19] Cecil Jane, *Liberty and Despotism in Latin America* (London: Clarendon Press, 1929), pp. 3, 14-15.

The extent to which the old order disintegrated varied greatly in the twenty Latin American republics. Using economic change, principally industrialization, as a measuring-stick, Chile, Argentina, Uruguay, Brazil, and Mexico were in the forefront. Then in the middle range of countries came Colombia, Cuba, Venezuela, Costa Rica, and Peru. In the remaining countries economic change was negligible.

Social upheaval, however, was not always related to industrialization. Only in Mexico and Bolivia, for example, were the old rural oligarchies destroyed, but they were strongly challenged by lower- and middle-income groups in Chile, Argentina, Brazil, Uruguay, Colombia, Cuba, Venezuela, Costa Rica and Peru. A more moderate, yet significant, threat from the lower social strata also appeared in Panama, Ecuador, Guatemala, and El Salvador. Only in Nicaragua, the Dominican Republic, and Paraguay were strong tensions lacking between aspiring new urban groups and the old oligarchy. Haiti and Honduras were unique in that landed oligarchies had never dominated their societies.

Sometimes, though by no means invariably, there was close correlation between political progress and socioeconomic change. Using the growth of democracy as a standard for measuring the coming of a new order, Uruguay, Chile, and Costa Rica ranked highest, followed by Mexico, Brazil, Argentina, Ecuador, and Bolivia.[20] None of the other twelve scored an appreciable advance in political progress.

The ways in which the old regime accommodated itself to the new order varied greatly. The most stubborn resistance came from the large landowners. Though their political control was gone, their economic power diminished, and their social monopoly broken, they successfully re-

20 See Russell H. Fitzgibbon, "Measurement of Latin American Political Phenomena: A Statistical Experiment," *American Political Science Review*, June 1951, pp. 517-523, for 1945 and 1950 ratings of ten experts.

sisted agrarian reform in all countries except Mexico and Bolivia.

The Catholic Church made a moderate accommodation to the new forces. The hierarchy, which at first tried to preserve the old system, was to some extent swayed by younger clergymen and Catholic laymen in bringing the church to adapt itself to the changing environment. To combat urban anticlericalism and to win support from organized labor, Christian Socialist parties were organized and Catholic trade-unions were set up in the major countries, particularly in the 1940's. In general, however, the power of the church as a political force declined after 1914. Yet the church proved to be an important factor in the resistance to, and the overthrow of, dictatorial regimes in Argentina in 1955, Colombia in 1957, and Venezuela in 1958, regimes which interfered with the liberty of the church as well as that of the people.

Finally, there are the armed forces to be considered. Their accommodation to the new order was by far the most profound and flexible of any of the three elements of the tripartite oligarchy. The evolution of the role of the military will be the central theme of the following chapters.

Chapter 3

THE ARMED FORCES AND THE SOCIAL REVOLUTION

In the crisis that has plagued Latin America since 1930 the role of the armed forces has followed broadly common lines in most of the countries of the area. As the pendulum swung from the traditional order to radical reform and back again, military officers appeared now on one side, now on the other, and were never very far from the seats of power. The great depression brought into sharp focus the conflicts between the traditional upper-group rulers and the new aspirants for power. Some army officers appeared on the scene as advocates of change. In the face of the threat from the left, however, in many countries the "oligarchs" willingly vacated the presidential palaces in favor of other army officers, the conservative generals on whom they counted to preserve the traditional order by force.

The trends were remarkably similar in so many countries, though differing often in their timing, that it is possible to discuss a general pattern between the role of the military and the developing social crisis. The span of three decades following the onset of the great depression may be divided into three main periods roughly as follows: (1) a period of unrest, coups and counter-coups, and generally unsuccessful challenges to the social order, from 1930 to the close of World War II; (2) a new cycle of revolt against the old order and social reform, marked in some cases by the appearance of a new civilian leadership and in others by a new type of military dictator, of which Juan Perón was the prototype, this period covering the decade following World War II; and (3) a period of reaction and counterrevolution, marked by a slowing or halting of the pace of social reform but also by the overthrow of some of the most oppressive dictatorships. This third period, which extended roughly from 1947 to 1957, overlapped the previous period, for the tide of social revolution began to recede in some countries before it had reached its crest in others, with elements of the armed forces generally engaged on both sides of the struggle. In the last few years Latin America seems to be entering still a different phase, one in which there are hopeful signs that social reform and political democracy may be able to move forward hand in hand. Here again the role of the military may be crucial, as it has been in the earlier periods.

Signs of the approaching crisis had been evident well before 1930, especially in the revolutionary experience of Mexico, where it took a generation after the outbreak of the revolution in 1911 to curb irresponsible military elements. In Chile in the 1920's the military attempted to arbitrate the developing social crisis. In September 1924, the Chilean army, which had long remained aloof from politics, stepped in to break the deadlock between the oligarchic Congress and the popularly-elected President, Arturo Alessandri. A few months later, a clique of young officers seized control of the armed forces and, shortly thereafter, of the government as well.[1] Major Carlos Ibáñez established a military dictatorship, and until the great depression this precursor of Perón was notably successful in combining authoritarian rule with policies aimed at meeting popular demands for greater social justice.

It was the depression, bringing the social crisis to a head nearly everywhere in Latin America, that provoked the general resurgence of militarism. In 1929, rightist military dictators were already in power in Cuba (Gerardo Ma-

[1] Alberto Edwards, *La fronda aristocrática: historia política de Chile* (Santiago: Editorial del Pacífico, 1952), pp. 259-264.

chado) and Venezuela (Juan Vicente Gómez). During the two following years eight more such regimes were set up. In Argentina, General José Uriburu, acting in behalf of the landed aristocracy, ousted President Hipólito Irigoyen's middle-of-the-road, civilian regime. Similar roles were played by Colonel Luís Sánchez Cerro in Peru, Colonel Luís Larrea Alba in Ecuador, General Carlos Blanco Galindo in Bolivia, and General Maximiliano Hernández Martínez in El Salvador. Attempted *coups d'état* nearly succeeded in Paraguay and Honduras. In Mexico, General Plutarco Elías Calles turned the left-of-center government to the right. By questionable electoral procedures, Generals Rafael Trujillo and Jorge Ubico took power in the Dominican Republic and Guatemala, respectively. In Chile, General Bartolomé Blanche Espejo and his colleagues forced Ibáñez into exile; in the period of unrest that followed, a group of army officers made common cause with the civilian Socialists to carry out a *coup d'état,* but after a brief period of radical reform was halted by a new rightist coup; a conservative reaction then set in and the Chilean military turned away from politics. In Nicaragua and Haiti at this time United States marines were still maintaining order. In the early 1930's, civilian-controlled governments existed only in Uruguay, Costa Rica, and Colombia.

Not all the influence of the military, however, was directed toward the support of the forms of conservatism. The revolts in Brazil (1930) and in Panama (1931) represented defeat for the traditional ruling groups, with the armed forces playing a decisive role although civilian politicians took the lead. The Cuban revolution that brought Fulgencio Batista to power in 1933 was unique in being a mutiny of the military rank and file, which toppled the old officer corps along with the government. Thenceforth, Batista and his noncommissioned cohorts, who became officers in the new army, ran Cuba and held the real power but saw to it that the new government was somewhat more attentive to the demands of previously neglected middle-

and lower-class groups. In both Paraguay and Bolivia, after the destructive Chaco War, successful but short-lived revolts took place during 1936 under the leadership of radical young officers inspired by ideas of social reform and authoritarian nationalism.

By the eve of World War II, however, the political picture in Latin America had generally reverted to the rightist-authoritarian pattern. The brief flurry of military-political radicalism that had appeared in a minority of the Latin American countries seemed to have spent its force. When the war broke out in Europe more than half the twenty republics were ruled by conservative military men: Bolivia (General Carlos Quintanilla), the Dominican Republic (General Trujillo), Ecuador (General P. Alberto Rodríguez), Guatemala (General Ubico), Honduras (General Tiburcio Carías), Nicaragua (General Anastasio Somoza), Peru (Marshall Oscar Benavides), El Salvador (General Martínez), Venezuela (General Eleazar López Contreras) and Paraguay (General Félix Estigarribia). Traditionalist civilian regimes, maintained in office by the armed forces, prevailed in Argentina, Panama and Haiti, and the army-backed Vargas and Batista dictatorships remained entrenched in Brazil and Cuba respectively. Thus the armed forces were playing key political roles in all the Latin American countries at this time except Chile, Colombia, Costa Rica, Uruguay, and Mexico. In the latter two countries, popularly elected military men (Generals Alfredo Baldomir and Lázaro Cárdenas) held sway.

The net effect of the war upon Latin American politics was to freeze traditionalist regimes in power as long as the security of the hemisphere was threatened. The wartime emergency provided dictatorial regimes with justification for outlawing political experimentation and major social or economic reform for the duration. Also, the United States, whose overriding consideration was strategic, did its best to maintain stability in Latin America, sought the cooperation of incumbent regimes which were willing to help the war effort, and provided them with military and economic aid.

Yet the war produced pressures that made the maintenance of the *status quo* progressively more difficult. The outbreak of hostilities in Europe seriously disturbed Latin America's economy. The immediate shock, due to the transportation squeeze, was felt in shortages, particularly of manufactured goods, but also of foodstuffs. The sudden interruption of imports from the United States and from Europe gave a great new impetus to industrialization, a trend stimulated by financial assistance from the United States. Despite wartime shortages of labor and equipment, Latin America's industrial establishment grew by leaps and bounds. New installations included steel mills, textile mills, paper mills, chemical factories, food-processing plants, highways, shipyards, and airfields.

Wartime prosperity, however, was not broadly based. Governments froze wages, prohibited strikes, even outlawed labor movements in some countries. The hardships suffered by the middle- and lower-income groups intensified social stresses and strains. It was merely a matter of time before popular pressures would again break through the dikes, bringing in a flood of political and social changes. Civilian foes of the *status quo* were joined by young officers.

The first breakthrough was the seizure of power in Argentina by Colonel Juan Perón and his colleagues in 1943. A new revolt in Bolivia later in that year was obviously an echo of the events in Buenos Aires, as well as a recrudescence of the radical junior-officer movement of the 1930's. The influence of *Peronismo* was to spread further northward in the next decade, affecting many countries of the Caribbean and Central America. Meanwhile, other and more democratic influences were making themselves felt. With the fall of totalitarian dictatorship in Italy and its impending destruction in Germany and Japan, authoritarian regimes were bound to seem anachronistic in Latin America, and a new burst of enthusiasm for popular democracy, added to the economic and social pressures, helped to topple many of the authoritarian regimes, even some of the more progressive ones. In 1944, traditionalist governments were overthrown in Ecuador and in Guatemala by popular revolutions led by young officers. Batista's power as *de facto* ruler of Cuba disappeared when his candidate lost to a popular coalition in the 1944 elections. In 1945 Vargas was forced to step down in Brazil mainly because of the army's prodding and popular pressures. Strong reform-minded parties came to power in Venezuela and in Peru in that same year. Later manifestations of the same trend were the revolutions of 1948 in El Salvador and Costa Rica and that of 1952 in Panama, the profound social upheaval that took place in Bolivia in 1952, and the Colombian army's coup which ousted the extreme right-wing regime of Laureano Gómez in 1953.

Colombia's revolution ended Latin America's postwar cycle of popular reform, generally through violent change. Twelve Latin American nations, containing 75 per cent of the population of the area, experienced it in varying degrees in the 1943-1953 decade. Five minor countries (Dominican Republic, Nicaragua, Paraguay, Honduras and Haiti) did not. In the Dominican Republic and Nicaragua, traditionalist *caudillos* in power ever since the early 1930's continued to hold sway. While Paraguay had briefly experienced a reform movement led by young officers following the Chaco War, such tendencies were subsequently kept under effective control by the partisans of the traditional order. In Haiti and Honduras, although the problems of poverty were enormous, the class structure was ill defined and social revolution did not break out. Reform-minded regimes held power in Mexico, Chile, and Uruguay, but in these countries the political role of the armed forces was not a determining one.

By 1953 the cycle of revolution and reform had already been overlapped by a new cycle of counterrevolution. As early as 1947, when the wave of social change seemed to be carrying all before it, political currents in some countries began to flow in the other direction. Sensing the threat of demagoguery, violence and extremism, the rising middle-class groups lost some of their enthusiasm for reform, as did many of the military officers. Traditionalist groups seized opportunities to reassert themselves. The reaction thus generated continued for an entire decade, until nearly every government of the reformist type had either been overturned or forced to adopt a more moderate course.

The seizure of power by Colonel Marcos Pérez Jiménez and his army friends in Venezuela and by General Manuel Odría in Peru, both in 1948, marked the beginning of the drift back to the right. El Salvador's "revolution" of 1948 petered out within a few years. Haiti and Cuba felt the effects of resurgent militarism in 1950 and 1952 respectively, although these were autonomous military seizures of power rather than counterrevolutions in the social sense. In Guatemala the revolt of 1954, which saved the country from the Communists, restored much of the old order. In Brazil, Vargas' apparent scorn for constitutional limitations and his emulation of Perón in demagogic appeals for the support of the masses led the army to force his resignation in 1954. Not long after, in 1955, came the assassination of Colonel José Antonio Remón in Panama and the fall of Perón himself, to be followed two years later by that of Colombia's strong-man, General Gustavo Rojas Pinilla. In all three cases the dictator was succeeded by a regime largely representative of the traditional ruling groups.

In this trend to the right, as in the trend to the left, the armed forces were cast in a leading role. Generally they stepped in, at the behest either of the oligarchy or of the frightened middle class, to halt further leftward evolution. Reformist rulers often lost a measure of popular support because of their methods or because they failed to deliver on demagogic promises. Yet there was no uniform desertion of them by the people. No true test took place at the polls. What generally happened was that the military intervened when either they themselves or civilian groups which had won their support were sufficiently provoked by the new leaders' softness toward organized labor, deliberate efforts to widen existing social cleavages, or irresponsible, undemocratic, and in some cases totalitarian methods of government. Often the military unmade the very revolutions they themselves had launched several years before.

That the drift to the right was not of purely military origin was evident from the appearance of similar political trends in countries where the military had become nonpolitical. In Mexico, under Presidents Miguel Alemán (1946-1952) and Adolfo Ruiz Cortines (1952-1958), the social revolution seemed to have slowed down or even halted. Even the radical government in Bolivia became more moderate after consolidating its position and after United States economic aid began flowing into the country in 1954. The 1958 elections in Costa Rica, Chile and Uruguay indicated that a conservative trend was still running in Latin America.

To assess the significance of the changing picture in these last three decades it is necessary to examine in some detail what role the military played in individual countries, taking note of differences that were of more than surface importance. An attempt will be made to explain and analyze the actions of the armed forces in each of twelve countries where they have played determining roles in the process of social and political change since World War II. The case of Mexico, where prewar developments were in many ways unique, but still of great importance as an example to the rest of Latin America, will be dealt with in detail in a separate chapter.

Argentina

General José Uriburu, installed as president following the revolution which overthrew the government of Irigoyen in 1930, at first relied principally on the armed forces and on the conservative landowning interests. Yet he and some officers began to doubt whether the armed forces could indefinitely conduct a holding action against an increasingly antagonistic public opinion. Influenced by Fascist writings, Uriburu attempted to set up a kind of corporate state based on a range of interests broader than those of the landowners. He was unable, however, to get support from the conservative groups, military and civilian, which had backed the 1930 revolution. After a year of futile effort, he was forced to hold elections which were won by General Augustín P. Justo. A firm supporter of the old landholding oligarchy, President Justo allowed the *estancieros* to take over administrative control of the government while the army stood guard to insure their dominance.[2]

The following years saw many efforts, none of them successful, on the part of other groups to gain or regain a voice in national politics corresponding to their growing economic and social importance. At the same time the tensions in Argentine society were heightened as the result of the war in Europe and the influence of foreign ideologies. The break finally came when restive elements in the army itself seized the initiative. In June 1943, the Group of United Officers (GOU), a colonels' clique led by Juan Perón, seized control of the armed forces and toppled the conservative government of President Ramón S. Castillo. The motives of the GOU were many. They had become disgusted with complacent generals and their alliance with the landed oligarchy in a political system they regarded as highly unsuited to Argentina's real needs. They also felt that the Castillo government had neglected the armed forces, had been indifferent to their needs for modern equipment, more men, and better pay. Many of the colonels were inspired by the initial triumphs of Fascist regimes in Europe.

With respect to the new military government's policies, there was initially a considerable variety of opinion and

2 Arthur P. Whitaker, *The United States and Argentina* (Cambridge: Harvard University Press, 1954), p. 60; George I. Blanksten, *Perón's Argentina* (Chicago: University of Chicago Press, 1953), p. 37.

a great deal of confusion. The jockeying for power amongst the victorious rebels continued for nearly two years before Perón emerged supreme and Argentine domestic and foreign policy became more clearly defined. From the very beginning of the revolt, however, one thing was certain. This was going to be a military government. The armed forces were going to run it and reap the benefits. A GOU manifesto, circulated a month before the revolution, stated:

> The first step to be taken, which shall lead us toward a strong and powerful Argentina, is to get the reins of government into our hands. Civilians will never understand the greatness of our ideal; we shall therefore have to eliminate them from the government and give them the only mission which corresponds to them: work and obedience.[3]

Accordingly, nearly all the cabinet posts, as well as the top administrative positions on both federal and provincial levels, were manned by officers in the armed forces.

In accordance with the GOU program, a huge military build-up began immediately. Appropriations for the armed forces in 1944 were nearly one billion pesos, more than double the amount spent in the last full year of the Castillo administration. In 1945, they amounted to nearly a billion and a half, a sum larger than the entire government revenue for that year. "Military rearmament," declared Perón in 1944, "is the objective to which the entire economy of the country and the life of all its people must be dedicated. If diplomacy cannot attain the political objectives decided upon, then the government will undertake to achieve them by force." [4]

The intended use of the new war machine was made clear by an earlier GOU manifesto:

> In South America, there are only two nations sufficiently big and strong enough to undertake leadership—Argentina and Brazil. It is our mission to make the leadership of Argentina

[3] Quoted in Blanksten, cited, p. 48.

[4] Stephan Naft, "Fascism's Newest Face," *American Mercury*, September 1947, pp. 285-287.

not only possible but indisputable. . . . Alliances will be our next step, Paraguay is already with us. We will get Bolivia and Chile. Together and united with these countries, it will be easy to exert pressure on Uruguay. These five nations can easily attract Brazil, due to its type of government and its important groups of Germans. Once Brazil has fallen, the South American continent will be ours.[5]

The realities of the new situation after World War II, however, were sufficient to deter even the most irrational of Argentina's advocates of "manifest destiny," and with the ascendancy of Perón as dictator at the end of 1945, the military build-up and the muscle-flexing abated. In the four years between 1945 and 1949, the size of the army was reduced by one-third (to 70,000), and the armed forces' share of the budget was cut to 25 per cent (down from just over 50 per cent in 1945).[6] By 1950, the building of military factories, barracks, and other installations had come to a virtual standstill. Meanwhile, the cabinet was progressively changed into a civilian body, and nonmilitary men once more began taking over other political offices.

The moving genius behind this de-emphasis upon things military was Perón himself, who, by gradually gathering popular civilian support, had made himself increasingly independent of his brothers in arms. Perón, alone among the 1943 revolutionary leaders, had been fully aware of the shift in the balance of economic power from the rural landowners to the urban industrialists and to labor. He was skillful enough to utilize the political potential of these latter groups. It was labor that had rescued him from a military purge in October of 1945, and once back in power he deliberately built up and used the trade-unions as a counterpoise to the armed forces, to deprive the latter of the role of sole arbiter of the political process. He armed and equipped and organized a workers' militia that was numerically stronger than the regular army, and

[5] Quoted in Robert J. Alexander, *The Perón Era* (London: Gollancz, 1952), p. 12.

[6] Same, pp. 118-119.

he built up a large national police force. Perón's aim was to be independent of all three groups, to manipulate and control them, to play one off against the other in such a way as to enhance his own power.[7]

Because Perón's supremacy was never so complete that he could ignore the army, he sought to weaken its power by corrupting its leaders with privileges and wealth. He made professional advancement dependent on loyalty to himself. Officers who played his game obtained lucrative administrative offices and quick promotions. Officers' pay was raised to unprecedented heights after 1945; by 1949 it was higher than in any other Latin American country. Special privileges for the favored included opportunities for graft in connection with government contracts, and licenses to import automobiles duty-free.[8]

While Perón was thus softening up the officer corps, he was trying at the same time to undercut their authority and influence. He encouraged rivalry among the three branches of the service. "So long as their surplus energies are used up in fighting one another, they won't have the strength to bother me much," he is reported to have said. The better to control the young officers, he took the power to appoint cadets out of military hands and placed it under the control of the Peronista political party. And he moved this monolithic organization into the barracks to convert the enlisted personnel into loyal political supporters.[9] All these efforts, however, successful as they were in prolonging the regime's life, created restlessness and resentment in the armed forces without decisively breaking their ultimate power to destroy it. And in the end Perón, who owed

[7] George Pendle, *Argentina* (London: Royal Institute of International Affairs, 1955), p. 74; Whitaker, cited, pp. 142, 170.

[8] Ernesto Sammartino, *La verdad sobre la situación argentina* (Montevideo, 1950), pp. 250-252; Silvano Santander, *Nazismo en Argentina: la conquista del ejército* (Montevideo: Pueblos Unidos, 1945), pp. 171-172; Alexander, cited, p. 118.

[9] James Bruce, *Those Perplexing Argentines* (New York: Longmans, Green, 1953), pp. 302-313; *Hispanic American Report,* March 1949, p. 19; Whitaker, cited, p. 141.

his original access to power to the armed forces, fell from power through a revolt organized and led by military officers.

Resistance to Perón had always been strongest in the navy, whose democratic traditions conflicted with Perón's increasing authoritarianism. The naval officer corps, unlike that of the army, tended to come from the rural oligarchy and the wealthier urban families, and hence was hostile to any regime bent on upsetting the nation's basic institutions. So unsympathetic was the navy to the GOU and its program, even in the very beginning, that the government after the 1943 revolution could find no high-ranking naval officer willing to accept the post of navy minister until March of 1944. As early as February of 1944 the navy launched a conspiracy to oust the Farrell-Perón regime. In August and September of 1945, high-ranking navy men were demanding and petitioning that Perón not be allowed to assume the presidency and that the "sovereignty of the people" be restored. And in October of that year the bulk of the navy joined a disgruntled army group that nearly succeeded in ousting Perón. Suppressed but not extinguished, the navy's resentment continued to smoulder as the regime lavished funds on the ground forces while refusing to purchase new naval combat units.[10]

Nor were the army and the air force by any means united behind Perón. After the 1943 revolt, high-ranking officers of the Castillo regime were purged, or retired and pensioned. A similar fate befell the anti-GOU colonels who had attempted during 1944 and 1945 to block the rise of Perón. Between 1946 and 1950, army and air force leaders, favored by Perón, willingly cooperated with him in making the Argentine government more nationalistic and authoritarian. However, as the powerful Peronista party and the militant central labor organization became increasingly important props under the dictatorship, the military,

[10] *New York Times,* March 1 and 2, 1944; Blanksten, cited, pp. 59, 312-316; Sammartino, cited, p. 249.

whose hitherto exclusive power position was being progressively undermined, became restless. Also, the devoted, nonpolitical professional officers were obviously irked by Perón's blatant attempts to make political instruments out of both the officer corps and the enlisted men.

When Evita Perón, noted for meddling in army affairs and for her pro-labor attitude, became a candidate for the vice-presidency in 1951, progressive disaffection in the armed forces came to a head. Still unappeased, even after they forced her to quit the race, rebel officers staged a revolt, which was led by retired generals but participated in by active officers in all three branches of the service. Lack of coordination among the rebel leaders, plus reluctance on the part of "Peronized" noncommissioned officers to join the conspiracy, saved the dictator. Leaders of the uprising were promptly purged, and an obedient congress granted Perón extraordinary powers over the promotion and retirement of all officers.[11]

Although he had successfully met the armed forces' challenge, Perón, for a variety of reasons, began to alter his policies after his re-election in November 1951. The military uprising, the economic crisis of 1951-1952, Evita's death in 1952—all these elements contributed to the moderation of Perón's extreme pro-labor policies. Offsetting his declining dependence upon the labor prop, Perón's respect for and cooperation with the armed forces grew. He now gave unusual attention to the demands of the navy. In 1952 Argentina purchased two light cruisers from the United States and the following year engaged a Japanese firm to build destroyers and frigates. Also, following his *rapprochement* with the United States in 1953, Perón demonstrated signs of willingness to sign a Mutual Defense Assistance Pact in order to meet the armed forces' demands for sufficient equipment to keep the Argentine military establishment at least on a par with Brazil's. In

[11] *New York Times*, September 29, 1951; *Hispanic American Report*, September 1951, pp. 28-29; Whitaker, cited, pp. 161-162.

addition, the numerical strength of the army began rising again after 1951.[12]

Despite this new catering to demands of the military, Perón's intractable opponents, especially in the navy, were not mollified. Also, his policy of moderation weakened the labor counterpoise. Further, the hundreds of purged officers were awaiting an opportunity for revenge. It came in mid-1955 at the height of Perón's feud with the Catholic Church. A June uprising nearly toppled the regime; a better coordinated movement three months later, in which all three services as well as retired officers and civilian commandos participated, accomplished the task. In a three-day revolt, the armed forces finally ended Perón's ten-year domination.

Politically, the September 1955 revolution, inasmuch as it toppled a dictatorial regime, was a liberating action. Socially, however, inasmuch as a heretofore labor-oriented government was now replaced by one supported by the middle and upper income groups in the society, it could be described as a counterrevolution.

General Eduardo Lonardi headed the new provisional government. He and many other officers forced into retirement by Perón now returned to active duty, and many Peronista officers, in turn, were retired. A military government was set up; an all-officer *junta* took charge in Buenos Aires, and military interventors took over the provinces. The heterogeneous groups that had united against Perón, however, were soon fighting amongst each other for control of the new regime. Lonardi, attempting to follow a moderate policy, was attacked for his hesitation in "de-Peronizing" the army and for his alleged favoritism of reactionary Catholic elements in the provisional government. Young officers led a new coup in November 1955 which ousted Lonardi and set up a new military *junta* headed by Provisional President General Pedro Aramburu.

This *junta,* however, was not exclusively an army re-

12 Whitaker, cited, pp. 230-231; *Hispanic American Report,* August 1953, p. 35.

gime such as took power in 1943. The navy, led by Admiral Isaac Rojas, had two of the five members of the *junta,* and the air force had one. The Aramburu regime energetically "de-Peronized" both the armed forces and the civilian political administration. But it was plagued by serious factionalism within the army and by intense rivalry amongst the three services. The army was torn by feuds between groups of junior and senior officers and by the conflicting ambitions of politically minded individuals. The navy, as a result, assumed unaccustomed influence, and the air force, too, gained in prestige.

In the continuing jockeying for power within and among the services, Aramburu showed a remarkable capacity to survive crisis after crisis. This he did by maintaining a thoroughly professional, nonpolitical attitude. His aim was to get the armed forces out of politics, to restore the military to its proper role of defending the country and preserving internal order. Overcoming seemingly insuperable obstacles, he progressed beyond all expectations along the rocky road to restoring civilian government in Argentina. The 1958 elections were conducted on schedule and normal constitutional processes were restored as the military *junta* transferred political control to a civilian regime headed by Dr. Arturo Frondizi.

Brazil

In Brazil, the young officers, the so-called *tenentes,* who came to power in the Vargas revolution of 1930, had begun their agitation for socio-political change soon after World War I. The discontent of the *tenentes* to some extent was a reflection of the nation-wide discontent of rising industrialists, professional groups, and urban labor over the rural and regionalist political domination of the wealthy states of Minas Gerais and São Paulo. Under this political system, the national army was subordinate to the armed police of the states. Also, the promotion-hungry *tenentes,* many of them trained by a French military mission, thought the senior officers were incompetent and insufficiently attentive to the junior officers' individual needs, as well as to those of the military organization.[13]

One *tenente* uprising occurred in 1922 in the Rio de Janeiro garrison in protest against the obviously manipulated election of President Artur Bernardes. Loyal troops, with some difficulty, crushed this movement, but a far more serious challenge occurred in 1924 when the young officers captured the key city of São Paulo. When senior officers crushed their uprising, the retreating young officers thereupon formed a guerrilla organization, which for three years harassed the central government from one end of Brazil to the other. This was the famous column led by Captain Luiz Carlos Prestes. The triumph of the rebellious *tenente* minority was finally achieved in 1930 when, joining forces with other defecting officers, they took part in the Rio Grande do Sul rebellion led by Vargas.

The *tenentes* were the most radical element in the new regime. Though the main body of the army was still controlled by high-ranking regulars, Vargas placed the *tenentes* in charge of many state governments, a move which caused considerable concern over a possible social revolution. The *tenentes,* however, were a radical minority in an essentially moderate coalition. For the Vargas revolution, though it represented a shift in the locus of power, was not actually a social revolution. Frustrated in their initial efforts to make it one, the *tenentes* began to lose their zeal for reform and were gradually reincorporated into the regular army. By threats of military intervention, they helped Vargas force the 1934 constitution through a procrastinating civilian constituent assembly, and in 1937 they quietly acquiesced when the dictator set up his semi-Fascist corporate state.[14]

13 General Eurico Gaspar Dutra, *O exército em dez anos do govêrno do presidente Vargas* (Rio de Janeiro: D. I. P., 1941), pp. 19-22.

14 Robert J. Alexander, "Brazilian Tenantismo," in *Hispanic American Historical Review,* May 1956, pp. 229-238; Lourival Coutinho, *O General Goes depoe* (Rio de Janeiro: Coelho Branco, 1956), pp. 240-243.

After the ousting of Vargas at the close of World War II, General Eurico Gaspar Dutra's government (1945-1950), either unaware of, or indifferent to, the nation's changing social realities, did virtually nothing to alleviate the economic hardships suffered by growing lower middle-class and labor groups. In fact, both the main political organizations, the Social Democratic party (PSD) and the opposing Democratic National Union (UDN), controlled by traditionalist elements, also ignored the mounting social problem. Nor did the armed forces show any great cognizance of it.

The man who recognized the political potential of the new social classes was the former president, Getulio Vargas. Resorting to demagogic techniques, he posed as the champion of the downtrodden, launched a new organization, the Brazilian Labor party, and began his comeback. The chief opposition candidate in the election of 1950, the one naturally favored by the armed forces, was General Eduardo Gomes of the UDN. Thus the 1950 elections became a severe test of the military's alleged devotion to constitutional processes. For Vargas was the man they had deposed in 1945; now he threatened to return to power at the head of a movement pledged to alter drastically the social and economic structure of the country, to transform its basic institutions. In a campaign conducted amidst threats and rumors of military coups, Vargas won and was allowed to take office.

Four years later, the armed forces of Brazil, backed by alarmed conservatives, intervened to oust his reform-minded regime. Though the generals had permitted him to assume the presidency in 1950, they had also kept an extremely short rein on him. Faced with a moderate-conservative opposition majority in Congress, he was powerless, by constitutional means, to deliver on his campaign promises. When his radical young labor minister, Jango Goulart, attempted to stir the workers to action early in 1954, the army stepped in and forced his dismissal. As the country's economic deterioration and political stagnation continued, Vargas tried desperately to intrigue his way out of his constitutional limitations by manipulating strikes and by directing the pressure of the masses against existing institutions. But the generals became increasingly restless. Late in 1954, after an air corps major had been killed, apparently by one of the president's henchmen, the army stepped in and forced Vargas to resign, whereupon he committed suicide.

The government then passed into the hands of the caretaker administration of Vice-President João Café Filho while the nation prepared for the 1955 elections. Conservative civilian and military leaders apparently expected Café Filho to suppress the radical labor and lower-middle political forces that the Vargas administration had unleashed, but he did nothing of the sort. He chose to leave the decision to the electorate. The election campaign was conducted in an atmosphere of political and social tension unequaled in Brazil's entire history. The armed forces and the traditional ruling groups hoped that party leaders would see the folly of Vargas' catering to lower-income groups, and instead join in supporting a respectable compromise candidate who would pose no threat to Brazil's traditional order.

In early January, Governor Juscelino Kubitschek of Minas Gerais was nominated by the moderate PSD. A former backer of the discredited Vargas regime, he was unacceptable to the armed forces. When, ignoring military disapproval, he refused to withdraw from the campaign, the traditional ruling forces in the moderate-conservative UDN party nominated General Juárez Távora, then one of the high chiefs in Café Filho's military household. In the spring of 1955 Kubitschek's PSD and the Brazilian Labor party (PTB) formed a coalition. Goulart became Kubitschek's running-mate. War Minister General Henrique Teixeira Lott, who had previously warned the colonels and generals against intervening in the campaign, now warned the PSD-PTB politicians that he could no longer be responsible for the army's actions if they persisted in their efforts to make Goulart vice-president.

In October 1955, after the Kubitschek-Goulart ticket emerged narrowly victorious, tensions in the armed forces reached a breaking-point. A military coup to prevent the Kubitschek-Goulart inauguration appeared inevitable. At this critical juncture Café Filho resigned. The presidency then devolved upon House Speaker Carlos Luz, who was known to be highly unsympathetic to the winning candidates. Luz promptly dismissed Lott as war minister, whereupon the latter seized control in order to prevent an expected military coup and to ensure the inauguration of Kubitschek and Goulart. He quelled incipient navy and army uprisings by arresting the leading rebellious officers.[15]

Constitutional processes were thus guaranteed and Kubitschek's inauguration ensured by Lott and the army. The new president, however, with the majority of the officers and the bulk of the conservative groups against him, was extremely dependent upon his military saviors. As a reward, they demanded, successfully, a near doubling of their pay soon after his inauguration. In obvious fear of the army, the Kubitschek administration refrained from encouraging the leftist political movement. Military opposition also seriously hindered Kubitschek's attempts to free the nation's economy from retarding nationalistic and monopolistic restrictions.

Bolivia

The long, destructive Chaco War and the unpopular peace terms helped precipitate a revolution that in 1936 brought a clique of radical young officers to power in Bolivia. Major David Toro and Colonel Germán Busch successively headed regimes that had social revolution as their goals. Nationalism was the prop behind these authoritarian

[15] The narrative and interpretation of 1955 events was constructed from the running account of the presidential election campaign carried in the *New York Times* from January 29 to November 12.

and demagogic but reform-minded governments. They catered to the downtrodden and pledged to build for them a new, modern nation. Toro and Busch based their dictatorial regimes on attempts to win mass support, but they were in no sense orthodox Fascists. Cárdenas and Vargas, not Hitler and Mussolini, set the example for them. These precursors of Perón ruled less than two years, but in that short time they revealed the potential power of an alliance of the military with popular forces.

After a five-year interlude of rule by traditionalist forces, a new junior officers' movement led by Major Gualberto Villaroel seized power in December 1943 with a program very similar to Perón's. As in Argentina, the idealistic young officers claimed to be leading the masses against the "domestic oligarchy" and the "foreign imperialists," and their movement was authoritarian and even Fascist in form, social and even proletarian in content. It represented a resurrection of the abortive social revolution of 1936-1938. This time, however, the young officers had the firm backing of labor and middle-group elements represented in the popular National Revolutionary Movement (MNR). Villaroel and the MNR head, Victor Paz Estenssoro, made war upon the "tin barons" and the landlords by launching a revolutionary program of social reform.

They did not, however, hold power very long. Using methods of violence and terror, the Villaroel regime did not endear itself to the Bolivian people, nor, being regarded as an offspring of the Perón dictatorship in Argentina, had it won much good will in the rest of the hemisphere. It was overthrown in 1946 in a bloody revolt in La Paz led by senior army officers. But the ensuing period of traditionalist rule was only an interval before a new revolution brought the MNR to the top once more.

Paz Estenssoro won the presidential elections of 1951. Threatened with the loss of power to radical forces from the left, President Mamerto Urriolagoitia made a desperate attempt to save the oligarchy by turning over power to a military *junta*. At this juncture the MNR began arming the workers, engineered the defection of the police, and in the revolution of April 1952 completely routed the army. The armed forces, which had remained loyal to the oligarchy, were now disbanded and in their stead the successful rebels were organized into a new army. To make certain that it did not get out of hand, as had occurred in Mexico, the workers' militia retained their arms and the police forces were thoroughly reorganized and strengthened. The wisdom of this policy from the standpoint of the regime was demonstrated when the new army made several attempts to intervene in political affairs. In each case the police and civilian militia prevented the resurrection in Bolivia of the political power of military leaders.

Meanwhile a sweeping social revolution began. The mines of the foreign and local tin barons were nationalized in October 1952, and in 1953 a beginning was made in the expropriation of large land-holdings and their distribution to the peasants. Labor was given special favors, and the familiar pattern of economic nationalism and state socialism soon made its appearance.

Peru

The ferment which followed World War II in so many Latin American countries also became apparent in Peru, long ruled by its traditional upper class. Here the armed forces did not lead the revolution, but their neutral attitude did allow popular groups to come to the fore. The reformist APRA (Alianza Popular Revolucionaria Americana) helped elect a middle-of-the-road president, José Luís Bustamante, in 1945. But he soon found himself caught between two extremist forces. The Apristas, who were urging drastic reforms, had a plurality in Congress, but the conservative opposition brought the legislative machinery to a standstill by refusing to form a quorum. Bustamante was in sympathy with reform, but he opposed APRA's demagoguery and the totalitarian tendencies of its leaders. He also understood the oligarchy and was well aware of its determination to maintain the *status quo*. He therefore tried to carry on with a military cabinet.

When the inevitable deadlock occurred, APRA and the oligarchy, both realizing that the dilemma would be resolved by force, began conspiring with the armed forces, the former with the senior officers, the latter with the junior officers and the enlisted men. General Manuel Odría, minister of interior, demanded that the Aprista party be outlawed, that its press be closed, that its leaders be imprisoned or exiled. When Bustamante refused, the military cabinet resigned and the senior officers began to conspire against him, egged on by the wealthy land-holders and exporters through the rightist press. APRA countered by instigating an abortive naval mutiny led by the petty officers, an action which brought the crisis to a head. On October 27, 1948, the key army garrision at Arequipa, under the leadership of General Odría, revolted. The Lima garrison, under General Zenón Noriega, joined in two hours later. The air force and the navy stood passively by while General Odría seized power and set up a military dictatorship.[16]

Odría's traditionalist sympathies were revealed when he explained that

> the fundamental reason for the existence of the revolutionary government I head is to eliminate the sectarian danger [i.e., APRA] that for more than twenty years, under four past regimes, has done nothing but commit crimes of every order against individuals and institutions. *Aprismo* has . . . threatened the individual, the family, and the home, the school and church, the military and civilian institutions, and the nation itself. APRA threatens the fundamental basis of the home, poisons the mind of the child and the youth, setting them up against their parents and their leaders, filling them with rebelliousness and insolence and contempt for the wis-

[16] José Luís Bustamante, *Tres años de lucha por la democracia en el Perú* (Buenos Aires: Bartolomé U. Chiesino, 1949), pp. 131-142, 246-279.

dom and experience upon which the greatness of a nation rests.[17]

He also charged that Bustamante had committed an unpardonable crime, that of deliberately trying to weaken the power and prestige of the armed forces, to reduce their numbers, and to undermine their unity. Bustamante argued that he reduced the army because its expansion in World War II had left it more than adequate for its mission in the postwar period. He had also tried to put the armed forces to work, to use them on public works and agricultural projects, so that they might participate in the economic development of the country. His worst mistake was his attempt to impose a cut in the military budget.[18] Odría held power for eight years, during which the armed forces increased their customary lion's share of the national budget and the oligarchy was secure in its dominant economic position.

Ecuador

As early as the 1920's, the Chilean example showed the way for idealistic young Ecuadorian officers to intervene in behalf of the people against the oligarchy. Frustrated labor and middle-class leaders joined forces with the conspiratorial Liga Militar, which conducted a successful coup in July 1925.[19] What appeared to be a broadly based revolution, however, turned out to be just another palace revolt, for the young military leaders soon forgot their great plans for complete renovation and reorganization of the nation. Instead, under the government of Dr. Isidro Ayora, they were content to enjoy the privileges and emoluments of political power.

It was not until May 1944, just before scheduled presidential elections, that the political thaw came to Ecuador,

[17] Quoted in Germán Arciniegas, *The State of Latin America* (New York: Knopf, 1952), pp. 84-85.

[18] Bustamante, cited, pp. 267-270.

[19] General Angel I. Chiriboga, *Fuerzas morales en el ejército* (Quito: Imprenta Nacional, 1932), pp. 50-54.

where the oligarchy had been in firm control since 1930. General Larrea Alba, who had won his spurs in the revolution of July 7, 1925, yielding to pressure from junior officers and to popular demand, forced President Arroyo del Río's resignation, set up a *junta* and invited José María Velasco Ibarra, presumably the people's choice, to take over the presidency. Captain Sergio Enrique Girón, one of the leading conspirators at the key Guayaquil garrison, explained:

We, the military men who made this revolution, did not receive orders from anybody. . . . Nobody was director, nobody was chief. . . . We did not subvert order. We transformed it. We did not make a barracks revolt. We made a true revolution, supported and inspired by the people, to whom we belong and whom we obey. . . . We, the men of the people, captured the government and set up a popular regime, the most democratic in this America.[20]

Then, late in 1947, the armed forces decided the time had come to save the country from what they regarded as the demagogic rule of Velasco Ibarra. He was unceremoniously ejected, whereupon a national unity coalition elected the more moderate Galo Plaza Lasso to the presidency. Subsequently the turbulence in Ecuador subsided, mainly because the social question, which had loomed so important, was declared out of bounds as a political issue. Several attempts to revive it failed to find broad support from the young officers. President Plaza, who held office from 1948 to 1952, maintained that the conspiracies of 1949 and 1951 against him failed because the armed forces "had adopted a new, responsible and patriotic attitude, . . . that they were no longer straying from the straight and narrow path of defense of their country and its constitution." [21]

Actually, political calm came to Ecuador because the armed forces no longer intervened to resolve the social

[20] See his *Revolución de mayo* (Quito: Editorial Atahualpa, 1945), pp. 10, 54-55, 122.

[21] Galo Plaza Lasso, *Problems of Democracy in Latin America* (Chapel Hill: University of North Carolina Press, 1955), pp. 37-38.

question. The military showed themselves willing to compromise with the old system, in which the white oligarchy dominated politics and the large land-holders controlled the nation's predominantly agrarian economy. In this system the armed forces constituted an autonomous institution quietly collecting 25 per cent of the annual budget and looking after its own affairs. Even perennial President Velasco Ibarra, who was returned to office in the 1952 elections, was unable to change that situation. Conflict developed between Velasco Ibarra and the officer corps when he attempted to purge it of "disloyal" elements who were blocking his attempts to launch a reform program. Stopped short in his efforts to build up an army completely dependent upon himself, he was able to reach a modus vivendi enabling him to complete in 1956 his legal term of office.

Venezuela

The contagion of social revolution spread to Venezuela in 1945. Here, the traditionalist president, General Isaias Medina Angarita, whose legal term was about to expire, made plans for perpetuating Venezuela's customary political pattern under which senior army officers ran the government as their personal domain. These plans went awry, however, when a group of restless and disgruntled young officers decided to rebel. The tremendous peculation at the top, the incompetence of the superannuated generals, the resulting stagnation of the armed forces, and, above all, the extreme slowness of promotion, had led to the formation of the conspiratorial Patriot Military Union. Its stated aim was to introduce political responsibility, universal suffrage, and constitutional reform, and to create a truly professional army.[22] In October 1945, the junior officers joined forces with the popular civilian opposition, represented by the Acción Democrática party, and in a relatively bloodless coup ousted the Medina regime.

22 Rómulo Betancourt, *Venezuela: política y petróleo* (Mexico City: Fondo de Cultura Económica, 1956), pp. 189-190.

True to their word, the young officers initially cooperated in establishing a broadly based civilian government. Only two members of the seven-man *junta* wore uniforms, and both of these, Major Mario Vargas and Colonel Carlos Delgado Chalbaud, were sympathetic with Venezuela's first popular revolution. Acción Democrática, which represented hitherto ignored lower and middle groups, launched a broad program of fundamental reforms. Under the aegis of the party's political and intellectual leader, Rómulo Betancourt, taxes on the foreign oil companies and the larger Venezuelan businesses were sharply increased; grafters who had made fortunes under previous regimes were apprehended, tried, and ordered to surrender their ill-gotten gains; labor was encouraged to organize, and its wages and welfare benefits were sharply increased; a thorough reorganization of the educational system was begun with an eye to reducing illiteracy; economic development and diversification programs were set in motion; a blueprint for land reform was drawn up. To get a verdict on their program, Acción Democrática went to the people. After providing for universal suffrage in the liberal, democratic constitution of 1947, it launched its candidate, the novelist Rómulo Gallegos, for the presidency, and elected him by an overwhelming majority. It appeared that Venezuela had truly entered a new era.

The year 1948, however, saw a military coup carried out in Venezuela similar to the one just perpetrated in Peru. The young officers who had launched the popular and liberalizing revolution of 1945 had become dissatisfied with Acción Democrática's radical program. After failing in several attempts, they engineered a *coup d'état* in November of 1948, ousting Acción Democrática. The army once more took charge of the government. There were two versions of this coup. According to the army,

An extremist faction of the Acción Democrática party came to control all civil power, and it then initiated a series of maneuvers designed also to dominate the armed forces, trying to sow among them discord and dissension; . . . they planned to call a general strike in order to get their way. This situation caused the armed forces to assume control of the government in order to stop the political chaos and the economic collapse of the country.

The armed forces dissolved Acción Democrática because it attempted to incite the people to conduct a general strike of a political nature, because it tried to destroy the institutional essence of the armed forces and convert it into an instrument of their designs, and because an extremist faction of the party was attempting to maintain itself in power by diverse means of social disintegration.[23]

According to Acción Democrática,

Despite a series of reactionary counterplots, Acción Democrática did not have an inflexible hostility toward the armed forces. . . . We had agreed to the concept of the existence of a regular army, adjusted to the needs and requirements of the nation, well endowed and well organized. Faithful to this criterion, the government under Acción Democrática extended to the armed forces support in technological improvement and in betterment of the living conditions of the officers and men. . . . But we recognized that the army's only function was that assigned it under legal democratic processes, that is, that of an institution of a professional and technical character, subordinate to the executive power, entirely removed from politics. . . .

But armed forces conspiracies continued. . . . Acción Democrática lacked the elements to arm the people in order to confront this subversion. . . . When the revolution came there were popular protests and strikes, but the war material of the army, used with Prussian brutality, ended the resistance. . . .[24]

Whatever the differences as to the facts and their interpretation, it was clear that the army had decided to halt the experiment in social revolution and to continue its long tradition of exclusive domination of Venezuela's politics.

[23] Venezuela, Oficina Nacional de Información, *Documentos relativos al movimiento militar de 24 de noviembre de 1948* (Caracas: Imprenta Nacional, 1949), pp. 19-20, 29.

[24] Betancourt, cited, pp. 461-470.

A military *junta* ruled until 1952, when Colonel Pérez Jiménez, after staging an election which was a farce, but nevertheless clearly demonstrated popular antipathy to him, assumed the office of president. Thus Venezuela once more returned to traditional military dictatorship.

Colombia

In Colombia the crisis first developed in 1946, when victory in the primary election of the Liberal party went to a radical politician, Jorge Eliecer Gaitán, who was strongly backed by labor. Thereupon, right-wing Liberals, alarmed at the rising power of the lower-income groups, joined hands with the Conservatives. The split in the Liberal party enabled the Conservatives, under Mariano Ospina Pérez, to return to power.

The economic and political aspirations of Colombia's newly awakened lower and middle groups were intensified by severe postwar inflationary pressures which the regime of President Ospina did little to alleviate. These economic hardships stretched political and social tensions to the breaking-point. In April 1948, the assassination of Gaitán set off a wave of mob violence. The country drifted into civil war.

As violence spread to the provinces, President Ospina, because he could not trust the loyalty of the police nor their effectiveness in quelling disturbances, was forced to rely increasingly upon the army. But here again the question of loyalty arose, for most army officers were of middle-class Liberal party families. Ospina, accordingly, gave preference in promotions to those with known Conservative party sympathies and assigned them to key commands. This was the first step in bringing the armed forces back into politics. The pace of the purge of Liberal officers was stepped up as the civil war became hotter. Increasingly the army was used to harass Liberals suspected of advocating violent measures and to intimidate Liberal members of Congress.

In anticipation of the presidential elections, Laureano Gómez, leader of the uncompromising right wing of the Conservative party, came back from exile. "Elected" while the country was under a state of siege in November of 1949, his reactionary tactics provoked widespread, violent opposition in the countryside. The blood-letting became worse. Gómez was determined to set up a Falange-type state in Colombia, converting the army into an instrument of right-wing Conservative rule. To this Ospina and the moderate Conservatives objected, for they hoped to win the 1954 elections. Also, they planned to work out a compromise with the Liberals in order to end the fighting. In this intraparty strife the armed forces, increasingly reluctant actors in the game of suppressing political opponents by killing them, sided with the Ospinistas. When Gómez, in June 1953, tried to get rid of the army's chief, General Rojas Pinilla, the latter took over the government. While it was a general who took the lead, his strongest support came from the junior officers.

The army's coup aroused great popular enthusiasm. Most of the guerrilla fighting in the countryside subsided as General Rojas promised to bring order and to hold elections as soon as possible. The moderate Conservatives expected to return to power shortly, and the Liberal party also saw possibilities for a comeback. Rojas Pinilla, however, saw his role as something more than that of an interim pacifier. Instead, he began to think of himself as a sort of Messiah; Perón-like, he began a program of broad social reform. He levied heavier taxes on the upper-income groups, adopted a social-welfare program, sponsored government labor unions, and launched a "third-force" political movement seeking support from the long-neglected lower and middle classes.[25]

When the leaders of the traditional parties saw that

[25] Vernon Lee Fluharty, *Dance of the Millions: Military Rule and the Social Revolution in Colombia, 1930-1956* (Pittsburgh: University of Pittsburgh Press, 1957), pp. 237-254.

Rojas' intentions were to perpetuate himself and the army in power and to lead a social revolution, they went into uncompromising opposition. Rojas reacted by tightening his dictatorship and by increasing substantially the size of the army. Where only 14,000 were under arms in 1948, there were over 32,000 in 1956. He raised the armed forces' share of the budget and lavished material benefits on the officers, a tactic which inevitably gave rise to widespread charges of graft and corruption from the parties. Also, despite the lack of initial success with a "third-force" movement, he continued efforts to build up mass support by representing himself as the savior of the people from exploitation by the oligarchy.

Political tensions came to a head in the spring of 1957 when Rojas made known his determination to continue in power beyond the expiration of his term of office in 1958. Early in May violence broke out in the capital, and a brief reign of terror ensued. The army, faced with the prospect of intensification of the nine-year-old civil war, turned against its leader. Rojas was ousted on May 10, 1957, and a new military *junta* took over, pending the holding of elections in 1958, and the return to civilian rule.

The leaders of the two traditional parties, after their narrow escape from military dictatorship and enforced social reform, quickly made peace. They worked out a formula, approved by the military *junta,* to give each party an equal share in control of the government through 1970. It was a return to Colombia's tradition of orderly constitutional government, generally welcomed after years of civil strife and arbitrary rule. The party leaders seemed, in many respects, however, to be turning the political clock back to 1930, to an Athenian type of democracy, to conditions prevailing before the left wing of the Liberal party attempted to win support from groups outside the elite. In this apparent hope, the military *junta* transferred power during 1958 to a civilian government headed by President Alberto Lleras Camargo.

Panama

The revolution of 1931 in Panama was significant for two reasons: first, it broke the traditional rule of the white aristocracy; second, it brought to the political forefront the national police, a body which held the balance of power between the traditional ruling aristocracy and aspiring middle-class groups.[26] During the 1930's, the role of the Panamanian police was essentially that of political arbiter; in the social struggle they did not take the side of any class or group.

Following Arnulfo Arias' coup in 1940, however, the Panamanian government embarked on an entirely new course. A ruthless opportunist and a demagogue, Arias appealed for political support to the hitherto-ignored lower classes, especially to the Negroes. His obviously dictatorial ambitions, his semi-Fascist leanings, his land reform proposals, and his exaggerated nationalism brought resistance from the oligarchy and from the national police. The latter forced him out in 1941, and during World War II conservative politicians held office with the backing of the police.

By 1947 the chief of police, Colonel José Antonio Remón, and his 2,000 well-armed and disciplined men had become the major force of Panamanian politics. Remón, an ambitious career officer of nonpropertied middle-group origins, after training at a military academy in Mexico, had joined the national police force in 1931. By 1947 he had climbed to its top command, and in the process he had also become the most potent political leader in Panama. This he demonstrated by making and breaking five civilian presidents in four years, before assuming presidential power himself.

Colonel Remón, in three years in the presidential office before his assassination in early 1955, represented a curious

26 John Biesanz and Luke M. Smith, "Panamanian Politics," in *Journal of Politics,* August 1952, pp. 389-397.

mixture of corruption and responsibility. He had elevated himself to the top in politics and, through assorted types of official graft and police racketeering, made a small fortune. On the other hand, when he became president in 1952, he insisted upon integrity in the hitherto corrupt bureaucracy, thoroughly reorganized the country's finances, and promoted agricultural and industrial development.[27] He sought to make the government the servant of all social classes rather than only the privileged. He introduced social-welfare measures and catered to the Negro vote.

Though Colonel Remón was probably the popular choice for president, upper- and middle-group opposition would have ousted him had it not been for the support of the police. These colleagues he kept loyal by material favors, by substantially increasing the size of the force to 3,000, and by converting it into a Guardia Nacional, thus elevating it in effect to army status.[28]

Guatemala

The beginning of the end of Guatemala's *ancien régime* came in June 1944, when the pent-up popular restlessness and antagonism found release in a national strike. The instinct of the dictator, General Ubico, was to drown the resistance in blood. Most of the other generals, aware of the young officers' sympathies for the rebels, decided to desert their erstwhile leader in an effort to save themselves. Accordingly, three of them, led by General Federico Ponce Valdez, seized power in an attempt to head off the threatened social revolution.

It was too late. Young army officers, many of them made aware by wartime training in the United States of Guatemala's need for reforms, now had their long-awaited opportunity. Together with the *ladino* (mixed blood),

[27] See John and Marie Biesanz, *The People of Panama* (New York: Columbia University Press, 1955).

[28] *Hispanic American Report,* June 1954, p. 16.

middle-class professional men and intellectuals of the capital, they plotted the overthrow of the generals. Success came on October 20, 1944, when the conspirators, using captured Lend-Lease equipment, seized the strategic Guardia de Honor fortress in the capital. Other military uprisings occurred in the provinces. A civilian-military *junta* was set up, and Dr. Juan Arévalo, a left-of-center intellectual, became the triumphant revolutionists' choice for president.

The new government quickly passed a rash of reform legislation, directed toward expansion of education, protection of organized labor, social welfare, industrialization, and agrarian reform. As to political reform the key obstacle was the army, long the determining factor in Guatemala's politics. The dual aim of Arévalo and his civilian colleagues was to transform the armed forces into devoted supporters of the social revolution and at the same time severely to restrict, by a system of checks and balances, their political power. The young officers were taught civic and social responsibility. Emphasis was placed on professionalism. Military installations were modernized, the armed forces were expanded in size, and the pay and benefits of both officers and men were substantially increased.[29]

As Arévalo's radical reform program got under way in 1944, the resulting political and social tensions gave rise to two distinct army factions—a leftist group led by the defense minister, Colonel Jacobo Arbenz, and a moderate faction led by the army chief of staff, Colonel Francisco Javier Araña. Only the assassination of the latter in 1949 postponed, for a few years, an ideological clash between the moderate-to-conservative army leaders, who thought the revolution was proceeding too rapidly, and the more radical military and civilian leaders. With Araña no longer on the scene and his supporters silenced or forced into exile, Arbenz was an easy victor in the 1950 presidential campaign. After his inauguration, the social revolution

[29] Guillermo Toriello, *La batalla de Guatemala* (Mexico City: Ediciones Cuadernos Americanos, 1955), pp. 184-185.

veered decidedly leftward; the energetic Communist minority got the ear of the new president and rapidly began to usurp control of the movement. Essentially agents of the U.S.S.R., they sought to destroy United States influence, to provoke a violent class struggle, and to spread communism into neighboring republics.

Although Arbenz was more easily duped than most of his military brothers, who were generally unresponsive to Communist overtures, they were somewhat naïvely unaware of the magnitude of the threat arising from the steady growth of communism within the Arbenz government, within the working class, which the Communists planned to arm, and among the Indian conscripts, whom they hoped to win over with gifts of land. Eventually the officer corps adopted a neutral attitude in politics; they neither interfered with the regime nor did they defend it when the crisis came in June 1954.

The shipment of Soviet-bloc arms to Guatemala gave the ousted pro-Araña army exiles, now led by Colonel Carlos Castillo Armas, their opportunity to return, for it provoked the United States government, which saw its vital strategic interests in jeopardy, to counter the Russian move by sending armaments to Guatemala's neighbors—armaments which quickly found their way into the hands of Castillo. When the latter crossed the border from Honduras, the Guatemalan army could still have driven him out. However, rather than shed their blood for a regime for which they had little enthusiasm, they made a compromise with Castillo's "liberation army" and ousted Arbenz and the Communists.

For three difficult years the middle-of-the-road military regime of Castillo Armas tried to restore to the disturbed country a semblance of order and moderation. It was easy for him, with army support, to crush the Communists and the radical left. However, it was quite another matter to uphold, even to a limited extent, the principles of the 1944 revolution in the face of the oligarchy's desire to make a comeback. For the overturn of 1954 was a genuine counterrevolution. Social questions were important in the thinking of both sides, though Communist participation in the Arbenz regime and the international aspects of Guatemala's position confused and obscured the local issues.

El Salvador

El Salvador's popular revolution, led by young officers and following the familiar post-World War II pattern, came in December 1948. It had nearly occurred four years earlier when the cumulative pressure of population upon limited rural resources, the rise of urban labor and middle-class commercial and professional groups, and the defeat and discrediting of military dictatorships elsewhere, upset the regime of General Martínez. The military uprising which deposed him in 1944 revealed serious discontent among the colonels, but out of the brief internecine struggle for power, the generals, under Salvador Castañeda Castro, emerged triumphant. He held power for four years by harsh, arbitrary rule under a nearly constant state of siege.

Initially, the revolution of 1948, spearheaded by radical-talking majors and colonels and backed by reform-minded intellectuals, appeared to signal the beginning of the end of militarism and feudalism in El Salvador. The five-man military-civilian *junta* announced plans for "honest government," for conversion of the army into "a faithful defender of the constitution," and for other sweeping reforms.[30] Major Oscar Osorio, one of the three military members, assumed the provisional presidency a month after the revolt; he was elected to a six-year term in 1950.

The address given by the minister of the interior, Colonel José María Lemus, on the third anniversary of the revolution, revealed the mentality of the colonels' clique that governed El Salvador after 1948. Lemus stated:

In order to conduct the 1948 revolution, the army had to with-

[30] *New York Times*, December 16, 1948.

draw itself from the influence of the existing political climate and identify itself with the popular will, in order to form for itself an adequate mentality, with the end of responding to the imperatives of the democratic world movement. . . . The army exists . . . not to enthrone tyrannies . . . [but] to observe the sacred institutional postulates of fulfilling the law and of being the guardian of the national sovereignty. . . . The army is not a static institution. . . . In effect the army is the force which represents the right of the people. . . . It is an institution with a conscience. . . . The army is the main bulwark in defense of the popular rights which were so valiantly fought for in the 1948 revolution.[31]

Perhaps the army was playing a new role. But it was still very much in politics.

It was not long before the young officers turned their backs on social reform. In response to the increasing popular clamor that the army, now that it had done its job, ought to get out of politics, or perhaps even be disbanded altogether, as in Costa Rica, Colonel Lemus replied:

Today's barracks . . . are the laboratories of conscience where soldiers are instructed in the use of arms to defend the national territory and legal rights of the people. . . . It is, therefore, treason to ask for dissolution of the army . . . for this would annihilate democracy and enthrone the system of the past which the revolution liquidated. . . . There is now an ideological [i.e., democratic] identification between the army and the people.[32]

The army colonels, however, enjoyed far more "democracy" than the people. In the 1950 elections the people had to choose between two colonels; in 1956 four of the five presidential candidates were colonels. The new military despotism, to be sure, was somewhat less retrogressive than the pre-1948 variety. There was more serious thinking about urgent national problems. Power and water systems were built, public-housing projects begun, and the

[31] Lt. Colonel José María Lemus, *Pueblo, ejército, y doctrina revolucionaria* (San Salvador: Imprenta Nacional, 1952), pp. 3-13.

[32] Same, pp. 10-13.

government's administrative machinery was overhauled for more efficient operation. The army, however, resisted diversion of any of its share of the budget for public projects. The regime, moreover, was essentially paternalistic. Urban, though not rural, labor could organize and bargain collectively, but only under strict government tutelage. Political power remained the monopoly of the armed forces. The colonels introduced modest welfare measures, but faced by firm resistance from the planters they no longer even mentioned agrarian reform or sweeping social changes. The net results of the 1948 revolution were the substitution of colonels for generals, and the introduction of slightly greater responsibility in the administration of government. The 1948 "revolution" thus did not turn out to be a revolution in any fundamental sense.

Costa Rica

In Costa Rica there occurred a revolution in the spring of 1948 that could not properly be classed as a left-versus-right struggle, for a broadly based democratic system had already existed for some time. The revolutionary movement was primarily antimilitaristic, and its program also called for greater political democracy and economic independence. The occasion of its resort to armed revolt was an attempt by those in power to thwart the democratic process. Otilio Ulate and the National Union party won the 1948 elections, but the incumbent, President Teodoro Picado Michalski, refused to hand over to the president-elect control of the military forces and the barracks in San José. When Congress subsequently voided the election, Ulate's partisans had no choice but revolution to attain what they regarded as political justice. José Figueres, their leader, organized a rebel army which defeated the regulars who still backed Picado, then set up a military "*junta* of liberation."

Figueres, incensed at the regular army's action, sought vengeance. In November 1948, he declared the army henceforth dissolved and ordered its main barracks in San José converted into a Museum of Fine Arts. "Why," he asked, "should a group of professional men assume the right to annul the popular will as expressed at the polls?" [33] He explained that Costa Rica was not a military country, that the army was no longer needed. The problem of internal order could be adequately managed by the 1,000-man national police force.

For a full decade the democratic, moderately socialistic regimes of Figueres and Ulate made good their claims that an army was totally unnecessary, despite invasions led by Costa Rican exiles from Nicaragua in 1949 and again in 1955. In both cases, emergency volunteer forces, aided by prompt intervention by the Organization of American States, were able to repel the attackers. Thus the armed forces were no longer decisive factors in the politics of Costa Rica. Besides giving relief from militarism in government, that nation has also avoided the huge budgetary drain that military expenditures entailed in other Latin American countries.

Cuba

The Cuban armed forces involvement in the nation's political and social revolution began in 1933. In August of that year, when sporadic antagonism to the irresponsible military dictatorship of Machado jelled in the form of a general strike, young army officers felt that the time had come to sacrifice their erstwhile master. However, it was too late for the officer corps to save their own skins simply by ousting the number one tyrant. They had become too closely associated with the graft, corruption, and brutality to escape the popular wrath. Within a month power passed into the hands of the men who actually wielded the bayonets. In September of 1933, the enlisted men, under the astute leadership of Sergeant Batista, seized control of the military installations and forced two-thirds of the six hun-

[33] *Hispanic American Report,* December 1948, p. 9.

dred career officers into retirement. Batista proclaimed himself a colonel, then proceeded to hand out commissions of lesser rank to the sergeants, corporals, privates, and a number of civilians.

The ousting of the incorrigible officer caste, however, did nothing to slacken the army's grip on Cuban politics. For the next eleven years Batista and the army ran Cuba. Seven civilian puppets sat in the presidential chair prior to Batista's election in 1940, while the *caudillo* issued orders from behind the scenes. For example, when President Miguel Mariano Gómez in 1936 resisted plans for an army-sponsored and directed rural education program, he was impeached by a legislature subservient to, and intimidated by, Batista's wishes.

Like Machado, Batista catered to the armed forces upon whose support his own supremacy always depended. He increased the size of the army by one-third (to 16,000), raised the pay of both his new officers and the enlisted men, created a new military academy, modernized military installations, and increased the armed forces' share of the national budget to 22 per cent (from 15 per cent in 1932). Army administrators and supervisors, temporarily ousted after Machado's downfall, again began occupying Cuba's high civil-service positions, and the customary graft, though now conducted in a more sophisticated manner, was transferred to the sticky fingers of the new military elite. Batista, himself, asserted his rights to the lion's share.

Batista, however, did give Cuban politics order and stability. Despite the corruption his government had sufficient resources to launch worthwhile health, education, and public-works programs. Batista made advances for Cuba in the field of social legislation and social welfare. After his initial crushing of the organized labor movement in 1934, he allowed it to rebuild under government tutelage in 1937. Labor's support, in turn, became vital to Batista in 1940 when he "resigned" from the armed forces in order to be elected to the presidency. While occupying the latter office he gave his regime a civilian façade by removing the army officers from most political and administrative offices, but his power was still dependent upon his colleagues in the armed forces.

At the end of his constitutional term of office in 1944, the *caudillo* surprised everyone by accepting the defeat of his hand-picked candidate. He then retired with his millions to Florida.

There then occurred an eight-year civilian interlude. President Ramón Grau San Martín courageously purged the military hierarchy of Batista's principal supporters, but neither he nor his successor, Carlos Prío Socorras, dared tamper with the armed forces' traditional share of the national revenues. Nor did they deem it advisable to put restrictions on the military opportunities for graft opened wide by Machado and Batista; in fact, their administrations were as noted for corruption as that of Batista. Both Grau and Prío made attempts to liberalize political institutions and bring the government into closer conformity with Cuba's democratic constitution, but the result was a sharp upswing in "gangsterism" and disorder. Prío, especially, was forced increasingly to use the army to preserve internal order, just as Batista had done earlier.

The notorious corruption in public life, the increasing violence, the restlessness apparent in the armed forces—all these things convinced Batista that the time was opportune for a comeback. He became an active candidate in the 1952 presidential race, but, as the election approached, he found himself running a poor third against Prío's candidate and another civilian aspirant. When it became apparent that he had no chance of winning, he began conspiring with the young officers. In a carefully planned coup they surprised and arrested the military chiefs and took control of the government in March of 1952.

Batista, however, soon found that the problem of running Cuba by fiat was far more difficult than it had been in the pre-World War II era. Particularly after 1955, his assumed omnipotence was seriously challenged. It began with student disturbances in late 1955, followed by army conspiracies, increasing terrorism and assassinations, and a successful invasion of eastern Cuba by radical young civilian revolutionaries led by Fidel Castro. The years 1957 and 1958 were marked by further army restlessness, a nearly successful naval revolt, and an expansion of Castro's guerrilla operations. Urban labor backed the dictator, as Argentine labor had backed Perón, while the middle groups and the peasantry hoped to bring him down and restore constitutional government. Only by enriching the faithful and purging suspects in the officer corps was Batista able to keep the loyalty of the armed forces, and only by conducting an increasingly rigid despotism was he able to withstand civilian pressures. Thus, characteristically, certain elements in the army perverted the popular democratic and social revolution and ended by seeking power for its own sake, a power spelling tyranny and corruption.

Throughout the latter half of 1958, the pressures against the regime steadily swelled toward the inevitable breaking-point. Castro's guerrillas descended from the rugged Sierra Maestra in the eastern part of the island, and with the help of the organized underground and the repressed populace began moving toward Havana. The regular army, in the face of mass antagonism toward the regime and repeated guerrilla successes, began losing its will to fight. Air force pilots began to desert rather than follow out orders to bomb defenseless cities. Faced with the distasteful prospect of having to conduct wholesale slaughter in an attempt to quell the swelling popular opposition, the army generals went to Batista and forced his resignation.[34]

The end came in the early morning hours of New Year's Day, 1959, as the dictator fled into exile. However, just as in the crisis of 1933, it was too late for the officer corps to save themselves. They were forced to bow to the unconditional surrender mandate of Fidel Castro, whose remarkable victory over the regulars had made him undisputed leader of the Cuban nation.

[34] *New York Times,* January 10, 1959.

Chapter 4

CURBING MILITARISM IN MEXICO: A CASE STUDY

PROBABLY NO COUNTRY in Latin America has suffered longer and more deeply than Mexico from the curse of predatory militarism. More than a thousand armed uprisings plagued this unfortunate republic in its first century of nationhood. Here were compounded nearly all the evils associated with undisciplined, irresponsible armed bodies of men on the loose. The word "army" in the popular mind more often than not was associated with crime, violence, ignorance and corruption.

The sword and the rifle were the weapons of politics as opportunistic officers disregarded the constitution, broke laws with impunity, and provoked civil wars. Political turmoil engendered economic chaos, rampant peculation of public funds, deficits in the national budget, and loss of public credit abroad. The vigor of the private sector of the economy, small business especially, was sapped by monetary mismanagement, burdensome taxes, and confiscations. Thus the parasitic military caste added appreciably to the already deep-seated miseries of the Mexican people.

Yet Mexico has been able to rid itself of the plague of militarism. A quarter-century ago no Latin American army was more political than the Mexican; today the armed forces are virtually out of politics. Mexico has moved from one extreme to the other.

Although Mexican militarism actually was not born until after the country achieved independence, by the end of the colonial era conception had taken place and gestation was well advanced. Spanish monarchs had long fostered the growth of a military caste by restricting commissions as a rule to men of social position and by endowing the officer corps with special legal privileges. Clever and ambitious young men of limited means found in the career of arms opportunity for self-enrichment.[1] Officership was not a profession, it was a privilege. A late eighteenth-century observer noted:

> . . . The king had more officers than privates . . . [and] most of the former purchased their place to mock justice, to escape paying debts, to indulge in gaming and live a life of libertinage under the protection of the epaulettes. . . .[2]

In such armies standards of military honor could mean little, hence it was easy for leaders of independence movements to persuade a large fraction of the officer corps to betray their sworn allegiance to the king in exchange for quick promotions and new opportunities for graft. During the revolution of 1821, many young captains in the Spanish army were advanced to generals in the Mexican army as a reward for inducing large numbers of privates to desert with them.[3]

The dissolution of royal authority accelerated the breakdown of discipline in the armed forces. Three months after independence was declared, an audacious young officer, Augustín Iturbide, led a march on the constituent Congress and set himself up as Emperor Augustín I. Thus began the tragic spectacle of ambitious, undisciplined, irresponsible army officers competing with each other for short cuts to wealth, power, and influence.

For nearly sixty years political processes in Mexico were

[1] Lucas Alamán, *Historia de Méjico* (Mexico City: J. M. Lara, 5 v., 1849-1852), v. 4, pp. 445-448.

[2] Hipólito Villaroel, *Méjico por dentro y fuero bajo el gobierno de los virreyes, o sea enfermedades políticas* (Mexico City: A. Valdés, 1831), p. 170.

[3] Ernest Gruening, *Mexico and Its Heritage* (New York: Century, 1928), pp. 289-291.

dominated by military violence. Hundreds of barracks uprisings and rebellions were led by army officers and backed by the political out-groups. Incumbent regimes were toppled at an average of better than one a year.[4] In 1821 there were nearly five thousand officers for the eight thousand enlisted men stationed in the capital. In 1823, when total government revenues were five million dollars, the budget of the armed forces was nine million. During Mexico's first quarter-century of independence, the military budget exceeded government revenues two out of every three years.[5]

The armed forces were completely beyond civilian control. The legal privileges and exemptions granted them in the colonial era continued in force. By threats of rebellion they got the lion's share of the national budget. The philosophy that predominated among the ambitious is described by Ernest Gruening as follows:

> . . . Good faith, merit, constancy and hard work were not only unappreciated but detrimental to an ambitious young man. Chicanery brought richer rewards. A lieutenant who participated in a half dozen *cuartelazos* [barrack uprisings] almost certainly emerged a general. A successful *levantamiento* [uprising] erased a previous defalcation. The risks were not great —except for a few hours—and far preferable to years of patient drudgery. Thus was the atmosphere of public life vitiated. Honorable men had no chance in it, for the successful tricksters wanted men of like stamp to further their common base ends. Even civilians were given high army commissions. So the officer caste grew, exempt from and above the civil law, an arrogant coterie of debauchees, reveling by night and conspiring by day.[6]

The most notorious of the predatory military adventurers was General Antonio López de Santa Anna. For over a quarter of a century he capriciously made and unmade

[4] Frank Tannenbaum, *Peace by Revolution* (New York: Columbia University Press, 1933), pp. 75-76, 92-93.

[5] Alamán, cited, v. 5, p. 499; Francisco Bulnes, *Las grandes mentiras de nuestra historia* (Paris: C. Bouret, 1904), pp. 210-211.

[6] Cited, p. 26.

governments. In fact, the domestic political history of Mexico up to 1855 is practically a narrative of General Santa Anna's revolutions.

In the 1850's and 1860's, a group of civilians led by Benito Juárez made some progress subordinating the military to civil authority. After a generation of conflict over this issue, a military man, General Porfirio Díaz, finally established control over the army and achieved political stability. Frank Tannenbaum explains that he did this "by replacing instability and disorganized violence with tyranny and organized violence." [7]

Pacifying and disciplining the hitherto untractable officer corps took patience, astuteness, and a wide variety of Machiavellian techniques. Díaz quieted rivals too dangerous to crush by providing them with unlimited opportunities for graft and plunder. Those that he was prepared to tackle he deliberately offended, then discharged and exiled. Gradually he ousted a quarter of the army's one hundred generals and dismissed some four hundred officers of lower rank. He attempted to purchase the loyalty of the remainder with generous salaries, expense accounts, and opportunities for self-enrichment. Further to insure their fidelity, he established a system of shifting commands in the nation's eleven newly organized military zones. To prevent any officer from gaining the allegiance of a large body of enlisted men, he extended the periodic change of officer duty as far down as the regimental level. Potential rivals he either "promoted" to governorships, or cashiered on charges of corruption. By 1892, after a dozen years of effort, the army was finally under Díaz' firm control.[8]

Díaz accomplished the miracle of disciplining the Mexican army not only by his remarkable courage, his astuteness and his administrative talents; in addition he owed

[7] Frank Tannenbaum, *Mexico: The Struggle for Peace and Bread* (New York: Knopf, 1950), pp. 81-82.

[8] Carleton Beals, *Porfirio Díaz* (Philadelphia: Lippincott, 1932), pp. 223-255, 287, 289; Hubert Herring, *A History of Latin America* (New York: Knopf, 1955), p. 342.

much to the great influx of foreign capital in the late nineteenth century, which came in partly as result of his pacification of the country. The new investments enabled the dictator to provide would-be rivals with the material benefits so essential to subduing their latent aspirations to power. Moreover, the rapid development of modern communications had made it far easier to stamp out incipient rebellions.

Díaz may have disciplined the military, but he failed to create an efficient and loyal fighting force. The armed forces were adequate, along with the *rurales* (mounted constabulary), for performing police functions and quelling isolated disturbances, but when in 1910 a popular revolution broke out the vaunted capabilities of the Díaz army and the asserted loyalty of his officer corps proved to be fictitious. The army in reality proved to be but a fragile shell.

On the eve of the revolution, when the total population was about fourteen million, the Mexican army consisted of some four thousand officers, twenty thousand enlisted men, and four thousand rural mounted police. Organized on a caste system, it was led by middle and upper-middle class white officers, most of whom were graduates of the Chapultepec military school. Although French influence was noticeable in the army and some of the equipment was German, Mexico did not entertain any foreign military missions and rarely sent officers abroad to study. Consequently, it lacked modern military techniques and equipment. The ranks were filled with primitive Indian conscripts, among them a good number of vagabonds, beggars, and criminals. The small navy was weak and insignificant.[9] Ostensibly, the mission of the armed forces was to repel foreign invaders; their actual mission was to crush

[9] Charles M. Jerram, *Armies of the World* (London: Lawrence and Bullen, 1899), pp. 206-207, 299; Thomas A. Janvier, "The Mexican Army," in *The Armies of Today* (New York: Harper, 1893), pp. 366-396; Percy F. Martin, *Mexico in the Twentieth Century* (London: E. Arnold, 1907), v. 2, pp. 42-43.

all internal opposition to Díaz and perpetuate the dictator in power. They lacked the capabilities for doing either.

The storm that broke in 1910 was not just another local rebellion or barracks revolt, but a fundamental social revolution with broad popular participation. Ultimately it was to bring about sweeping changes in Mexico's economy, its social organization and its political structure. Nevertheless, the country was doomed first to return to chaotic pre-Díaz conditions. Again irresponsible militarism was to hold sway over politics and to prey upon the nation's economy and civilian society.

The electoral dispute of 1910 was the spark that set aflame the latent popular antagonism to the Díaz regime. Under the leadership of middle-group citizens spontaneous uprisings began in scattered areas. When the weakness of the regular army became apparent, the movement began to snowball. An increasing number of officers deserted the regime and joined the revolutionary forces, impressed by their power and by their popular support. Their object obviously was to emerge on the winning side.[10] Thus, with the help of the regulars, the Díaz regime was overthrown and Francisco Madero assumed the presidency. Almost immediately, however, he was plagued by the problem of the army. Only those regulars who were loyal to Díaz had been crushed. Most of the army regulars, who had joined the rebels in ousting Díaz, now claimed their rewards. They were challenged, however, by revolutionary citizen-generals demanding to be made generals in the regular army.[11] Madero made the mistake of siding with the regulars and disbanding the revolutionary army. His reward was assassination at the hands of former Díaz henchmen;

[10] Gruening, cited, p. 302; Tannenbaum, *Mexico: The Struggle for Peace and Bread,* cited, p. 50; Jesús Silva Herzog, *Un ensayo sobre la revolución mejicana* (Mexico City: Ediciones Cuadernos Americanos, 1946), pp. 28-29.

[11] Charles L. Cumberland, *Mexican Revolution: Genesis under Madero* (Austin: University of Texas Press, 1952), pp. 159-160; Silva Herzog, cited, pp. 28-29.

thereupon General Victoriano Huerta attempted to reimpose a Díaz-type regime.

This action not only stirred to action the outraged former revolutionary generals, but stimulated the rise of new leaders as well. Thus the Constitutionalist army was formed in March of 1913. In this force were almost no regulars, but many civilian leaders like Alvaro Obregón who had displayed a natural talent for soldiering, and skilled military adventurers like Pancho Villa. A former state governor, Venustiano Carranza, assumed command of the movement. The revolutionary force drove down from the north, virtually annihilated the regulars, and took command of the capital.

But the citizen-generals were no more immune to political rivalry and ambition than their more class-conscious predecessors. Almost immediately the victors were squabbling over the spoils. Militarism returned to Mexico with vengeance as Pancho Villa, whose private army was even larger than the entire regular army had been under Díaz, challenged Carranza's authority. But by making use of nonpolitical, professional officers, and by enlisting the support of urban labor and the peasants to whom he promised reforms, Carranza was able to crush Villa in March of 1915.

Though Carranza was now dominant, he by no means had absolute control. The nation was armed to the teeth and equipped with a superabundance of improvised generals. The regular army had disappeared, but there was no real national army to take its place. Instead, there were a whole series of separate revolutionary armies, each claiming and exercising a large degree of autonomy.

Carranza, after desperately trying to establish firm centralized control of the army, was finally forced to sanction a certain measure of regional autonomy. Then, too, he was overly tolerant of the excesses committed by a large, irresponsible group of "loyal" young officers in the capital. This, along with Carranza's attempt to dictate his successor, turned Generals Obregón, Calles, and the bulk of the army against him. Driven from office, he was murdered by one of his closest military colleagues.[12]

Nineteen hundred twenty, a crucial year in the evolution of Mexico's armed forces, marked their last successful coup. The militarism of the revolutionary period had reached its high point. Thereafter the tide ran out. The Mexican army, which had been one of the most political and unprofessional in all Latin America, had become by 1940 one of the most nonpolitical and professional. Credit for this reform must go mainly to four strong revolutionary generals (Obregón, Calles, Amaro, and Cárdenas), who together spent an entire generation in accomplishing this extremely difficult task.

What was the army like in 1920? After ten years of revolutionary turbulence the curse laid by militarism on the Mexican political scene was at its worst. Carranza had been unable to bridle the generals. Around 80,000 men were under arms, more than double the number in 1910. The army, which still consisted of poorly organized, badly disciplined, semi-autonomous revolutionary bands, was notoriously overstaffed. Its volunteer ranks were filled with a motley assortment of adventurers, vagabonds, bandits, and loyal followers of various revolutionary leaders. It lacked regulation uniforms, arms, training, and tactics. Its numbers rose and fell with fluctuations in the ambitions and power of its leaders.

The officer corps, a most unprofessional body, was headed by the scandalously young, bellicose generals of the revolution. Though Díaz-trained professionals were scattered through the various units, they wielded relatively little influence in comparison to the victorious political officers of the revolution. The latter, of course, were completely without professional training and were ignorant of modern military science.[13]

[12] Gruening, cited, pp. 311-315; Tannenbaum, *Mexico: The Struggle for Peace and Bread,* cited, pp. 62-63.

[13] Vicente Blasco Ibáñez, *El militarismo mejicano* (Valencia: Prometeo, 1920), pp. 177-192; Virginia Prewitt, "The Mexican Army," *Foreign Affairs,* April 1941, pp. 609-612.

The main tasks facing the central government were somehow to curb the regional *caudillos,* to cut down the heavy military expenditures, to reorganize the army and to build it into a truly national institution. To inaugurate this difficult program there was probably no better man than General Obregón, one of the best of the revolutionary generals, who had succeeded Carranza as president. His heroic role in the revolution had gained him widespread popular support and great prestige in the army. He alone commanded sufficient respect, combined with the necessary force of character, to have a chance of tethering the young mustang generals of the revolution. Somehow he had to convince them that the army was no longer a revolutionary instrument, that henceforth their careers depended upon their loyalty and service to the incumbent government.[14]

Obregón moved cautiously, but deliberately, to establish control at the center. He first incorporated all revolutionary generals into the regular army, putting them on the federal payroll. These attempts to extend his authority, however, provoked resistance among a number of generals who believed their real interest lay in a continuance of a semi-autonomy and unbridled militarism. In 1923, the Obregón government was very nearly toppled by a generals' conspiracy led by Adolfo de la Huerta.[15] Obregón promptly followed up his narrow victory by a thorough purge of all suspects. After many officers had been shot and others sent into exile, a number of the vacancies thus created were filled by young professionals from the newly organized officers' training-school. For Obregón, in addition to curbing militarism, had energetically promoted professionalism. Already, in 1917, under Carranza, he had set up a general-staff school, in which officers of the revolution received technical training from officers who had served in Díaz' army. And when he became president in

[14] Tannenbaum, *Mexico: The Struggle for Peace and Bread,* cited, p. 63; Gruening, cited, pp. 319-322; Prewitt, cited, p. 612.

[15] Gruening, cited, pp. 319-322; Tannenbaum, *Mexico: The Struggle for Peace and Bread,* cited, p. 63.

1920, he reopened the old Colegio Militar at Chapultepec for newly enlisted officers, with a three-year curriculum offering specialized training for the infantry, the cavalry, and the artillery.[16] In addition, he dispatched promising young officers to Spain, France, Germany, and the United States to study modern military methods and techniques. He also succeeded in easing the military burden on the federal budget from 142 million pesos in 1921 to 117 million in 1924, by reducing the size of the army, and by curbing graft and corruption. Despite this progress, militarism was to remain a major problem for his successors. For in the course of crushing the Huerta revolt, Obregón found it expedient to promote twenty-three generals and create fifty-four new ones, in order to ensure their loyalty.[17]

General Calles' views on militarism, though similar to Obregón's, were somewhat more advanced. Obregón had relied for his success on personal prestige, but Calles, far less a hero among the revolutionary officers, initially sought to de-emphasize *personalismo* and instill in the army a sense of loyalty to their profession and to their country. This, he correctly believed, was the only real cure for the disease of militarism. The secretary of war selected to transform Mexico's semifeudal army into a truly national body was Joaquín Amaro, a young Indian general of the revolution whose pro-professional and antimilitaristic zeal was unmatched.

In the six years during which Amaro had a free hand to straighten out the army he did a truly remarkable job.[18] Wisely avoiding a direct challenge to the old revolutionary generals whom he was determined ultimately to break, he began his reforms in the ranks, by improving recruiting standards, living conditions, and military equipment. To cut down costs, he disbanded the most unreliable armed

16 Prewitt, cited, p. 613; Fritz T. Epstein, *European Military Influences in Latin America* (manuscript in possession of author in Library of Congress, 1941), p. 206.

17 Gruening, cited, pp. 322-323.

18 Carleton Beals, "The Indian Who Sways Mexico's Destiny," *New York Times*, December 7, 1930, sec. 5, p. 8.

groups and discharged the least desirable individuals in other groups. By 1930 he had reduced the army from about 75,000 to 50,000 men and had slashed military expenditures from 107 million pesos to 70 million. He put the troops to work, employing them on road-building and other public-works projects.[19] He also launched an educational and recreational program, hoping it would pay off in patriotism and loyalty to the central government rather than to the regional *caudillos*.

To discipline and organize armed peasants so that they would be a dependable military force in times of internal crises, the cooperation of the officer corps was necessary. Again General Amaro avoided a direct onslaught on the revolutionary generals; instead he bored in from the bottom. He stepped up the training of young officers abroad and sent missions to France, Spain, Italy, and the United States to study foreign military organization and methods. Upon returning to Mexico, they became Amaro's advisers, assisting him to build up a more efficient general staff. The first step toward this goal was the creation in 1926 of a Commission of Military Studies; the last was the organization in 1932 of a War College, under French professional influence, to train superior senior officers for general-staff duty.[20] Meanwhile, the newly organized Colegio Militar was rapidly improving as the officer trainees returned from abroad to provide modern technical instruction to the cadets. The latter, upon receiving their commissions, were deliberately assigned to regiments of doubtful loyalty, the object being to interpose a shield of loyal officers between the revolutionary general and his private army.[21]

19 Same; Prewitt, cited, p. 613; Gruening, cited, p. 322; Mexico, Ministerio de Guerra y Marina, *Memoria* (Mexico City), 1930/31, p. 10, 1931/32, p. 10.

20 Epstein ms., cited, p. 206; *Memoria*, 1930/31, cited, pp. 9-10; Mexico, Ministerio de Guerra y Marina, Dirrección General de Educación Militar, *Los estudios de la escuela superior de guerra* (Mexico City: Imprenta Nacional, 1934), pp. 24-25, 65, 73-175.

21 Tannenbaum, *Mexico: The Struggle for Peace and Bread,"* cited, p. 91; Beals, "The Indian Who Sways Mexico's Destiny," cited, p. 8; Virginia Prewitt, *Reportage on Mexico* (New York: Dutton, 1941), p. 76.

As soon as Amaro's reforms were well advanced, General Calles was ready to challenge the generals. He deliberately provoked them by launching a policy of shifting commands. This decisive move in breaking the force of *personalismo* and militarism met with resistance as Calles and Amaro had expected, but they were ready for it. When the first uprising came, in 1927, they promptly crushed it and dismissed all the conspiring generals. In 1929 another revolt took place, the General Gonzalo Escobar rebellion, with the same results. This time thousands of loyal peasant troops came quickly to the government's assistance.[22]

The success of the Obregón-Calles reforms is revealed by the progressive decline in the number of disloyal officers. In the outbreak of 1923 nearly half of the officers went over to the rebels, in 1927 less than a quarter; a decade later, the final major uprising attracted practically no support from regular officers. In breaking the power of the regional *caudillos* Calles had surmounted the most dangerous obstacle to genuine military reform. To his successor, General Lázaro Cárdenas, he left the task of completing the job. There was still much to be done, but the day of the military chieftain, the regional *caudillo,* had passed.

After crushing the Escobar rebellion Calles rapidly consolidated his dictatorship. He arranged for a "figurehead" to succeed him, remaining until 1934 the real power behind the scenes. Most people expected the Callista dictatorship to continue, but Cárdenas, the new president and also a general of the revolution, soon asserted, and won, his independence. Cárdenas insisted on deepening the revolution by sweeping social and economic reforms, whereas Calles would have limited the government's task to pacifying the country and consolidating the completed revolution. The break came in June 1935, when Cárdenas openly refused to accept Calles' suggestions on economic and political policies. The outcome depended primarily on the

[22] Prewitt, "The Mexican Army," cited, p. 613; Beals, "The Indian Who Sways Mexico's Destiny," cited, p. 8.

army. Calles still had the support of most of the active revolutionary generals, but Cárdenas had the backing of a few of the more influential ones, plus the young elements in the army—both officers and men. In addition he had much broader popular support. The tension continued to mount in the latter half of 1935 until December 15, when Cárdenas suddenly began dismissing pro-Calles senators and top generals, including General Joaquín Amaro. The victory was completed in April of 1936 when Calles and a number of supporting generals were forced into exile.[23]

Cárdenas knew he had little chance of getting the army's cooperation in his plans for land and labor reform. For one thing, many revolutionary generals had utilized the opportunities of the continuing turmoil to become large property owners and big businessmen themselves. Naturally they would oppose reforms that might affect their vested interests. Then there was the growing conservatism of men like Amaro, devoted to the profession of arms, who felt that Cárdenas' radical policies would give rise to domestic disturbances and thus undo the great progress already made toward pacification of the country and consolidation of the revolution.[24] Thus Cárdenas, anticipating army resistance to his policies, began to build up powerful labor and agrarian organizations to serve as counterpoises. He played down the role of the military as guardians of internal order, emphasizing instead their functions in education and public works. Refusing to increase the size of the regular army, he proposed instead to organize all peons in federal army reserves and advocated the formation of an independent labor militia. He revealed his fear of ambitious generals by shifting commands frequently, by building up support in the ranks through new material and

[23] *New York Times,* June 23, sec. 4, p. 11; December 16; December 22, sec. 4, p. 6, 1935; April 11, 1936; Tannenbaum, *Mexico: The Struggle for Peace and Bread,* cited, pp. 74-76, 82-84.

[24] *New York Times,* December 22, 1935, sec. 4, p. 6; Frank Kluckholn, "The Army Keeps Hold in Mexico," in same, May 29, 1948, sec. 4, p. 6.

educational benefits, and by providing promising young soldiers the opportunity to become officers.[25]

Cárdenas also did his utmost to spur professionalism and to remove the army from politics. In 1934 he inaugurated a six-year program for "the moral and professional advance of the army." The following year all infantry officers below the rank of colonel were given examinations in military science; those who failed were sent back to school. In 1936 he made competitive technical examinations requisite for officer promotion; the same year he issued a *reglamento* which proscribed all forms of political activity for officers. The following year he made it mandatory that officers on active duty give up all civilian employment.[26]

His master stroke at the army's political power came in December 1937 when he organized a new federated revolutionary party composed of four equal sectors—labor, peasant, military and popular. When his critics accused him of bringing the army into politics he replied: "We did not put the army in politics. It was already there. In fact, it had been dominating the situation, and we did well to reduce its influence to one vote out of four." [27] Now the army could always be outvoted. Cárdenas and the party leaders could curb its accustomed political strength by balancing it against the other three forces.[28]

The president's military reforms and his radical land and labor policies provoked a certain amount of rightist reaction. General Nicolás Rodríquez, leader of the "Gold Shirts," an incipient Fascist movement in northern Mexico, tried to start an uprising but could get no army backing. The movement was easily crushed by the Cárdenas

[25] Kluckholn, cited, p. 5; *New York Times,* July 18 and August 17, 1935; Prewitt, "The Mexican Army," cited, p. 614.

[26] Mexico, Ministerio de Guerra y Marina, *Memoria,* 1933/34, pp. 10, 13, 1934/35, p. 14, 1935/36, p. 16; Mexico, Presidente, *Reglamento general de deberes militares* (Mexico City: Imprenta Nacional, 1936); Prewitt, "The Mexican Army," cited, p. 614.

[27] William C. Townshend, *Lázaro Cárdenas* (Ann Arbor, Mich.: George Wahr, 1952), p. 216.

[28] Prewitt, *Reportage on Mexico,* cited, pp. 167-169.

regime; its leader was arrested and cashiered. Similarly, General Laura Rocha's "anti-Soviet" campaign in the western states of Guadalajara and Jalisco against Cárdenas' "socialistic" agrarian and educational reforms was more annoying than dangerous to the stability of his regime.[29] A far more serious threat came from General Saturnino Cedillo, the last of the regional *caudillos*. Breaking with Cárdenas over both personal and policy differences, Cedillo in 1937 resigned from the cabinet and returned to his native state of San Luís Potosí where he began drilling a personal army, estimated at 8,000 to 15,000 armed peasants. But again the army remained loyal and Cárdenas, taking command in the field in the spring of 1938, had little trouble in crushing the uprising, thereby enhancing the prestige and authority of the central government.

Despite their unwillingness to join an armed revolt, some of the top revolutionary generals and a certain number of the new professional officers continued to balk at and protest against Cárdenas' radical land and labor policies. They were especially apprehensive about the new breed of extremist labor leaders, like Lombardo Toledano, and about the formation of a uniformed workers' militia which outnumbered the army by nearly two to one. A congressional bloc, led partly by revolutionary generals, bitterly fought the Cárdenas-sponsored legislation proposing to strengthen the agrarian organizations and the labor unions.[30] The army's fear of the rising power of labor was revealed in the following public statement released by a group of army colonels on June 29, 1938:

> Lombardo Toledano cannot hide now that he seeks the dissolution of the revolutionary army, and one proof of this is the formation of the so-called workers' militia in order to install a proletarian dictatorship in Mexico. The army is tired of the anti-army calumny by labor leaders like Lombardo who are seeking to fool the workers into starting a fight like that in Spain. The Mexican public may have the secure knowledge

[29] *New York Times,* February 11, March 24, August 12, 1936.
[30] Same, May 2, 1938; Kluckholn, cited, p. 5.

that the military officers will put an end to the calumny and violence of perverse leaders who are exploiters of the working class. In good time the army officers will answer their aggressors. We wish it to be known that if our brother officers, in defense of our armed institutions, punish Lombardo we are not guilty since we have been provoked.[31]

Army-labor tensions threatened a crisis in the summer of 1938. In a very real sense the issue was control of the party, the revolution, and the state. The battle was between the old revolutionary army generals in the north, who had been dominant since Carranza's victory in 1914, and the rising new political elements (the peasantry and the urban workers) in the central region. The latter, having grown to maturity during the mid-1930's, were now, with Cárdenas' backing, challenging the generals. Toledano's central Confederation of Labor (CTM) boldly attacked General Juan Yocupicio, the antilabor governor of the state of Sonora, and demanded his dismissal. The Revolutionary party, no longer controlled by the generals since Cárdenas reorganized it in four sectors in late 1937, moved to expel "congressional" generals who seemed to be resisting labor-agrarian advances. The CTM's aggressiveness in Monterrey, Mexico's leading industrial center, prompted General Andreu Almazán, the regional military commander who was the highest-ranking officer in the army and one of the ablest of all the old revolutionary generals, to call on Cárdenas and urge him to curb the activities of pro-labor groups.[32]

When Cárdenas refused to intervene in behalf of his old colleagues, the lines were drawn for the political battle centering on the election of 1940. On one side, now outvoted and therefore outside the official party, were ranged the old leaders of the revolution and the conservative landed and business interests. Their candidate was General Almazán. Thirty-four high-ranking officers, mostly old generals of the revolution, took leave from active service to

[31] *New York Times,* June 30, 1938.

[32] Same, July 17, August 11 and October 16, 1938.

campaign for him. The government party also had a general as its candidate, Manuel Avila Camacho, Cárdenas' secretary of defense. But Avila Camacho was no revolutionary hero; instead he represented new labor and agrarian forces. Cárdenas appears to have chosen him to run because his influence with younger officers gave him the best chance of combating, in the army, the support still enjoyed by the clique of old revolutionary generals.

General Almazán and his supporters were well aware that they had no chance of winning elections managed by the incumbents. Consequently, they began making charges of electoral fraud early in the campaign. They accused the Cárdenas regime of "imposing" an unwanted official candidate on the people. They issued warnings and veiled threats of revolt, but the bulk of the army, in contrast to its past attitude, now seemed thoroughly bored by politics. The result was that the threats of Almazán and his supporters proved empty. General Avila Camacho and his labor-agrarian backed party were proclaimed easy victors over the revolutionary generals and their conservative supporters in the 1940 elections. After several minor post-election conspiracies had been easily quelled,[33] the shift was complete. Control of Mexico's politics had been taken away from the generals of the revolution and placed in the hands of the labor-agrarian forces. Avila Camacho delivered the final blows to politically minded generals soon after his inauguration when he eliminated the military sector from the government party, broke up the military bloc in Congress, and placed a number of revolutionary generals on the retired list.[34]

With militarism finally throttled and internal order no longer a serious problem, the Mexican army could now devote its attention to its orthodox function—namely, to protect the nation against possible foreign enemies. And

33 Same, January 4, February 12, July 4, August 11, August 20, September 14, October 2, and October 3, 1940.

34 Howard Cline, *The United States and Mexico* (Cambridge, Mass.: Harvard University Press, 1953), p. 276.

it was primarily for this purpose that the armed forces were built up, with United States assistance, during World War II. Under President Avila Camacho the armed forces were further reorganized, modernized, and professionalized. With political stability, accelerated economic development, and the increasing strength and influence of middle-class and professional groups, military officers played an ever-declining role in public affairs.

In 1946 and 1952 the party in power put up civilian candidates which easily defeated the still present and ever-threatening political generals of the opposition. The 1958 elections were again won handily by the civilian candidates without serious incident. By this time the die-hard generals of the revolution were no longer in evidence.

Compared with other Latin American armies, the Mexican today is a model institution. In accordance with the constitution, it devotes its energies principally to two fundamental functions: (1) the maintenance of internal peace, and (2) the provision for external defense. Incidentally, it performs an important function in collaborating in the country's public-works program. It builds barracks, schools, and hospitals, manages reforestation and irrigation projects, and helps keep the roads in good repair. It does not carry out its internal-security duties autonomously, as in so many Latin American countries, but acts only under the orders of the president and the authority of Congress as provided in the constitution.

In accordance with the law, military personnel in active service surrender their political rights. They may neither participate in public political discussions or meetings, venture their opinions publicly on political matters, nor attempt to exercise political influence over their subordinates. For such illegal action the law provides penalties, including dismissal from the service.[35]

The armed forces are by no means completely removed

[35] Javier Bazán Pérez, *El ejército en la constitución y en la política* (Mexico City, 1952), pp. 11-54; William P. Tucker, *The Mexican Government Today* (Minneapolis: University of Minnesota Press, 1957), p. 194.

from the business of government, however. All the commanders of the nation's thirty-three military zones are political in the sense that they are agents of the central government. They keep the state authorities in line and preserve order during elections. The growing strength of parties independent of the central government reveals, however, that the tyrannical rule of the zone commanders over the state governors and manipulation of elections by the army is rapidly becoming a thing of the past. Although some high officers are very influential in the Mexican government today, the military men are definitely in the minority. In 1958, only seven out of twenty-nine state governors and only two of eighteen cabinet ministers (defense and navy), were military men.[36] Inside the ruling party and inside the government itself civilian professionals predominate; they are the real policy-makers. The army is under their control. On issues that do not concern the military establishment they can act without consulting the armed forces, and they can, and do at times, oppose it on military issues. For example, despite the armed forces' desire for outside assistance and modernized equipment, the civilian authorities overruled the military and rejected the proposed Mutual Defense Assistance Pact with the United States.[37]

In accordance with the limited functions and influence of the military, the civilian authorities have deliberately kept the military establishment small (around 50,000 over the past quarter-century) while the rest of the nation has grown rapidly. Consequently, the armed forces have received a declining percentage of the national budget (only about 12 per cent in 1957 as compared with 21 per cent in 1940). They absorb, also, a smaller percentage of the gross

[36] Tucker, cited, p. 193; Walter H. Mallory, ed., *Political Handbook of the World, 1957* (New York: Harper, for the Council on Foreign Relations, 1957), pp. 134-135.

[37] *Hispanic American Report,* September 1950, p. 13; January 1952, p. 8; July 1953, p. 10.

national product than do the armed forces of any other Latin American country except Costa Rica.[38]

Though the Mexican army ranks very low in Latin America with respect to its political influence, its professional rating, based on modern methods of organization, instruction and discipline, is high. Since the beginning of World War II the United States armed forces have served as Mexico's model for the organization of the army, its arms, methods of instruction, and discipline.[39]

The officer corps, only 3,500 strong, comes mainly from conservative middle-class families. A competitive entry examination and a 500-peso admission fee screen out the uneducated and the poor. Officership is now an established and respected profession. The young men plan their careers carefully and obtain promotions through professional competence rather than through political influence as in the past. No longer are their aspirations blocked by "revolutionary generals" with no knowledge of modern military methods.

The capabilities of Mexico's armed forces, although limited by their size and by shortages in equipment, are adequate for their principal mission—preserving internal order. For defense against threats from a major foreign invader, Mexico knows it can count on the United States.

For an underdeveloped Latin American country that is trying to modernize, it is important that the armed forces neither act as a serious drag on the economy by inflated budget requests nor pervert and corrupt politics. The Mexican armed forces now do neither. Discipline and control are firmly in the hands of a government and a political party, both of which are dominated by civilians. Inasmuch as the political influence of the officer corps has continued to decline over the past quarter-century while professionalism has risen, it is difficult to see how in the foreseeable

[38] *Inter-American Statistical Yearbook* (New York: Macmillan, 1940), pp. 512-541.

[39] Prewitt, "The Mexican Army," cited, p. 612; Tucker, cited, pp. 193-194.

future militarism can again plague Mexico. The counteracting trends are firm and steady and unlikely to be reversed. Mexico is over the hump. Fortunately, it has solved the problem of militarism. That is a major reason why it has become one of Latin America's most progressive nations.

In dealing with militarism, Mexico has set an example which other Latin American nations might be well advised to follow. Its experience has shown that, once a major social revolution has taken place, determined executives can launch a comprehensive program to mould the armed forces into a disciplined, professional army that would shun political activities. The task involved a liberal use of Machiavellian techniques to break the power of the citizen-officers of the revolution and a well-planned educational program designed to instill in the new young officers the concept of the "good soldier." An integral part of the project to achieve civilian supremacy in politics was the development among the urban workers and the peasants of counterpoises to the armed might of the military. The task took a generation to accomplish, but the results have proved more than worth the effort. For the past generation the entire nation, including the armed forces, has been reaping the rewards of this basic political reform and will almost certainly continue to do so.

Chapter 5

THE CHANGING ROLE OF THE ARMED FORCES: AN ANALYSIS

Militarism and Politics

EARLIER CHAPTERS have shown how the last few decades of rapid change and social crisis in Latin America brought the armed forces back into a position of political prominence they had not held since the nineteenth century. At the time of World War I, the fraction of the total area and population that was dominated by the military was declining, and by 1928 only six Latin American countries, containing but 15 per cent of the total population, were ruled by military regimes. Then, abruptly, following the onset of the world depression in 1930, there occurred a striking relapse into militarism.

A rough measure of this phenomenon, though not always foolproof, was the number of presidents in uniform. Brazil, with its civilian traditions, managed to avoid it. But in Argentina, to take a different example, after nearly half a century of civilian rule, eight out of ten presidents between 1930 and 1957 were generals or colonels. To take a single year, in 1954 thirteen of the twenty republics were ruled by military presidents. In those countries which had never developed a civilian tradition in politics, like the republics of the Caribbean and Central America, the military tradition not only continued but was even reinforced.

This re-emergence of the armed forces upon the Latin American political scene was a by-product of the area's developing economic and social crisis, which the political institutions were not strong enough to contain. In the resulting political chaos the armed forces again and again were provoked or called upon to intervene. Their motives for so doing were not always the same. The devoted professionals might intervene in the name of their legitimate duty to preserve internal order, while the latent militarists might be motivated only by political ambition, and still a third group, the idealistic officers who believed it their duty to provide social justice, might compete with the other two.

The militarism of the postwar period, like that of the 1930's, has been principally a reflection of demands made upon the armed forces by antagonistic classes—by the traditional order attempting to maintain the *status quo* and by new social forces attempting to alter it. Examples already described will illustrate the point. In some cases, such as Argentina in 1930 and Peru in 1948, the armed forces intervened at the behest of the beleaguered civilian oligarchy. In others they acted on behalf of rising popular forces, as in Guatemala in 1944 and Venezuela in 1945. In Colombia, in 1953, the army took over when a stalemate appeared in the conflict of civilian groups. In El Salvador, where the strength of the civilian oligarchy declined after 1930 without a concomitant growth in responsible labor and middle-class groups, power went by default to the army, the only organized, disciplined force available for administering the affairs of the nation.

The environment in Latin America invited military rule. The decadence of the oligarchy, the political immaturity (not to mention the poverty and illiteracy) of the new groups aspiring to power, the lack of any strong, well-integrated group aside from the armed forces—all these combined to encourage militarism. In the words of one recent author:

If there is no agreement on the right to command or the duty to obey, either because of ethnic heterogeneity or in consequence of an internal schism, naked force must remain the argument of last resort, and the distribution of military might must then be the principal determinant of the social structure.[1]

Had the armed forces remained neutral, or had they been unable to exercise effective control, unruly civilian elements would probably have made Latin America even more unstable than it actually became. The threatened use of force, for example, by rival, extremist civilian groups, such as the White Guard and the Red Militia in Chile, the pro-Prestes partisans and the Integralistas in Brazil, and the fascistic Gold Shirts and the labor militia in Mexico, made it most difficult for the regular army to remain aloof from politics.

Whenever the armed forces assumed political power, whatever their actual motivation, they maintained they were doing so only because the civilian government had failed. Ostensibly they were motivated by only the purest of patriotic intentions. In their own eyes, grave national circumstances made their intervention imperative.[2] Indeed, ever since independence, the military had developed the firm conviction that it was their duty to step forward in times of internal crisis to save the nation from itself. The changing social scene had not affected this basic concept, except in the few countries like Chile, Uruguay, and Colombia where professionalism had really taken root.

The armed forces were the arbiters of politics because it was they who controlled the means of violence, the *sine qua non* for political change in most countries. Advances in armament technology and improved military capabilities made them increasingly confident of their overwhelmingly superior power over unruly civilian elements; accordingly, they were less hesitant in putting that power to use. In addition, the newly modernized armies had no

[1] Stanislaw Andrzejewski, *Military Organization and Society* (London: Routledge and K. Paul, 1954), p. 128.

[2] For a typical military view, see Colonel Sosa de Quesada, *Militarismo* (Havana: Instituto Civico Militar, 1939), pp. 25-57.

real military mission to perform. They were underemployed; the absence of international wars, other than the Chaco struggle and Peru's border conflicts with Ecuador and Colombia, confined their military activities to routine peacetime maneuvers. Such meager military demands left surplus energies for extramilitary activities, and the social crises of the period since 1930 have offered unlimited political opportunities for the more clever, ambitious and energetic officers.

Finally, developments abroad—Nazism, fascism and Franco's victory in Spain—gave encouragement to militarism in Latin America.[3] Some officers, like Uriburu in Argentina, were attracted by pro-Fascist propaganda. Others, like Germán Busch and his colleagues in Bolivia, were indoctrinated in national socialism by German military advisers. The political appetites of still others, Perón, for example, were obviously whetted by travel and study in Europe. Quite naturally, considerations of national security during and after World War II encouraged the officer corps everywhere to assume a larger role in national affairs. Latin American officers could not help but be impressed by the prominence of military men in the governments of the great powers, and not least in the United States.

Militarism was contagious. The example set by Perón, and particularly his techniques, did not go unobserved by Major Arbenz in Guatemala, for instance, or by General Rojas Pinilla in Colombia. Similarly, General Odría's successful coup in Peru in October of 1948 probably served as an example for Colonel Pérez Jiménez, who emulated him the following month in Venezuela.

The Officer Corps

Essential to a deeper understanding of the social significance of the resurgence of militarism is a closer examination of the role of the military leaders. For, as might be

[3] Eduardo Santos, "Latin American Realities," *Foreign Affairs*, January 1956, pp. 254-255.

expected, Latin America's twentieth-century economic, social, and political metamorphosis was clearly mirrored in the officer corps. The dramatic struggles that occurred between the old and the new, between farm and city, between vested interests and newly organized labor, resulted in institutional upheavals in the armed forces as far-reaching and profound as those that occurred in civilian society.

After World War I, as we have seen, there began to appear in the lower echelons of the officer corps representatives of the rising urban middle groups. The sons of industrialists, bureaucrats, and urban professional men began to acquire the educational background and the modern, progressive outlook that made them superior cadets in the military academies. As in the past, men who chose a career in arms continued to come from the middle class, but the military representatives of these new urban groups, unlike the traditionally rural-oriented officers, had no ties with either the landed oligarchy or the church hierarchy. Consequently, they had, at least initially, little enthusiasm for perpetuating the role of the armed forces as a guarantor of the traditional social order.

The social identification of the new-type officer with the urban groups where he originated was probably the fundamental cause of the junior-officer uprisings that occurred in Latin America's armies in the second quarter of the twentieth century. In general, the ideological conflict was between the old and the new generation, between the generals, on the one hand, and the majors, captains, and lieutenants on the other, with the colonels often pulled in both directions. Such cleavages were nothing new in Latin America; what was new was their origins in social conflict.

Almost invariably, Latin America's popular revolutions of this century were led by the young officers. They became the sponsors of fundamental change and reform, the underminers of traditional institutions, the proponents of public-welfare measures. Democratic political institutions were of less concern to them. Indeed, they were often the leading advocates of militarized, authoritarian government and were apt to speak scornfully of "decadent" democracy. Their revolutionary zeal was by no means entirely altruistic, for changes in the make-up and role of the armed forces meant unparalleled opportunities for promotion. Militarization of government and extreme nationalistic policies meant new and important jobs for them, as well as expansion and enrichment of the state apparatus upon which the military was dependent for its income.

The new militarism, therefore, went much deeper than in the past. It was much more complex, as new social forces (labor and middle groups) and new military factors (politically influential navies and air forces) were added. Thus, those who stood for the old-type military dictatorship, backed only by the landed oligarchy and the upper clergy and often favored by foreign commercial or financial interests, had to face an entirely new, modern type of military competitor for political power.

Generally speaking, the new leader did not create the new sources of power. More often than not, the environment called forth the man, who rode to power at the head of a popular reform movement. A typical example was that of Arbenz in Guatemala. The new social philosophy was not primarily the brain child of the leader himself. His articulate expression of popular demands, demands in which he himself probably did not believe, was a weapon, a technique utilized for the enhancement of his personal power.

The new leader's relationship to the armed forces, the institution out of which he rose to power, was a curious one. He did not rise to be the head of a revolution by his own individual initiative, as had the *caudillos*. Rather, he represented a substantial cross section of the junior or middle-rank army leadership, concentrated in a conspiratorial clique, like the Group of United Officers in Argentina or the Patriotic Military Union in Venezuela. These young officers thought of themselves as enlightened members of a new, modern generation. Regarding the generals as unimaginative and behind the times, they sought to bring the armed forces into more sympathetic relations with the rest of the society. They were also interested in power, which could be had by gaining popular support, by playing the role of saviors of the downtrodden masses.

To win his battle against the oligarchy, the revolutionary leader had to pose as a representative of the lower- and middle-income groups. He had to make them believe that the enhancement of his power would lead to a parallel advancement of their interests. If the people responded to his vilification of the old regime and his Messianic promises, he was well on the way to the establishment of a kind of plebeian dictatorship, whether or not he had the majority of the people behind him. Opposition leaders could be effectively handled by simply condemning them as enemies of the people. Particularly troublesome elements, such as the conservative press, could be suppressed by organized violence, generally by police or security forces acting in "the people's" interest.

Every successful new leader announced a revolutionary reform program reflecting popular demands. The people supposedly would rule; they were the state; their new leader was its representative. He proposed to rebuild the national economy along modern lines, gave at least lip service to demands for agrarian reform, promised to curb the power of the landlords and the foreign capitalists, and pledged greater benefits to workers and peasants in the form of higher wages, better housing, and expanded social security.

In a typical case, the beneficiaries of these material gains were content with the vicarious enjoyment of political power through identification with the military dictator; but his colleagues were not. They had originally brought him to power; he was still dependent upon them. To decrease this dependence and thereby enhance his own power, he appealed even more to the people. Generally, to this end he built up organized labor as a counterpoise to potential rivals in the armed forces. The alliance with labor, the technique used by Perón, Arbenz, and others, was often as essential to the cause of fundamental reform as it was to the leader's drive for power. For in the frequent cases where his military colleagues began to lose their enthusiasm for drastic change soon after the revolution succeeded, labor was caught in a dilemma. Unless it shared in the aspiring dictator's drive for supreme power, achievement of its material and social demands was impossible. Generally, the lower classes chose to go along with him, as the only hope for more "economic democracy."

The first of these new-type military rulers, officers who rose to power as leaders of popular reform movements, was General Carranza in Mexico, who in 1915 appealed to the new social forces and gave lip service to—but did not fulfill—their demands. His successors, Generals Obregón and Calles, were more attentive to such demands. Prior to 1930, Major Ibáñez of Chile was the only other leader of the new type on the Latin American scene. Between 1930 and 1957, eleven of the fifty-six military men who held the presidential office in the twenty Latin American republics for as long as a year might be so described: Major Ibáñez (1930-1931), Colonel Perón (1945-1955), Colonel Rafael Franco (1936-1937) of Paraguay, Colonel Busch (1936-1938) and Major Villaroel (1943-1946) of Bolivia, General Rojas Pinilla of Colombia (1953-1957), Colonel Remón of Panama (1952-1955), Colonel Arbenz of Guatemala (1950-1954), General Cárdenas of Mexico (1934-1940), Sergeant Batista of Cuba (1933-1944), and Major Osorio of El Salvador (1948-1956). In three countries young officers who had conducted revolutions sustained reform-oriented, civilian-led regimes in power. This was the situation in Brazil under Vargas (1930-1945), Venezuela under Betancourt and Gallegos (1945-1948), and Ecuador under Velasco Ibarra (1944-1947).

Generally opposed to the military "reformers" were the senior officers. Their god was stability, and as its defenders they frowned upon social and political experimentation. They might be more partial to democratic institutions than their younger rivals, but this was likely to be the narrowly based "democracy" which had been allowed to function within the traditional order. Their political philosophy was understandable. Having arrived at the top of their profession, they were affected by the conservatism that came with rank, age, status, and the attainment of comfortable material circumstances. The exalted rank of general enabled them, unlike the junior officers, to enter politics without sacrificing their professional position.

In the events of the years 1947-1957 already described, every one of the reformist military regimes was overthrown, usually either by conservative army officers or by young officers, originally leaders of the revolution, whose zeal for reform had withered before the winds of labor-leftist extremism. Reactionary movements brought to the fore officers whose mission it was to halt the social revolution, although they were never completely successful, for the changes wrought by the reform regimes were generally too fundamental to be undone. In most cases labor-leftist political activity was sharply curtailed or prohibited, and although most of the social and material gains already attained were preserved, no new ones were forthcoming. In economic policy, however, the military leaders of the counterrevolution generally stole much of the industrializing, modernizing, and nationalistic programs of their predecessors.

It is difficult to make reliable generalizations about the socio-political attitudes of the officer corps in a single country, let alone in Latin America as a whole. Some military leaders did not conform to any type. The lines between groups were fluid, and there was seldom any permanent resolution of the struggle among those vying for power. Sometimes revolutionary young officers would win control, only to lose it to their more conservative seniors, as in Chile between 1925 and 1932. Sometimes senior officers would attempt a liberating revolution, as in Colombia in 1953. Sometimes junior officers originally liberal would turn conservative, as in Brazil between 1930 and 1945 and in Venezuela between 1945 and 1948. Sometimes the same officers that originally sponsored a military dictatorship would later bring it to an end, as happened when Perón and Rojas Pinilla were ousted.

Struggles within the officer class were complicated by ideological cross-currents and fierce personal and professional rivalries. Many officers in the lower ranks who talked of social reform really wanted increased pay and more rapid promotion. At times some of the senior officers, convinced of the inevitable political triumph of the new social forces compromised with them in order to preserve their own positions. This occurred, for example, in Guatemala in 1944. In the larger countries, generals interested in keeping pace with modern military technology in order to improve the capabilities of the armed forces, sometimes supported the new nationalism and industrialization.

Sometimes the three services were split along divergent political lines. The situation in Argentina under the Perón regime, for example, was most complex. There the army was the most powerful and the most politically inclined of the three branches of the armed forces. Within the army, whose officer corps had a middle-class background, there were two groups: one—the dominant—was nationalistic, socialistic, and politically minded; the less powerful group was more democratic in its outlook, inclined to accept the *status quo,* and relatively nonpolitical. A similar division characterized the navy, whose officers came from the upper middle class and the landed aristocracy. But in the navy, the democratic rather than the nationalist group held sway. Consequently, Perón never really had the navy on his side.[4] To compound the confusion, the air force was split about evenly. Only the police force, built up by Perón himself, revealed no broad internal divisions.

Throughout Latin America the armies were the strongest and the most politically active of the three services. They reflected social tensions most accurately, and therefore they were more seriously wracked by internal splits.

4 Jorge Abelado Ramos, *América latina: un país* (Buenos Aires: Ediciones Octubre 1956), p. 193.

Air forces had no significance in Latin America until World War II and have not yet achieved a major political role. Navies (important only in Brazil, Argentina, Chile and Peru), though less politically minded than armies, usually remained unified, fundamentally conservative institutions. A naval career, consequently, carried more social prestige.[5] The aristocratic tendencies of naval officers, however, often were moderated by the democratic views of the British and United States officers who were their professional advisers. Conversely, before World War II, authoritarian attitudes of some Latin American armies were reinforced by the influence of German, Spanish, and Italian military missions.

The Pattern of Revolution

In a number of Latin American countries, as we have seen, the pattern of revolution underwent radical change in the second quarter of the twentieth century. The former comic-opera, barracks-type revolts were superseded by revolutions of a genuinely social character, in which the military were usually forced into taking a stand. The general picture was one in which the young officers, also frustrated in their ambitions, made common cause with the rising popular groups. Together they collaborated in bringing down, by force, the *ancien régime*. Revolutions of this type arose in some countries from direct military initiative, as in Bolivia in 1936; in others, e.g., Guatemala in 1944, the young officers were inspired to revolt by civilian groups who were pressing for reform. In Argentina, in 1943, the colonels' clique took action in the belief that it had a continuing mission to manage the renovation of the nation. In Colombia in 1953, on the other hand, they intervened with reluctance and only after the traditional civilian leadership had amply demonstrated its incompetence.

However deep the causes, many of these twentieth-

[5] This was not true in Colombia, however.

century revolutions appeared, on the surface, very much like the old palace revolts. Nearly always, preceding a revolutionary attempt, there was plotting by "disloyal" officers. As in the past, a secret clique did the organization and planning. In Bolivia in 1936 it was the Logia Santa Cruz, in Argentina in 1943 the Group of United Officers, and in Venezuela in 1945 the Patriotic Military Union. The leader of the conspirators circulated a reform program designed to attract his colleagues. Then, as the tensions inside the armed forces increased, officers who had no real desire to intervene in political processes had to weigh carefully the probable outcome of the impending crisis and make their gamble. Loyalty to the incumbent regime would be rewarded if the rebellion failed, punished if it succeeded. Neutral, innocent bystanders were apt to be suspected by both sides.

The revolt generally began with the carefully prearranged seizure of a key garrison, either in or near the capital. If a sufficient number of outlying garrisons joined the initial uprising, an assault was made upon communication centers, the presidential palace, and loyal military installations. If the revolt succeeded, the Junta Revolucionaria or a Junta Militar was set up as a transitional regime, allegedly administering the transfer of power to a "constitutional" government.

The *junta's* job was to remove from their official posts both the military and the civilian partisans of the defeated regime, in order to guard against counterrevolution. Usually the revolutionary *junta* reorganized all branches of the administration, decreed a certain amount of reform legislation, and, after an interim rule of one to three years, arranged for elections designed to restore a constitutional government satisfactory to the military leaders and more or less consonant with the wishes of supporting civilian groups. But the transitional period was generally far from smooth. Conspiring officers, no longer united against a common foe, found the aftermath of victory filled with conflicts, ideological and personal. In the jockeying for power, *junta* membership frequently shifted to reflect the changing balance of the forces, military and civilian, which had sponsored the revolution. There was always the temptation to stay in power and to postpone indefinitely any free election or return to civilian government.

Such were the surface manifestations common to nearly all twentieth-century Latin American revolutions. To determine whether they were of the "palace" variety or represented broadly based social movements, one must look at the forces supporting the rebels and their programs. Generally speaking, a *sine qua non* for fundamental revolution was a prior upheaval in the armed forces in which junior officers seized power from their superiors, as, for example, in Chile in 1925 and Brazil in 1930, in Argentina in 1943, and in Venezuela in 1945. When a revolt occurred without such an overturn in the armed forces, the revolution was generally superficial, a mere changing of the guard without social or economic reform. Such was the case in 1930 in Argentina, in 1943 in Bolivia, and in 1948 in Peru.

Despite the existence of popular pressures it was still no easy matter to conduct revolutions in the face of resistance by armed forces united in their loyalty to the government. On the contrary, the technological advance in weaponry—the machine gun, the tank, the airplane—and the development of modern systems of transport and communication notably increased the repressive power of the armed forces. Except in Cuba, Lenin's dictum that "no revolution of the masses can triumph without the help of a portion of the armed forces that sustained the old regime" applied to Latin America in the twentieth century. Each day, as armament grew more elaborate, as police organizations adopted modern equipment and new methods of surveillance, the possibility of successful civilian uprisings or local rebellions became more remote.

But the frequency of revolutions in Latin America underwent no notable alteration. For the new repressive powers of the armed forces were offset by defections of key officers or groups of officers. For example, as recently as January 1958, the heavily armed, dictatorial regime of General Pérez Jiménez in Venezuela was toppled with surprising ease when naval and air force officers made common cause with popular forces. What technology and modernization had done was to make it certain that the armed forces would always play a dominant role, on one side or another, in any revolutionary contest.

Contrary to what one might expect, the social revolutions, except for the unique upheavals in Mexico and Bolivia, were no bloodier than the palace revolutions. This was because the masses of the population, though they exerted pressure, did not generally participate in the actual fighting. Except in Colombia in the decade following World War II and in Mexico a generation earlier, social change fortunately took place in Latin America without civil war. For this result, the continued use in the twentieth century of nineteenth-century revolutionary techniques was largely responsible.

It was sometimes possible to launch insurrections and to keep them going although the armed forces remained loyal to the government. This could happen, however, only when the terrain suited the conduct of guerrilla-type warfare and when the rebels received clandestine support from sympathetic civilians.[6] These conditions enabled the famous Prestes column in Brazil in the mid-1920's to hold out successfully for more than three years against the government forces. Similarly favored Colombian guerrilla forces continued to operate for more than a decade after World War II. More recently, the rebel forces of Fidel Castro successfully defied the Batista regime. In these cases the strategy of the rebels was to wear down the morale of the government forces by long-term operations on an ever-increasing scale until defections or frustration made victory possible. Although this technique had heretofore not proved successful in defeating an incumbent regime,

[6] See Katharine C. Chorley, *Armies and the Art of Revolution* (London: Faber, 1943), pp. 49, 61.

Castro's forces were able to carry though to victory in the first days of 1959.

Enlisted men played no leading or determining role in the social revolutions. Unlike the situation in Russia in 1917, extensive fraternization between regular troops and revolutionary elements of the civilian population did not occur in Latin America, for the commanders effectively isolated the men in the ranks by confining them in barracks, bases, and various military installations. Also, the illiteracy and general political apathy of the rank and file tended to make them docile instruments in the hands of the officer corps. As a result, many civilians tended to build up an emotional resentment to anyone in uniform and to condemn all soldiers as defenders of a hated regime.

Only in one brief period, the early 1930's, when economic depression brought discontent over loss of pay and deterioration in living conditions, did the men in the ranks become restless, and then in only a few countries. In 1931, the soldiers of the Fifth Regiment in Peru made an abortive attempt to seize the government; the sailors' mutiny in Ecuador in April of 1932 likewise failed. Success came in only one instance, in Cuba in 1933, when the enlisted men, led by Sergeant Batista, overwhelmed the officers, took over the government, and made themselves officers.

This Cuban experience was the single exception to the general rule that the Latin American officer corps kept the loyalty of the common soldiers and maintained discipline. Officers recognized that their own position depended on a contented rank and file, hence they usually ousted civilian governments which refused to provide for them adequately. Some reformist military presidents, in an effort to diminish their extreme dependence upon the officer corps and build up a defense against conspiracy, cultivated the men in the ranks with extraordinary emoluments and favors. Their aim was to secure from the enlisted men primary loyalty to the chief of state rather than to their immediate military superiors. But it did not work. Perón,

Arbenz, Batista, and other military dictators who tried this technique ultimately failed.

Civilian revolutionaries, however, were sometimes able to gain support from special groups within the military. In several countries the military cadets, whose careers had not advanced sufficiently to give them a predominantly military outlook, and whose youthful idealism could be exploited by astute political crusaders, were attracted to revolutionary causes. In Colombia in 1948 and Bolivia in 1952, the police, who were in much closer, day-to-day contact with the civilian population than the armed forces, made common cause with the rebellious populace.

Revolutions were most sweeping when the regular army, the ultimate guardian of social order, was overwhelmed, as in Mexico in 1914, Bolivia in 1952, and Cuba in 1958-1959. These, however, were not primarily planned revolutions, but spontaneous outbursts of popular antagonism manifested in violent uprisings. Only in these three countries, moreover, was it possible in the aftermath of victory to deal with the basic problem of land reform, a matter which even the most radical military reformers elsewhere avoided. Genuine agrarian reform in Latin America was perhaps impossible without the destruction of the officer corps, recruited as it was from the middle and upper-middle social ranks which believed firmly in the sanctity of private property. A reform regime that attacked the latter soon forfeited the good will of the officers, as was demonstrated in Venezuela in 1948 and Guatemala in 1954.

Nature of the New Militarism

Militarism, an endemic political phenomenon in Latin America, has had two sides. It has been both progressive and predatory. The military have generally shown no great concern for such concepts as representative government or individual civil rights. That is not surprising. In a region of backward economies, extreme social stratification, and great political apathy among the masses, with little tradition of orderly, democratic, constitutional procedures, governments have necessarily rested upon force. Inevitably, therefore, the armed forces have played a determining political role, be it for good or for evil, for progress or for reaction.

Some military regimes, especially the reform-minded ones that came to power after World War II, have had a decisive influence in promoting economic development and social change, and indirectly even in furthering political democracy. The late Vernon Fluharty has described the significance of this type of militarism in Colombia, a not untypical example:

> Rojas Pinilla has turned the clock forward on social achievement for the masses. He gave them status and a sense of their importance, if only because his government has emphasized their welfare. That lesson they will never forget, and nothing less will be acceptable from other governments to come. . . .
>
> In this sense, paradoxically, the military dictator is making a substantial contribution toward democracy. Every social, educational, political, and economic gain in status is a step toward the creation of the substantive basis upon which true popular democracy may one day rise in Colombia. . . .
>
> Ultimate accomplishment of this process may require many Rojas Pinillas. . . . But the military dictatorships make their necessary contribution, a lasting one, with their emphasis upon substantive democracy. Nothing can be the same after they have come, spoken to and for the masses, and gone their way. It does not even matter, in the long run, whether they were sincere in their solicitude for the people, or merely self-seeking. The important thing is that the masses will not forget. They will slowly grow into the new concept that they, too, are men, and they will demand more from the parties in the future than ever they dared demand before.
>
> Sooner or later those demands will be met. . . . Even though it may appear negative and temporary, this contribution is a gain for the future of popular democracy in Latin America.[7]

[7] Vernon Lee Fluharty, *Dance of the Millions: Military Rule and the Social Revolution in Colombia, 1930-1956* (Pittsburgh: University of Pittsburgh Press, 1957), pp. 316-317.

Until the appearance of reform-minded young officers, governments in Latin America had paid little attention to the masses. Although the new-type military leaders were anything but practitioners of genuine democracy, their new policies tended to bring about greater equality in income and social position, without which political equality could never have a solid, long-term basis. Many of the military regimes, moreover, regardless of whether they had popular backing or were reform-minded in a social sense, achieved a certain amount of material progress by fostering industrialization, the development of communications and public-works projects, and by enforcing political stability.

An officer's professional training often equipped him for the ministry of communications or of public works or other technical posts. In Brazil it was the army that explored the virgin interior, set up telegraph and wireless stations, developed agricultural colonies, and helped the Indians to advance in civilization. The army undertook similar tasks in Peru in the 1940's and in Bolivia in the 1950's. In Mexico and Argentina it played a key role in economic development by opening up new roads and constructing schools and hospitals. In Cuba, after 1936, it assumed a pedagogic and social function when it took charge of the new Escuelas Rurales Cívico-Militares designed to combat illiteracy and improve rural living conditions. In Chile, during World War II, the army helped alleviate the import crisis by manufacturing agricultural implements and bicycles.[8]

It can be also said in behalf of the armed forces that they often played an antidespotic political role, intervening to terminate the tyranny of one of their own errant colleagues or to supply a corrective to the excesses of civilian politicians. For example, they brought an end to the Vargas dictatorship in Brazil in 1945 and that of Perón in Argen-

[8] José Cavero Bendzú, *El ejército en las democracias hispanoamericanas* (Chorillos, Peru: Imprenta de la Escuela Militar, 1944), pp. 7-10.

tina a decade later. To take an earlier example, they served the cause of genuine political democracy in Chile in 1924 when they stepped in, on behalf of the people, to break the deadlock between popular President Alessandri and the oligarchic Congress.

In many cases, genuine patriotism and a desire to prevent political excess have been the dominant motivations for military intervention in politics. The stabilizing role of the army in Brazil has been aptly described by Alan Manchester:

> That the nation has been able to survive the incredibly rapid transition to industrialization without discarding its basic political structure is due in no small part to the army. Under the leadership of the General Staff the army has been the stabilizing factor which has stopped the political pendulum from swinging too far from the center. It terminated the dictatorship when the need for that regime was over and stood aside while the civil leaders laid the foundations for a real democracy. It stepped in again when the political leadership swung too far to the opposite extreme. It has played a conservative, stabilizing role since its rise to decisive influence in 1930.[9]

What might be called the predatory side of militarism, however, far overshadowed its beneficent and progressive aspects, even when military regimes rode to power on a program of social reform. One has only to compare their actual exercise of power with the legal provisions defining the position and function of the armed forces. The constitutions of the Latin American countries contain clauses along the following lines:

(1) The president of the republic is the commander in chief of the armed forces.

(2) The armed forces are a professional, nonpolitical body, which may not deliberate on matters relating to the service.

[9] "Brazil in Transition," *South Atlantic Quarterly*, April 1955, p. 175.

(3) The fundamental aim of the armed forces is to guarantee the defense of the nation, to maintain internal order, to guarantee constitutional rights, and to enforce the laws.

Yet in most Latin American countries the president was effectively commander in chief of the armed forces only when he was a military man who had come to power by revolution. Duly elected civilian presidents were generally powerless to call erring generals to order; the latter considered successful politicians ephemeral rulers, whereas an officer's position gave him continuing and assured power until his retirement. With few exceptions, the armed forces were in fact not strictly professional, no matter what the law said, and they were anything but "nonpolitical." They "deliberated" on all matters, but particularly "on matters relating to the service," that is, on their needs for funds, manpower, and equipment. Finally, they frequently flouted the constitutional rights they were supposed to "guarantee" and ignored the laws they were pledged to enforce. Whatever role the armed forces played in a revolution itself, the new civilian government was never permitted to alter the armed forces' traditional role as the ultimate arbiter of political disputes, to trim their customary share of the budget, or to interfere with their pay, benefits, discipline and promotions. Reform regimes were obliged to confine their reform activities to nonmilitary matters. Presidents Bustamante of Peru and Gallegos of Venezuela learned this lesson the hard way in 1948. Similarly, Presidents Velasco of Ecuador and Vargas of Brazil in the 1940's and again in the early 1950's failed in repeated attempts to exert executive authority over their respective nation's armed forces.

In brief, the armed forces have generally held themselves above the law. True, there might be lengthy constitutional discussions between the lawyer-politicians and the officers, but the latter always won with the incontrovertible argument of force. The central issue was: Are the functions of the armed forces delegated to them by the state, or do they already possess, inherently and permanently, rights and functions independent of those specified in the ephemeral constitutions?[10] The armed forces in most Latin American countries insisted, as regards military matters, on being a state within a state, demanding complete autonomy for the armed forces. As to politics, with the exception of only a few countries, they were in fact above the state in claiming for themselves the inherent right to change governments at will.

Accordingly, the military arrogated to itself the power of deciding when constitutional rights had been violated and when the time had arrived to enforce the law. Though there were obvious cases where military intervention was needed to curb the excesses of military or civilian *políticos,* in most instances its justification was highly questionable. On all too many occasions the armed forces acted arbitrarily and in utter defiance of the duly constituted authorities and the popular will. A particularly notorious case occurred in 1948 in Venezuela, when the armed forces took it upon themselves to substitute a military *junta* for a popularly elected government. Then, in 1952, when the military were overwhelmingly defeated in an election, they simply refused to honor the popular mandate. Similarly, in Peru in 1948 and in Cuba in 1952 military leaders overthrew democratic governments, then kept themselves in power by force in the face of popular opposition.

Predatory military governments could maintain their rule only by tyrannical methods; accordingly, they set up bodies of secret police, ostensibly "to enforce the law," but actually to throttle opposition. While such rulers were actually stifling freedom and democracy, political expediency often prompted them to conduct their despotisms behind a constitutional façade. Most Latin American constitutions sanction, in time of grave national emergency, the declaration of a state of siege, making legal the "temporary" suspension of constitutional rights. Under such

[10] Javier Bazán Pérez, *El ejército en la constitución y en la política* (Mexico City, 1952), pp. 16-17

conditions, after all the potential rival parties and candidates have been effectively suppressed, a military dictator can be elected "democratically," without opposition. This was the technique used effectively by Generals Odría, Rojas Pinilla, and Batista.

Military training obviously did little to equip an officer with the skills necessary for running a modern state. Because his professional career isolated him from the main currents of society, his understanding of national problems was apt to be defective. And as technical advances made military affairs more complicated and as new economic tasks and social responsibilities had a similar effect on the tasks of civil administration, it became each day more difficult for a soldier to become also a statesman. Eduardo Santos, a political leader concerned with democratic values and procedures, has written:

> The military profession is poor schooling for learning the difficult art of government, for to govern well means to interpret, to reconcile, to respect the rights of all, to give freedom of expression to every opinion, to abide by the laws and never subordinate them to personal caprice, to have the courage to rectify mistakes, to ask for and listen to advice, to have patience, to realize that one owes one's power to the will of the people. . . . All this is difficult for the military to understand and accept, accustomed as they are to the blind obedience of their inferiors, the dry voices of command, and the narrow horizon of their profession, which rarely encompasses the element of humanism.[11]

As he wrote this in 1956, the ex-president of Colombia was witnessing, from exile, an example in his own country of how a fine professional soldier could prove utterly inept in the business of running a government. Rojas Pinilla, a devoted, conscientious, career man, had risen to the number-one post in the army by sheer dint of energy and professional excellence. As one of the more promising middle-grade officers, he had been selected for advanced

[11] "Latin American Realities," cited, p. 256.

training abroad. Having brilliantly led the Colombian Battalion in the Korean War, upon his return he became minister of defense. Unhappily, his country, ever since 1948, had been in the throes of a near civil war, with crime and violence widespread. Confronted by a deadlock between the Liberal and Conservative parties, public opinion demanded that something be done to stop the bloodletting.

The only individual in a position to act was Rojas Pinilla, who seized the reins of power with broad popular approval. But, since he had no experience in the complex business of governing, he was forced to seek advice from other generals; and he also compounded his difficulties by often stubbornly following mistaken civilian advice. He knew how to meet opposition only with force. His crude efforts to launch a popular political movement of his own ended in failure. Each day he marched more rapidly down the path of error. Frustrated by repeated failures (a severe blow to his pride), he became increasingly tyrannical, thus rekindling furious civil strife in the countryside. In 1957 public opposition had reached the point where his military colleagues had to unseat him.

Below the presidential level, also, the competence of military men for high political posts was open to serious question. In the aftermath of the military revolts that occurred after 1930, and particularly after those of 1948, there was a tendency to assign to men in uniform cabinet posts heretofore held by civilians.[12] It was not surprising that the Fascist-inspired revolutions in Bolivia in 1937 and Argentina in 1943 should produce all-military cabinets, but the trend was noticeable elsewhere too. The war ministry had always been an army post, but under the Ibáñez government in Chile in the mid-1950's, for example, the ministries of labor and interior, also, were headed by army officers. In Venezuela, after the 1948 revolution, army officers headed the interior and communications ministries,

[12] Jesús Silva Herzog, "Las juntas militares de govierno," *Cuadernos Americanos* (Mexico City), July-August 1949, pp. 9-10.

and acted as governors of the Federal District. The extreme was reached in Peru with the all-military cabinet of General Odría, in which colonels headed the ministries of public health, education, labor, interior, treasury, and justice, and a rear admiral conducted foreign relations. Obviously, these officers' professional training did not include the schooling in medicine, economics, law, politics, diplomacy, and public administration that their official tasks demanded. Mexico under Cárdenas had an all-military cabinet, but the ministers had no real responsibilities. Cárdenas appointed old revolutionary generals merely as figureheads, so as to be better able to control them. Actually, competent civilian technicians ran his ministries.

Despite the fact that young officers led social revolutions in many republics at certain stages of their history, especially in the 1943-1953 decade, the conclusion is inescapable that, on balance, the armed forces have represented a static or reactionary social force in Latin American politics since 1930. Military regimes which really promoted reform were the exception; political intervention by the armed forces was more often than not a conservative holding action, even to the point of dissolving popular political parties by force.

As suggested earlier in this chapter, moreover, even when idealistic young officers led a genuine social revolution, in the end they nearly always perverted and distorted its aims. Reform-minded military leaders generally came to power with a majority of the people behind them. During a brief honeymoon, drawing on their reservoir of popular support, they launched ambitious projects of economic development and enacted social-welfare measures. Yet, somehow, such regimes moved away from political freedom and eventually from social reform as well. It was as though the new military rulers were psychologically unprepared to accept authentically popular solutions to their nation's problems. Why?

Let us describe a generalized case which is hypothetical but quite typical. A young officer leads a military *coup d'état* and announces a program of reform. His head is then turned by his sudden attainment of tremendous personal power; he is reluctant to let it go. Then, too, his revolutionary zeal is nearly always greater than that of his colleagues, whose ardor for reform cools fast in the aftermath of victory. Consequently, the social program begins to slow down. Also, the victors, in accordance with accepted traditions, demand spoils, and the illicit enrichment of the new military elite, including the reform-minded dictator, soon makes his government appear to the populace more and more like that of its exploiting predecessors. The dictator's mounting problems are complicated by his political incompetence and his often ill-conceived, ruinous economic policies. All of this gives new courage to the traditionalist opposition, increasingly joined by many who had originally supported the liberal revolution. Faced with mounting resistance, the dictator tightens his control and increases its brutality in a desperate attempt to hold power. Ultimately, the armed forces split, and when that happens the days of the dictator are numbered.

Such was the fate, in a general way, of Ibáñez (1930-1931), Franco (1936-1937), Busch (1937-1938), Villaroel (1943-1946), Perón (1945-1955), Arbenz (1950-1954), and Rojas Pinilla (1953-1957). Neither they nor their military colleagues gave proof of possessing the ability, or the determination, to solve their nation's problems in an orderly, progressive fashion.

Reform-minded military rulers showed little competence in dealing with economics. They were particularly inclined toward ruinous financial policies. Almost invariably they were poor planners. Their drive for economic independence often led to over-hasty industrialization programs. The case of Perón in Argentina is a good example. His short-sighted emphasis upon industry led him to foster it at the expense of agriculture, the principal source of funds for investment in industrialization. Lopsided economic policies brought the nation to the brink of disaster. In the comparable case of Colombia, Rojas Pinilla's ambitious programs of public works and economic development left the country near bankruptcy.

One of the chief impediments to real economic progress in nearly all Latin American countries, whether the regime was military or not, was the inflated demands the armed forces made upon government revenues. Traditionally, since the turn of the century, the armed forces' reported share of the national budget has averaged about 20-25 per cent annually in most Latin American countries.[13] Official figures of war and navy departments, however, do not tell the whole story. Sizable appropriations for the armed forces, amounting to perhaps 5 per cent of the total budget, were often concealed in appropriations for the ministries of interior, public works, and communications. In Paraguay, after the military coup of 1954, the share of the armed forces went up to 50 per cent, and in Colombia and Cuba, due to the civil wars, military budgets also rose sharply. In the total Latin American picture, however, these increases were at least partly counterbalanced by sharp declines in Mexico after 1938, in Bolivia following the 1952 revolution, and in Costa Rica following the abolition of the army in 1948.

Although budgetary percentages generally remained constant, the expenses for Latin America's armed forces in absolute figures grew tremendously. This was because total national expenditures, with the rise of statism and big bureaucracies, had risen rapidly. For example, national budgets were several times larger in 1958 than in 1939. To some extent the armed forces' increase reflected the high cost of modern military equipment.

The resources that annually went into the armed forces' salaries and equipment obviously contributed little to the

[13] According to the *Inter-American Statistical Yearbook* (New York: Macmillan, 1940), pp. 512-541, the armed forces' percentages of the national budgets were as follows: Argentina—18, Bolivia—30, Brazil—24, Chile—26, Colombia—16, Costa Rica—9, Cuba—22, Dominican Republic—17, Ecuador—22, El Salvador—21, Guatemala—19, Haiti—24, Honduras—19, Mexico—21, Nicaragua—11, Panama—0, Paraguay—38, Peru—23, Uruguay—12, Venezuela—12.

economic development of a country. Civilian reformers like Arévalo of Guatemala, Paz Estenssoro of Bolivia, and Betancourt of Venezuela found it hard to condone expenditures which seemed so wasteful—wasteful because in their view the armed forces had no commensurate military function to perform: there was no danger of invasion, and the maintenance of internal order was being capably handled by the nation's police forces. In addition, the continued high military budgets served to enhance the political power of the military. Yet these were fixed expenditure items which no government, either civilian or military, could alter. The minister of war or of defense, always a representative of the armed forces rather than of the government, made it unmistakably clear that the military would brook no curtailment in their traditional budgetary share. Whenever a military regime was established there usually occurred a further build-up of the armed forces, with stronger emphasis upon military items in the budget. Only in the four Latin American states where civilian governments had brought their armed forces under control (Mexico after 1938, Bolivia after 1952, Costa Rica after 1948, and Uruguay since before World War I) were substantial reductions made in the military's percentage of the budget.

Inflated expenditures for the armed forces absorbed funds needed for technical progress. Except in a few countries, military men tended to eschew engineering and public-works functions. And certainly the side effects of predatory militarism—tyranny, ruinous economic policies, and intensified social cleavages—hampered technical progress. In some cases peculation, graft, and corruption were still more injurious.

In the Latin American tradition, military dictators used their office for purposes of illicit enrichment. Almost inevitably military dictatorship led to corruption. Not that civilian governments were clean in this regard, but the record of some of the military regimes is rather more spectacular. Immediately after a successful revolution the most pressing demands on the national treasury came from the new leader's military supporters. This was usually the first stage of corruption. The second came when the problem arose of consolidating power through the attainment of popular backing for the regime. For this purpose funds were needed which would be free from legal control. Established political parties already had resources of this kind, but military regimes did not, and so they naturally dipped into the national treasury.

A new leader generally did not hesitate for long to join his associates in their peculations; in some cases he set the example. Nearly all military rulers prepared for the inevitable day when, their power having collapsed, they would have to live out their days in exile. The conduct of Venezuela's military dictators was brazen but none the less typical. The corrupt pattern was fixed by General Juan Vicente Gómez, who during his long rule appropriated for himself hundreds of millions of dollars from the public treasury and substantial amounts for his family and military associates. After his death in 1935, his successors, Generals Eleazar López Contreras (1935-1941) and Isaias Medina Angarita (1941-1945) carried on the dishonorable tradition. Each, during his term of office, made off with about $13 million, then, following the 1945 revolution, retired in New York.[14] Yet the young officer who helped lead that revolution (Pérez Jiménez), and emerged as dictator in 1948, far outdid his predecessors.

In the five-year period from 1954 to 1959 Latin America's fleeing military dictators carried out of their countries hundreds of millions of dollars. Indications are that Perón escaped with as much as $700 million, Pérez Jiménez with more than $250 million, Batista with $50 million in 1944 and $200 million in 1959, and Rojas Pinilla, Paul Magloire, and Arbenz with smaller, yet sizable fortunes. Meanwhile, those still in power were providing for their

[14] Venezuela, Ministerio de Relaciones Interiores, *Sentencias del jurado de responsibilidad civil y administrativa* (Caracas: Imprenta Nacional, 1946), v. 1, pp. 303-334; v. 2, pp. 3-46.

retirement. General Trujillo, in the neighboring Dominican Republic, had over the years perfected his systematic graft until his annual income was estimated in the neighborhood of $30 million. In similar fashion, corrupt use of political power has made the Somoza family of Nicaragua one of the richest in Central America. But thievery by the heads of state was only part of the story. Under the Perón regime, favored generals like Humberto Sosa Molina and Franklin Lucero became multimillionaires. Colonel Pulido Barreto, Pérez Jiménez' ordnance chief, amassed millions from parking-meter collections and transportation concessions.[15]

Not all politically powerful military men were dishonest, nor was corruption limited to military leaders.[16] Colonel Remón of Panama, though he had enriched himself considerably as police chief, was a model of integrity in the presidential office. Also General Ubico of Guatemala (1930-1944) and certain leaders of the armed forces in Brazil earned reputations for honesty. But these examples were exceptions to the general rule that peculation on a large scale was characteristic of militarism.

Corruption in high places, like the inflation of military budgets, hindered economic development. As Stanislaw Andrzejewski has observed, the armed forces' "parasitic appropriation of the surplus produced by the economically productive civilian sectors of the society was one of the

[15] The figures here are merely rough estimates gleaned from a variety of newspaper reports. Obviously, statistics on the volume of peculation are unreliable and cannot possibly be well documented. For figures, there is little to rely upon save the charges of the victorious opposition. However, the notorious affluence of the exiles and their accumulated properties, both at home and abroad, provide irrefutable evidence of illicit gain of great proportions.

[16] Batista justified his 1952 coup with the charge that his corrupt civilian predecessors, Grau San Martín (1944-1948) and Prío (1948-1952) had misappropriated over $200 million. Also, it was estimated that Mexican President Miguel Alemán and the high officials of his administration had deposited $500 to $800 million in foreign banks between 1946 and 1952. See *New York Times,* September 19, 1952; March 24, April 9, April 28, 1953; March 25, 1954.

most powerful factors inhibiting technical progress."[17] This "surplus," in countries with exceptionally predatory military regimes, like those in the Dominican Republic, Nicaragua, and Paraguay, might be any amount in excess of the bare subsistence requirements of the mass of the population. Corruption was contagious; its spread caused would-be investors and entrepreneurs to lose confidence. The breakdown of many a nation's economy under corrupt military dictatorships was hastened by the flight of private capital.

Growth of Professionalism

There was, however, at work in Latin America a strong counterforce that reacted against militarism. This force was professionalism, which, despite the post-1930 upsurge of militarism, continued to build upon the initial advances that took place largely under the influence of European military missions around the turn of the century. Another and more basic factor in this trend was the antimilitaristic pressure exerted by the civilian population. In Mexico in 1914, in Costa Rica in 1948, and in Bolivia in 1952, the people destroyed militarism by violent revolution. And though in Mexico and Bolivia it reappeared in the post-revolutionary period, civilian authority eventually emerged supreme. In twentieth-century Uruguay, civilian leaders tethered the militarists, restricting them to proper military functions, notably the preservation of internal order.

In some other countries the armed forces retreated at least partially from the political arena and thus into a professional status as a result of pressure from hostile civilian groups. In Chile and Colombia the armed forces had developed a nonpolitical tradition. In each case the military intervened on one occasion (in Chile in 1924 and in Colombia in 1953) to arbitrate a current political crisis, and in neither case did intervention achieve its objective.

[17] Cited, p. 162.

Popular animosity, aroused by bungling and failures, ultimately forced the military to abandon politics (in Chile by 1932 and in Colombia by 1957). After 1955, similar antimilitaristic pressures exerted by the mass of the people were evident in Argentina, Brazil, Peru, Ecuador, Venezuela, and Cuba.

Since the military, however, still had a monopoly of physical power, the principal impetus toward professionalism had to come from within the armed forces. In almost every country the military organization was torn by two struggles: One reflected the country's social crisis; the other, but equally important, was the contest between the professionalists, the group of officers who held that the military should confine themselves to military duties, and the militarists who insisted on playing politics. In the first quarter of the century the former seemed to be in the ascendent, but in the period of continuing crisis that began in 1930 the militarists held sway. Only in the last few years, with the collapse of military dictatorships in Argentina, Peru, Colombia, Venezuela, Haiti, and Cuba, largely because many officers saw which way the wind was blowing and themselves aided in the overthrow of irresponsible military regimes, do the professionalists again appear to be gaining the upper hand.

Curiously enough, militaristic regimes gave stimulus to professionalism, not, to be sure, by the example they set, but because the dictators themselves feared the militarism that had given them power and might take it away again. For this reason rulers like Perón and Pérez Jiménez encouraged professionalism, advising young officers to stick to their military business and stay out of politics.

A growing element in the officer corps was becoming conscious of the proper role of the armed forces in the nation's affairs. The concept of the "good soldier" began to be more clearly understood, and was reinforced by travel and training in Western Europe and the United States and by the activities of foreign military missions in Latin America. Officers began to recognize that modern military technology required increased specialization, that genuine military *expertise* called for the digestion of a tremendous body of knowledge and years of training and experience, that gaining the technical proficiency necessary to qualify as a superior professional soldier was a full-time job that left no room for dabbling in politics.[18]

The rise of military professionalism was not an indigenous phenomenon. Rather, Latin America's armed forces were continuing their acceptance of ideas and programs already adopted in more advanced countries. During the 1930's German professionalist influence continued to prevail in southern South America; French missions were active in central South America (Brazil and Peru), and Italian missions, particularly in Ecuador and Bolivia. The United States, which did not establish military missions until the eve of World War II, achieved a monopoly of such activity in Latin America soon after hostilities began. The attitudes of United States officers toward their profession and their role in society, and indeed the very training in the arts of war which they imported, could not have failed to influence in some degree the outlook and the attitudes of their Latin American colleagues.

[18] The growing volume of professionalist literature emanating from the pens of Latin American officers well illustrates the steady growth of a professional *esprit*. See, for example Colonel Guillermo Prado Vasquez, *La carrera del oficial* (Santiago, 1952) and General Tomás Rueda Vargas, *El ejército nacional* (Bogotá: Comacho Roldán, 1944).

Chapter 6

THE LATIN AMERICAN MILITARY TODAY

For full understanding of the significance of the role the armed forces are playing in contemporary Latin America, analysis must proceed on two planes other than the strictly military—the political and the social—which are not always closely correlated. For example, an ostensible shift of political power to a civilian from a military regime, or vice versa, does not inevitably mean a change in social philosophy or basic orientation. For in many cases the transfer of political offices between the military and the civilians merely represents a step in the continuance of consolidation of a previous revolution or counterrevolution. The issue of military rule versus democracy, as we have seen, may cut across the issue of the traditional order versus social reform.

Obviously, an openly military regime invariably exercises a great deal of social control. And, even when civilians occupy all the top political offices, the armed forces may still exercise considerable influence behind the scenes, both because of their potential power and because of their known identification with, or antagonism toward, certain groups and classes in the society. For example, recent years have witnessed a pronounced trend away from leaders in uniform in executive branches of Latin American governments. In 1954 thirteen presidents were military; by early 1959 only four remained: General Trujillo in the Dominican Republic, General Stroessner in Paraguay, General

Miguel Ydígoras Fuentes in Guatemala, and Colonel José María Lemus in El Salvador. This does not necessarily mean that the role of the armed forces has been correspondingly reduced. On the contrary, the armed forces have continued to wield political power in all but three or four countries; in most of them they are making their powerful influence felt against a possible recurrence of the cycle of social revolution that characterized the 1943-1953 decade. Any general conclusions, of course, have to be tested by the situation existing in each individual country, and by looking beneath the surface of political appearances.

The recent apparent antimilitaristic trend has been running since 1954. Although it is still too recent to justify definite conclusions, the natural civilian reaction to a decade of flagrant and open militarism is one obvious explanation. But it was a reaction, in most cases, that required for success the support of elements of the armed forces. In the alternation in trends toward and away from military rule in Latin America the pendulum since 1954 seems to have swung in the latter direction, as it has before, with the added consideration that civilian regimes now coming into office have a wider popular basis for democratic government than existed in the past.

The trend began in Panama in 1955 with the assassination of Colonel Remón, an event which brought the movement toward social reform to a halt as the traditionalist first families, under President Ernesto de la Guardia, came back into office again. In Nicaragua, the assassination of General Anastasio Somoza in September of 1956 ended his career as the military ruler of that backward state, but disturbed little else; the dictator's two sons now rule the country. In Haiti, General Paul Magloire ran afoul of the same obstacles that plagued his predecessor—economic problems, graft and corruption on public works projects, resistance to his plans to continue in power beyond his constitutional term of office, and, in addition, a general strike. The army, influenced by popular antagonism to the regime and by the fact that the United States gave no encouragement to Magloire's plans for unconstitutional succession, willingly sacked their erstwhile leader, who retired to Jamaica at the end of 1956 with a large portion of his ill-gotten gains.

In Peru, General Odría's retirement and the election of Manuel Prado in 1956 demonstrated that the alliance of the oligarchs with the military leaders had collapsed. Odría's arbitrary policies and his harsh treatment of some members of the oligarchy had chilled their ardor for continued cooperation with the military. Also, the armed forces appear to have had some qualms about their ability to subdue indefinitely popular pressures for reform. Accordingly, in 1956 they retired from the presidential palace.

In Honduras, during 1957, the armed forces turned the government over to the civilians. A preliminary step had been taken in 1948 when General Carías, a dictator for sixteen years, resigned. The subsequent orderly election of Juan Manuel Gálvez, like Carías a leading politician in the conservative Nationalist party, indicated that Honduras was moving toward more stable and responsible government. The Gálvez regime promoted modernization of the Honduran economy and endeavored to substitute for *personalismo* the support of more broadly based political groups. Unhappily for the Nationalists, who in one guise or another had been in control since 1932, most of the emerging lower and lower-middle groups sided with the Liberal party in the 1954 elections. The result was that none of the three contestants won a majority. Thereupon, Vice-President Dr. Julio Lozano, with the blessing of the army, assumed the top political office. The effect of this action was to split the Nationalist party, as General Abraham Williams broke with Carías and set up an independent party. A third element adding fuel to the political fire was the activity of Dr. Ramón Villeda Morales and the Liberal party, which had won a plurality in the 1954 elections.

The upshot of the increasing political tension was a revolt of a group of junior officers. A major, a colonel, and a general comprised the *junta* which took over in 1956 after having deposed Lozano. The junior officers called for elections to a constituent assembly in October 1957. These elections were decisively won by the Liberals, whereupon the armed forces stepped aside and allowed Villeda Morales to assume the presidency; but they did not remain very far in the background.

The election of civilian regimes in Argentina and Colombia in 1958 and the transference of power from military *juntas* to moderate civilian regimes merely represented consolidation of the counterrevolutions against Perón, in 1955, and Rojas Pinilla in 1957. A later, and in many ways more surprising, upset came in Venezuela in January 1958, when the dictatorship of General Pérez Jiménez, which was apparently firmly entrenched, succumbed to naval and air force opposition backed by the populace. In the Venezuelan case, however, it was the new civilian regime issuing from elections held later in the year, rather than its military predecessor, which stood for social reform. The most recent and most spectacular upheaval of all occurred in Cuba, in which the civilian opposition, led by Fidel Castro's guerrillas, not only ousted the dictator but overwhelmed the armed forces.

Despite the clear trend away from military dictatorship, it is dangerous to generalize about the area as a whole, or any regional part of it, for the role of the military is not identical in any two countries. At the one extreme is Costa Rica, which abolished its army; at the other is the Dominican Republic with its absolutist military dictatorship. In between there are eighteen gradations.

Making due allowances for the difficulty of fitting living and changing societies into clearly defined categories, it is still possible to distinguish a broad pattern. The twenty republics can be broken down into three groups, roughly equal in number though not in importance. In one group the armed forces dominate politics; in the second their role is transitional; in the third they stand aside from political activity. In the first and third groups, the role of the armed forces is well defined and more or less stable. In countries of the transitional group, however, a struggle is going on between the officers who want to run the government, and those who want to keep hands off. The issue of militarism is a matter of dispute in the country at large and within the military establishment itself. In both the political and transitional groups the military exercise a profound influence upon movements directed toward social change and reform; in the nonpolitical group they affect the social problem very little, if at all.

Group I: Countries in which the Armed Forces Dominate Politics—Dominican Republic, Nicaragua, Paraguay, El Salvador, Haiti, Honduras, Panama

The seven republics in which the armed forces have traditionally been, and unquestionably still are (with the possible exception of Panama), the dominant political force have many common characteristics. All are small countries—small in population (together they have only 13.5 million people, 8 per cent of Latin America's total), and small in area (only 332,000 square miles, 4 per cent of the total). All seven have tropical climates, heterogeneous populations, high rates of illiteracy, low per capita incomes, and primitive agricultural economies. They are the most backward, least developed countries in Latin America. Their social structures are characterized by a high degree of stratification. Land and other forms of wealth and privilege are concentrated in the hands of the few; the middle group is relatively small, and the politically inert mass of the population exists at a bare subsistence level. The twentieth-century popular revolutionary stirrings by which the rest of Latin America has been deeply affected were felt but briefly in Paraguay after the Chaco War, in Panama during World War II, in El Salvador after the end of that conflict, and in the remaining four countries hardly at all. Such are the conditions in which irresponsible militarism thrives, and militarism, by its predatory activities, in turn exaggerates the depressing features of the economic and social milieu in which it operates.

In two of the seven countries in this group old-fashioned *caudillismo* still flourishes. The most primitive type is found in the Dominican Republic. General Trujillo, when he assumed power in 1930, ushered in a period of political stability and economic progress unparalleled in the history of the republic. Revolutions no longer break out, for the well-paid army is a disciplined, loyal, and efficient force. Material progress is steady. New highways have been built, harbors modernized, power plants constructed, agriculture diversified, industrialization promoted, schools built, illiteracy reduced, hospitals erected, and disease attacked.

The reverse of the coin, however, reveals the most brutal and stifling dictatorship in all of Latin America. It is completely personalistic; it has no ideological base. It rests on military force. The constitution describes the government as "civil, republican, democratic, and representative," but actually it violates all these principles. Elections are peaceful affairs, for there is only one party and only one candidate. Opponents of the regime are usually labeled "Communists." Incarceration, assassination, or exile is the reward for active opposition.

A fifth of the nation's sugar and brewery business is in the dictator's hands, and he has monopolies, or near monopolies, in domestic aviation, in sales of arms, tobacco and television sets, in shoe manufacturing, milk pasteurization, and cement production. Other income is provided by dress shops, newspapers, manufacture of furniture, and dealing in lumber, insurance, and real estate. General Trujillo has also begun taking over for purposes of self-enrichment hitherto-favored foreign investments, including United States sugar interests. All in all, it is a system which has produced stability, avoiding the chaos of periodic revolutions, but it is based purely on armed force, on *personalismo,* and on a complete absence of responsibility to the people.

General Anastasio Somoza, who set up a dictatorship in Nicaragua just three years after the evacuation of the United States marines in 1933, turned Nicaraguan politics back to the era of the nineteenth-century *caudillos.* He maintained order, keeping the loyalty of the Guardia Nacional, with material rewards. But like Trujillo he decided that the presidential office entitled him to the best land in the nation. He used his monopoly of the means of violence to promote the interests of his family. By systematic graft he accumulated vast commercial and agricultural holdings, making the Somozas one of the wealthiest families in the Americas.

Something remained of the national income to advance national interests. Agriculture was modernized, communications developed, schools built, and power facilities constructed. Yet almost nothing was accomplished in alleviating the great poverty and misery of the mass of the people, or in giving them any political responsibility. Elections were rigged; Congress was a rubber stamp; justice was rendered, Solomon-like, by the highly partisan dictator. The press was muzzled, opposition political parties throttled, and trade-unionism prohibited.

Was such a tyranny laying foundations for a violent popular upheaval? The assassination of the dictator in September of 1956 did not provide the answer to that question, for his sons carried on the *caudillo* tradition without major disturbance. Luís, formerly presiding officer of Congress, became president; his brother Tachito headed the *guardia.* The Somoza family and the *guardia* continued to dominate and exploit Nicaragua in the manner to which they had long been accustomed.

The five other countries where predatory militarism still prevails (Paraguay, El Salvador, Honduras, Haiti, and Panama) are only slightly less primitive politically than those with old-time *caudillismo,* and therefore somewhat less stable. They are more advanced only in the sense that their regimes are not so exclusively personal. The countries they run are not family estates. The presidents have to rely for their survival on the solid institutional backing of the armed forces. Only two of the five (Paraguay and El Salvador) had outwardly military governments in 1959. Military regimes came to an end in Panama in 1955 and in Honduras as recently as 1957, while in Haiti a civilian president was elected in 1957. But all five continued to be essentially soldiers' republics, with nearly exclusive military control of political processes.

The armed forces of all five nations, like the Roman Imperial Guard, intermittently and openly take power for the sake of their institution. These modern praetorians, like their forebears, identify themselves with no particular class and are devoid of any discernible social philosophy. They are a conservative force, nevertheless, because they insist upon order, preventing malcontent or reform-minded elements from creating political instability. Invariably they react negatively when their vested institutional interests or their role as political arbiter are threatened. They are sometimes willing to allow a civilian to occupy the presidential palace, provided he makes no disturbing changes.

In Haiti, following the collapse of the Magloire dictatorship in 1956, several provisional governments rose and fell because of the intense rivalry among aspirants to the presidency. Through all the energetic maneuvering of civilian groups, the army remained in the background managing affairs and probably determining their outcome. In the September 1957 election, victory went to Dr. François Duvalier, a popular candidate with a moderate reform program. His tenure of office depends, however, not on what he does for the welfare of the country but rather upon how well he looks after the army. The president has little independent authority. The army continues to sit firmly in the political saddle.

In Panama the police are still a powerful political force. Although the first families provide heads for the executive branch of government, the police (now called the Guardia Nacional), remain the key force behind the scenes and the nation's ultimate political arbiter. The civilian authorities dare make no major changes in policy without first clearing them with the military.

The young-officer coup that occurred in Honduras in 1956 seemed to indicate that revolutionary reforms might be in the offing, for the elections of October 1957 had resulted in a clear victory for the popular forces behind Villeda Morales and the Liberal party. That the military had no intention of relinquishing their strong political role became apparent, however, in their proclamation on the eve of that election that henceforth they would "assume the irrevocable functions of permanent guarantors and zealous keepers of the integrity of the country's institutions." Thus President Villeda Morales and the Liberal party were forewarned that they must expect armed intervention if they are unwilling to modify rather drastically their plans for fundamental reforms in Honduran social institutions. The same threat of military intervention has forced the Communists, who have recently begun to exploit unrest in this retarded republic, to move with caution.

In El Salvador the armed forces are in complete charge of the nation's politics and administration. President Lemus and his military colleagues manage the machinery of government, maintain political order, preserve the social *status quo* and their own institutional interests, while incidentally promoting a moderate amount of state-sponsored economic development.

In Paraguay flourishes the most extreme case of predatory praetorianism in all of Latin America. In May 1954 General Alfredo Stroessner seized power and set up a pure military regime. The armed forces thereupon declared a moratorium on civilian political activity. Meanwhile, they helped themselves to half the government's total revenues. The conservative Colorado party, which welcomed the military take-over because it blocked the revolutionary

Febreristas and the Liberals, still believes that it, rather than the armed forces, should rule. But the latter give no indication that they might be willing to relax their political grip.

Group II: Countries in which the Armed Forces Are in Transition from Political to Nonpolitical Bodies—Cuba, Guatemala, Venezuela, Peru, Ecuador, Argentina, Brazil

The second group of countries, those in which the political role of the armed forces is undergoing change and transformation, is the most important. The seven countries included in this group contain over 60 per cent of the area's total population, more than 70 per cent of its total land area, and the great bulk of its natural resources.

In this group of countries a most serious crisis exists. Every one of them has felt the revolutionary stirrings of this century, the demands from below for economic and social (including rural) emancipation. As we have seen, some elements of the military (except in Peru) allied themselves with rising popular forces, launched successful revolutions and, at least initially, backed programs of fundamental reform. Then, in response to rightist alarms and counterpressures, the armed forces re-entered the political picture to halt the leftward trend (in Ecuador in 1947, in Peru and Venezuela in 1948, in Brazil and Guatemala in 1954, and in Argentina in 1955). Although in some cases they later withdrew from overt political activities, in all seven countries the role of the military still looms large in the background, for the political system remains unstable and the forces of social revolution threaten to break out again.

The armed forces are torn in three directions. One group of officers wants to retain a dominant role in politics in order to resist further labor-leftist evolution, or at least to slow it down. A second group wants to leave politics to the civilians. Some members of this group are devoted professionals; others, disillusioned over the failure of men in uniform to resolve the social crisis, simply feel that this is a time to stay on the sidelines. The third group, now everywhere in eclipse, except in Cuba, is made up of young officers biding their time to identify themselves with the masses and the cause of social revolution.

These divisions are important; they can lead to conflict. Yet there exists at the same time a growing sense of solidarity within the military establishments, a feeling that the day of the militarist-politician is passing. Thus the second group of officers described above should gain in strength as the armed forces in these seven countries evolve from a highly political institution toward one that is politically neutral.

In Cuba, where the regular army was defeated and disbanded by the victorious revolutionaries in January 1959, Fidel Castro's liberation army has now become the island's dominant political force. True, the revolutionary program calls for unconditional subordination of the military to the civilian authorities, and to this end plans have been announced for a complete reorganization of the armed forces with a view to forever separating them from political activities. However, just as in the aftermath of the destruction of the regular armed forces in Mexico in 1914 and in Bolivia in 1952, the liberation army will undoubtedly play a potent political role in implementing the revolutionary program. The new army, of course, has already been indoctrinated with the ideology of the revolution. It is too early to predict when, or whether or not, Castro's thesis of civilian control will ultimately become effective in Cuban politics.

In Guatemala, Castillo's assassination in the summer of 1957 did little to resolve the struggle for power between rightist and moderate elements. When a moderate civilian candidate won the October 1957 election, the military-led, rightist political faction stirred up so much resistance that the armed forces felt obliged to nullify the election and to re-establish the rule of the *junta*. Then in early 1958 the conservatives, led by General Miguel Ydígoras Fuentes, having won on their second try, made the general president.

Although Ydígoras has recently veered toward the center, and the moderates in the army now seem to be running the government, the political situation is far from stable. Events since 1954 have revealed that a substantial cross-section of the officer corps, and undoubtedly a majority of the population, still cling to many of the principles of the popular revolution of 1944. The dominant elements in the armed forces, however, continue to arbitrate the nation's politics.

Venezuela, described over a century ago as "a barracks" by its founder, General Simón Bolívar, has pretty much remained a barracks ever since. The history of the nation could be told in the lives of its military dictators; the unchallenged supremacy of the armed forces has been the chief characteristic of the nation's politics. Despite the collapse of Pérez Jiménez' military dictatorship in January 1958, and the election of a civilian president the following December, the armed forces are still potent in the affairs of government. Because of the long tradition of political omnipotence on the part of the military, the officers who shun political office are probably still in the minority. The curse of militarism is far from being lifted in Venezuela.

In Peru the civilian government of President Manuel Prado is conservative but sufficiently democratic to provide renewed opportunities for the Apristas to reactivate the temporarily stalled social revolution. But in the armed forces there is always a faction ready to intervene to check radical change, either at the instigation of the oligarchy or if their own traditional privileges and emoluments are put in jeopardy by civilian groups.

In Ecuador the group of nonpolitical officers is apparently stronger than in Peru. Since 1948 they have progressively retired from active participation in political activities; the presidential elections of 1952 and 1956 took place under civilian control. There remained, however, politically minded officer groups, both on the right and on the left, ready to resume active roles in governmental processes should social reform again become a burning political issue.

In Argentina, right-wing militarists represent a continuing threat to the recently elected civilian regime. President Arturo Frondizi's sin in their eyes, is that he rode to electoral victory in early 1958 on the strength of support received from the Peronistas, the faction that the armed forces had overthrown and hoped to eject from politics by the revolution of 1955. The president's dilemma is that he must reward labor with political privileges and material gains if he wishes to retain its support, while, if he favors this element too much, he will provoke a new rightist military coup. Provisional President General Aramburu, Frondizi's predecessor, declared in his farewell address that the armed forces would henceforth steer clear of political intervention. However, the officers who are uninterested in politics are not the dominant group in the army. Frondizi himself, moreover, adopted a moderate course and an austerity program which made the Peronistas anything but happy, and he was forced to use the army to break strikes which they organized. Nevertheless, the dominant politically minded faction stands ready to intervene when these officers decide that "irresponsible policies" (that is, pro-Peronist or pro-labor) are becoming too pronounced.

The position of the Brazilian armed forces is in many ways unique. Politically, they are above partisan politics. As supreme guarantors of constitutional processes, they sit in judgment over presidents, judges, legislators and all nonuniformed mortals. When it becomes necessary to correct a political situation which they regard as illegal or unconstitutional, they do not descend to the street level, operating with brute force. Rather, they quietly issue a dignified ultimatum, from which there is no appeal, and which all astute politicians have learned to respect. In other words, a president's policies, especially if they involve significant innovations, are, in practice, subject to veto by the military.

The Brazilian constitution declares that the armed forces are agents of the executive branch of government, that Congress shall provide their appropriations and approve promotions, and that their only functions are to defend the nation against external threats, preserve internal order, and guarantee constitutional processes. In reality, however, the armed forces of Brazil act with nearly complete autonomy. They constitute an institution that is above the state. Although they are in theory under the command of the president and under authority of Congress, the latter dares not cut their requested appropriations or reject their recommendations for promotions.

The outward appearance of unity and the restriction of political influence to a silent, mysterious force in the background have had the effect of concealing severe conflicts within and among the services, particularly in respect to the nation's social problems. The conservative senior officers, the dominant element, are inclined to act as guardians of the *status quo*. They frown upon the new middle and lower groups whose attempts to increase their share of the national income by political or social action they believe threaten the nation's basic institutions. This attitude is not the result of class consciousness or antagonism toward the rising new groups, for in fact most of these officers come from families more akin to the new forces than to the wealthy rural landowners and the urban industrialists. It is rather that this group opposes social change because it disturbs internal order, which it is the military's mission to preserve. It is this military group that is responsible for the Kubitschek government's hewing to a moderate, cautious line.

There is, however, in the Brazilian military hierarchy a substantial element that wants to give the civilians a freer hand, at least so far as nonmilitary matters are concerned. This group is led by devoted professionals who fear lest their institution acquire a reputation for irresponsible militarism. Joined with them are those who doubt, in view of the futile interventions in politics by the armed forces in 1945, 1954, and 1955, that the military are capable of resolving the nation's developing social crisis. There is also a third group which believes that the military must give leadership to the insistent popular forces, and perhaps even manage the nation's social revolution.

Group III: Countries in which the Armed Forces Are Nonpolitical—Colombia, Chile, Mexico, Bolivia, Uruguay, Costa Rica

The final group includes those countries in which the armed forces have completed, or virtually so, their transition from dominant factors in government to a politically neutral professional status. These six countries contain about a third of Latin America's total population and a quarter of its land area. They range from big Mexico (second largest in population and third in size in Latin America) to tiny Costa Rica (second smallest in population and fourth in size). Included in the group are predominantly white countries (Uruguay, Chile, and Costa Rica), predominantly Indian countries (Bolivia and Mexico), and a *mestizo* country (Colombia). The six countries are of particular importance because they are the most democratic politically, both a cause and a result of the absence of militarism. They set an example; they point the way for other Latin American nations to follow toward orderly solutions of grave national problems. In four of these countries the basic problem of bringing the masses into the body politic has been largely resolved, in Mexico and Bolivia by violent revolution, in Costa Rica and Uruguay by peaceful evolution.

In the two countries where the social crisis still awaits further resolution, Chile and Colombia, the armed forces occupy a unique position. They are autonomous bodies, dominated and controlled by devoted professional officers. The latter do not openly espouse the cause of any class nor do they express any social or political philosophy. In both countries the armed forces have traditionally kept aloof from politics—in Chile since the early nineteenth century and Colombia since the early twentieth century. Only in grave national crises (in Chile in 1925 and in Colombia in 1953) have they intervened. Their failure in both cases taught them a lesson. Having burned their fingers in attempt at extramilitary functions, they soon withdrew from politics and resumed their traditional professional orientation.

Yet neither in Chile nor in Colombia are the armed forces now really under the control of the civilian government. True, governments can call on the military to preserve internal order, but where institutional military matters are concerned the civilian authorities have no control. The military's representative in the government, the defense minister, makes it understood that the armed forces' customary 20-25 per cent of the national budget must not be revised downward. A sort of gentleman's agreement exists. If the government allows the armed forces to function unmolested and to look after their own affairs, it need have no fear they will seize control.

The situation is less stable in Colombia than in Chile because the former's recent civil war left major social questions unresolved, and because in Colombia civilian groups were inclined toward radical programs. Chile, too, has a long way to go in social change, but peaceful democratic evolution is more in conformity with that nation's traditions than violent revolution and authoritarian rule.

Only in the four countries where a substantial social change has taken place and where, as a result, a new social equilibrium has been achieved, are the armed forces under the control of the civilian authorities. In these countries the presidents can call erring officers to order. The professional groups are dominant in the armed forces, and militarism is rendered further impotent by strong, loyal police forces plus an effective counterpoise in organized labor. The most revealing indication of civilian authority is to be found in budget figures. In these countries the armed forces get appreciably less than the customary 20-25 per cent of the national revenue. In Bolivia they get only 15 per cent, in Mexico 12, in Uruguay 11, and in Costa Rica nothing.

In Bolivia endemic militaristic tendencies of the new revolutionary army have been progressively curbed. Although six years have not sufficed to obliterate completely the militaristic habits of a century and a half, the government has control of its army and is progressively eliminating the remaining vestiges of praetorianism. In order to combat militarism, it was necessary for a time to put loyal supporters of the pro-government Movimiento Nacional Revolucionario in key commands, but, now that the rightist military threat is virtually gone, the Bolivian armed forces are moving toward the professional ideal. A word of caution, however, seems necessary in Bolivia's case. Because of the long militaristic tradition and severe economic difficulties, it is always possible that in time of crises the military may again assume a strong, or even dominant, political role.

In Mexico, as related in an earlier chapter, militarism has been dead for over a generation. The troublesome generals of the revolution are no more. A strong professionalist tradition has grown up, and the armed forces respond dutifully and without question to orders given by the civilian authorities. Mexico has unquestionably solved its problem of militarism. That nation's political stability, its social equilibrium, and economic progress have made that solution an enduring one.

Uruguay took the unique path of peaceful evolution rather than violent revolution in achieving civilian control over its armed forces. Militarism began to die out toward the end of the nineteenth century. The country's extraordinary economic and social progress in the twentieth century has been paralleled by the assumption by the armed forces of a professional, purely military role. In Uruguay the armed forces at present are neither above the law nor beyond civilian control. The defense minister is uniformly a civilian. The career in arms is voluntary; there is no conscription. Personnel of the small professional army, air force, and navy are isolated in military bases and other installations. The armed forces play only a minor, a disciplined, and a completely subordinate role in the Uruguayan state.

Finally, there is Costa Rica, a unique case. The Figueres regime destroyed the army in the 1948 revolution, and since it had no meaningful military function to perform—the police have had no difficulty in maintaining internal order, and OAS peace machinery has taken care of external threats—the nation gets along quite well without armed forces.

Conclusions

It becomes obvious, when the contemporary role of the armed forces in the various Latin American countries is compared with their past role as described in previous chapters, that in all the important countries of the area the political role of the military either has changed decisively already or is presently undergoing fundamental change. The inescapable historical conclusion is that, although there have been short-term cyclical undulations in the pattern of military as opposed to civilian rule, the long-term secular trend is away from the former and is moving toward civilian government.

As late as the turn of the present century, eight of the thirteen countries now included in Group II (transitional) and Group III (nonpolitical) would have been included in Group I (political domination). These include Cuba, Guatemala, Venezuela, Peru, Ecuador, Colombia, Mexico, and Bolivia. The other five, Argentina, Brazil, Chile, Uruguay, and Costa Rica, were then at different points in the transitional stage. In none of the countries of the area were the military really nonpolitical. Yet during the course of the twentieth century, particularly since 1930, the armed forces in Colombia, Chile, Mexico, Bolivia, Uruguay, and Costa Rica have become nonpolitical organizations; those of Cuba, Guatemala, Venezuela, Peru, and Ecuador have begun their transition from political to nonpolitical; and those of Argentina and Brazil have moved into the middle-to-advanced stages of the transitional process. Only in seven relatively unimportant countries (Paraguay, Haiti, Dominican Republic, Panama, Honduras, El Salvador, and Nicaragua) is militarism not on the way out or already out.

Because there is little immediate prospect that the countries now in Group I will be able to rid themselves of the shackles of militarism, and because the countries now in Group III will probably henceforth remain free of the militaristic curse (with the possible exception of Bolivia), those countries in Group II assume overriding importance in contemporary Latin America, not only because they contain three-fifths of the population, but also because these countries are currently in the throes of the military-civilian struggle for power. The future of Latin America as a whole may be largely determined by the duration and outcome of this struggle. For complexly intertwined with the latter, but dependent upon it in many ways, are such major issues as that of dictatorship versus democracy and that of evolution or revolution in the process of social change. It is, therefore, a struggle of the greatest importance for the United States, one which is bound to affect this country's position in Latin America and which we shall ignore at our peril in determining and carrying out our policies.

Part Two

MILITARY ASPECTS OF THE LATIN AMERICAN POLICY OF THE UNITED STATES

Chapter 7

EVOLUTION OF POLICY, 1898-1959

LATIN AMERICA'S UNQUESTIONABLE importance to the United States has many aspects. Since the inauguration of the "good-neighbor" policy the United States has come to value ever more highly the political support of the other American republics, and in economic matters the stake of the United States in Latin America's trade, its economic development, and its good will has continued to grow. In recent years, however, it is the strategic factor, Latin America's vital importance to the security of the United States, that has given special emphasis to such matters as the defense of Latin America against the internal and external threats of communism, access to the area's strategic raw materials, the use of its military bases, and the cooperation of its armed forces in the common problem of defending the hemisphere.

The reasons for concentrating attention, in the consideration of United States policy which follows, upon strategic problems and the security aspects are twofold: first, because these problems have been the major concern of the United States in Latin America since the cold war began; and second, because of the peculiar and pronounced effect that resulting measures undertaken by the United States or on its initiative appear to be having upon the internal political and social role of the Latin American armed forces. Latin America's domestic upheavals have unavoidably become involved with the international crisis faced by the entire hemisphere. Thus, current United

States policy in the military field may be exerting a significant influence upon nearly all the problems and issues discussed in Part One of this study.

For an adequate understanding of the background of the military aspects of U.S. policy, and of the relationship to that policy of the role of the military in Latin America, it is necessary to go back to the beginning of the twentieth century, the period of United States intervention in several American republics.

Intervention and Its Consequences

The emergence of the United States as a world power following the Spanish-American War and the threat of encroachments in the Caribbean area by European powers made security a key consideration in the United States' policy toward Latin America.

Concern for the rights of U.S. creditors and for the safety of U.S. property was the reason most frequently cited for the active policy of intervention in five Latin American countries in the early decades of this century. But the primary motive was to stabilize chaotic political situations that loomed as a threat to this nation's security. In the Caribbean, the fear of European intervention was the main reason for United States action; in Central America, the safety of the Panama Canal was at issue. In every military intervention the formula for the establishment of stability was the same, namely, to restore order in the finances and to build up responsible armed forces that would preserve internal order and thus ensure orderly constitutional political processes. This latter part of the task was entrusted directly to the United States armed forces on the spot.

In 1906 the United States army began the process in Cuba. The marine corps extended it to Haiti in 1915, to the Dominican Republic in 1916, to Panama in 1918, and finally to Nicaragua in 1926. The series of occupations did not come to an end until the last of the marines left Haiti in 1934.

CUBA

Cuba became independent of Spain at the turn of the present century, largely as a result of assistance from the United States. During the years 1898-1902, United States occupation authorities worked to prepare the island for nationhood. They helped to rebuild Cuba's war-torn economy, to develop a communications system, to inaugurate a health and sanitation program and public-works projects, and to promote the expansion of education.

The most urgent and delicate task was to establish internal order, for the long wars of independence had left thousands of Cubans armed to the teeth. In exchange for a $3 million bonus for his veterans, provided by the occupation authorities, General Máximo Gómez disbanded his revolutionary army. In its stead was organized a rural guard of 1,600 men. After Cuba had adopted a constitution that granted the United States the right to intervene to insure responsible government, and had installed a duly elected administration, the U.S. army withdrew in 1902. It was assumed that Cuba, with its rich store of raw materials, its human resources, and the training for self-government provided by the occupation authorities, was ready to take on what the United States regarded as the responsibilities of nationhood.

The new republic was not long in showing how erroneous this assumption was. Cuba, it seemed, was destined to suffer the same growing-pains endured by its elder Latin American sisters four generations before. Immediately after the United States occupation authorities departed, deterioration set in. Political processes, despite the progressive constitution, took on the character of a primitive struggle for spoils and power.

The Estrada Palma administration (1902-1906) was too weak to resist veterans' pressures for more bonuses. To keep the rural guard loyal, it was forced to grant material benefits and political favors. When the inevitable revolt came in 1906, the rural guard, now increased to over three thousand, proved no match for twenty thousand revolutionists. The beleaguered government called for assistance from the United States.

Under the second occupation (1906-1909), law and order were re-established, and an effort was made to provide for future political stability. The principal task was to nip incipient militarism in the bud. The rebel forces were disarmed and disbanded, and the rural guard, which had become corrupted by mixing into politics, was thoroughly reorganized. United States army officers purged the militarists and professionalized the guard. To take it out of politics, they set up a promotion system based exclusively on merit. Because the small, scattered guard detachments had been unable to quell uprisings, a permanent army was organized in 1908. With the armed forces (army and rural guard combined) now increased to five thousand and a new government elected and installed, the United States army withdrew in 1909.

The second military occupation, however, was followed by worse conditions than the first. The administration of José Miguel Gómez (1909-1913) was notoriously corrupt. Its answer to the opposition's protests was to double the size of the armed forces, by which it maintained a tyrannical rule. Under Gómez' successor, Mario García Menocal (1913-1921), conditions grew worse. He also used the army, which he strengthened still further, as a political tool. Under the corrupt government of President Alfredo Zayas (1921-1925), army officers moved increasingly into administrative posts hitherto occupied by civilians. The nadir was reached under the regime of Gerardo Machado (1925-1933), which degenerated into an irresponsible military dictatorship. How the reorganized armed forces, led by Fulgencio Batista, dominated Cuba for the greater part of the following quarter-century has already been related.[1]

[1] See above, pp. 97-100.

This long history of militarism obviously cannot be laid at the door of the United States and its military occupation many years before. But it is obvious that the intervention did nothing to save Cuba from the curse of irresponsible army rule.

HAITI

Haiti, in the seventy-two years preceding the United States military occupation, was plagued with predatory militarism. For practically the entire period from 1843 to 1915, the nation suffered under the heel of illiterate Negro generals. Twenty-two dictators, an average of one every three years, took turns in tyrannizing the populace. Governments rose and fell as the result of military intrigues, popular uprisings, and conspiracies of the mulatto elite. The monotonous succession of ignorant, corrupt generals was occasionally broken by mulatto reformers. They lasted only until they infringed on the traditional right of the military caste to feed at the public trough. The nation made little material progress in the period; nothing was done to relieve the poverty and ignorance of the black masses.

Between 1908 and 1915 the long-unstable political situation threatened to turn into utter chaos. Military adventurers succeeded to the presidential office with bewildering rapidity, and the tumult and bloodletting in each upheaval became increasingly serious. Finally, by 1915, the nation was bankrupt; orderly political processes had disappeared, the German and French governments were making threatening gestures and demanding participation in control of the customs. At this point, the United States sent in the marines.

The aims of the United States military occupation (1915-1934) were to preserve Haitian independence, to protect American property rights, and to establish a stable, responsible government. For this last purpose, the occupation authorities set up puppet presidents and congressmen, selected from the educated mulatto elite, who rubber-stamped broad political and economic reforms. Haiti was given a new constitution, its finances were reorganized, public-works programs were inaugurated, a health program was launched, and opportunities for graft were reduced.

To give such reforms permanency, it was deemed essential to reorganize the armed forces, which were chiefly responsible for the previous chaotic conditions. Accordingly, American marine officers trained a 3,000-man volunteer constabulary, which took the place of the pre-1915 army of 6,000 men. It was intended that the constabulary would confine its functions to maintaining order; it was to be the servant rather than the master of the state. Preparations for ending the military occupation began in 1930 with the election of Sténio Vincent, an educated mulatto, as president. The transfer of control of the constabulary from the marine officers to Haitian professionals was accomplished in 1934, whereupon the American forces retired.

Vincent, with a disciplined armed force under his control, extended his term to 1941, and the momentum of the United States reforms was sufficient to elect Elie Lescot, another educated mulatto, as his successor. Gradually, however, the Negro army moved toward recapture of its pre-eminent position in politics. In addition to the natural inclination of the officers to vindicate their social position, they were egged on by the Negro masses. The latter were increasingly aroused by the failure of mulatto leadership to improve the people's lot, by increasing evidence of graft, inefficiency, and mismanagement in high places, and by the progressive undoing of the economic and political reforms of the occupation era.

In the face of a general strike, the army in 1946 ousted Lescot and permitted the election of Dumarsais Estimé, an anti-mulatto Negro, to the presidency. The Negro military, especially the officers of the 500-man Palace Guard, had clearly become once more the arbiters of politics. Now, however, as a result of their training during the occupation by U.S. forces, bloody revolutionary uprisings came to an end. The disciplined military remained unified instead of fighting each other as in the past, gave orders to erring and wayward politicians, and kept jealous guard over the armed forces' political and material interests.

As corruption rapidly became rife inside the Dumarsais Estimé regime, the president responded to the deepening economic crisis by decreeing martial law. His undoing was his inflated political ambition, which the army would not tolerate. When in 1950 he attempted to amend the constitution to provide for his continuation in office, the Palace Guard, led by the same group that installed him four years previously, ousted him. The army strong-man, Colonel Paul Magloire, was then duly elected to the presidency. The Magloire regime, casting aside the veil of civilian government, was an outright military dictatorship. The army had become the only real political power in Haiti, and so it has remained.[2]

THE DOMINICAN REPUBLIC

The Dominican Republic, in the seventy-two years between 1844 and 1916, had forty-three presidents, mostly army generals. In this period in which thirty-nine successful *coups d'état* were carried out, only three presidents (Generals Pedro de Santana, Buenaventura Baez, and Ulysses Heureaux) obtained sufficient control over the national army and the local *caudillos* to last out their full terms of office. The last of these, General Heureaux, came to power in 1882. For seventeen years he conducted one of the most bestial, irresponsible tyrannies of the history of Latin America. With an oversized and generally loyal army, he bilked the citizenry and squandered the wealth

[2] The military elite were the 40 officers and 500 men that made up the Palace Guard in the capital. They in turn were reinforced by 400 officers and 4,500 disciplined men throughout the country. Most of the officers were black, all were literate, and all were graduates of the military academy at Frères. To the nation's armed forces was reserved 20 per cent of the national budget. See Selden Rodman, *Haiti the Black Republic* (New York: Devin-Adair, 1954), pp. 41-42.

of the country. His financial mismanagement was notorious.

The aftermath of the Heureaux regime was typical. When he was cut down by an assassin in 1899, the unfortunate republic was plunged into anarchy. For a generation irresponsible, opportunistic *caudillos* rose and fell with bewildering rapidity. With the nation in chaos and French intervention threatening, the United States moved in. It set up a customs receivership in 1905, and in 1916 the marines occupied the republic.

United States military rule (1916-1924) was designed to bring order out of chaos. Finances were reorganized, public-works projects undertaken, and sanitation programs inaugurated. As in Cuba and Haiti, the key to future political stability and economic progress was thought to be a thorough overhauling of the hitherto undisciplined and irresponsible army. Accordingly, the marines set to work reforming it. To United States officers must go the credit for creating the first regular standing army in the Dominican Republic and organizing it along up-to-date, professional lines. The result was to relegate the militias of the regional *caudillos* to a condition of impotence.

Thus, when General Horacio Vásquez was elected president in 1924, just before the marines departed, political stability seemed assured, and the nation was entering a unique era of peace and prosperity. Vásquez, however, attempted six years later to alter the constitution in order to perpetuate himself in office. This move provoked a rebellion which the army could easily have crushed, but General Rafael Leonidas Trujillo, an astute officer of lower middle-class origins, whom the marine officers had left in charge of the newly organized Dominican army, deliberately allowed it to succeed. Having proclaimed himself a candidate for the presidency, he was "elected" in May 1930, and ever since has been master of the nation.

PANAMA

The republic of Panama is quite unlike any other nation

in Latin America. It was the creation of the United States government, which insured the success of the Panamanian revolution against Colombia in 1903 so that a canal, owned and controlled by the United States, might be built across the isthmus. For the first three decades of its history Panama was, in fact if not in law, a protectorate of the United States; because of its strategic importance, it was never completely free of United States influence. Politically it was little more than a "canal state." A third of its population of less than one million lived along the canal and provided the leaders who ran the nation. The rural two-thirds of the population counted for virtually nothing, either politically or socially.

Treaty arrangements gave the United States the right to intervene to preserve Panamanian independence, to maintain order, and to protect the canal. And in the turbulent early history of the republic this right was frequently exercised. Panama inherited from its Colombian origin the usual conflicts between Liberal and Conservative parties; it inherited also army intrigues in politics. A small revolutionary army, plus Colombian troops which had been bribed to desert, made up Panama's armed forces. The two political parties, run exclusively by the first families of Panama, agreed upon a coalition president. Less than a year after independence, disgruntled liberals induced the army chief to attempt a *coup d'état,* which was prevented only by the timely intervention of the United States minister. He applied diplomatic pressure to force the unruly army to disband. Inasmuch as Panamanian independence was guaranteed by the United States, an army was obviously unnecessary to cope with threats of invasion. It was replaced by a police force sufficient to preserve internal order.

Within a few years, however, the police were just as quarrelsome, corrupt, and politically minded as the former army. They were soon caught up in the intense rivalry among first-family cliques competing for the spoils of presidential office. Only the threat of United States intervention preserved even a modicum of political order. Then in 1912, there emerged a strong-man, Dr. Belisario Porras, who dominated Panama for the next twelve years. By adroit maneuvering, he accomplished the unique feat of serving out a full term of office (1912-1916). Under Porras' successor a police intrigue upset the republic's uncertain stability, bringing about, in 1917, a brief intervention by United States marines. The following year, when Porras attempted a comeback, political turmoil broke out again. Once more, in came the marines, and in the 1918 elections Porras emerged victorious.

To obviate the need for future interventions in Panama, the United States had recourse to the same methods it had applied in the Caribbean republics. Marine corps officers thoroughly reformed the Panamanian police, aiming to make it a responsible profession which would avoid politics and limit its activities to preserving internal order in behalf of duly elected governments. At the same time, the United States military instructors introduced modern weapons and methods, thus insuring that the national police would be overwhelmingly superior to any revolutionary force.

The reform was successful. Porras, supported by the police, consolidated his position, won the election of 1920, and served out a second full term of office (1920-1924). In 1925, the threat of revolt brought in U.S. troops briefly for the last time. Then for several years the oligarchy rotated the presidential office among its leaders, ruling for the benefit of their class, while the efficient, disciplined police maintained internal order.

Following the defeat of the oligarchy in the revolution of 1931, the police assumed for a decade the role of arbiter between the old aristocracy and aspiring middle groups in the society. In the 1940's they exercised their growing power more openly, ousting five "unsatisfactory" civilian presidents in the years between 1948 and 1952. In that year, their chief, Colonel Remón, took charge of the government.

NICARAGUA

Nicaragua, the fifth country to come under United States military occupation, had found itself since 1893 under the rule of Dr. José Santos Zelaya, the first long-term strong-man in its history. In sixteen years of tyrannical rule, his constant meddling in the affairs of his neighbors maintained international friction in the Central American area at a high level. He contracted large loans in Europe, thereby raising the specter of intervention in case of default on payments, and spoke glibly of selling exclusive canal rights through Nicaragua to Great Britain or Japan.

Such a situation the United States, with its growing strategic stake in the isthmian area, could not permit indefinitely. Accordingly, it gave material support to his opponents, and Zelaya was finally overthrown in 1909. There then followed a generation of puppet rulers, who maintained themselves in power only because of United States backing. For example, when War Minister General Luís Mena attempted to oust Dr. Adolfo Díaz in 1912, two thousand United States marines were landed to protect Díaz. Once the revolt was quelled, 100-odd marines remained as "legation guards."

Affairs proceeded so calmly and smoothly after the 1912 intervention that in 1925 the Coolidge administration decided it safe to withdraw the "legation guards." Almost immediately, however, political strife broke out with a vengeance. Early in 1926 two thousand marines landed. Again, as in 1912, they came to protect "dependable" Conservative leaders against the attacks of "irresponsible" Liberals. A puppet president took office once more.

At this juncture the Coolidge administration, obviously embarrassed by the fact of marine corps rule and by the charges of imperialism from all corners of Latin America, launched a program designed to terminate the occupation and obviate the need for future intervention. Henry L. Stimson was sent as mediator. He persuaded both factions to agree to turn in their arms and to allow the marines to supervise the next election. The unruly, politically inclined, regular army was disbanded and replaced with a United States-trained professional constabulary, which would (hopefully) uphold democracy and constitutionalism. Five years of intensive training by marine officers produced a highly efficient, disciplined Guardia Nacional, which was more than adequate for the preservation of internal order. The presidential elections of 1928 and 1932, held under United States supervision, demonstrated that the Liberal party, traditionally hostile to the United States, was indeed the majority party. However, inasmuch as it had shown a new sense of responsibility, and because the *guardia* was now in a position to keep all politicians and would-be revolutionaries in line, the marines were finally withdrawn in 1933.

But the Guardia Nacional, which had been built up to insure honest, orderly government, soon took advantage of its superior power and discipline to take over the government and exploit the nation. General Anastasio Somoza, a former mechanic and storekeeper who had risen under marine corps tutelage to the leadership of the Guardia, refused to take orders from the Liberal president, Juan Batista Sacasa. For three years after the marines departed the latter sat precariously in the presidential chair. Finally, in 1936, Somoza ousted him and assumed the presidency. Thereupon, the nation was run as the private preserve of the Somoza family and the Guardia Nacional.

Thus, in all five cases the policies of the United States backfired. Only if real and permanent improvement could have been brought about in the occupied countries would the military interventions possibly have been worth the price of widespread protests and antagonism which they aroused against the United States throughout Latin America. In fact, the ultimate result of each attempt to build up responsible, nonpolitical military establishments was to enshrine the new officer corps as a political elite. United States military reforms, because they unified and made efficient armed bodies hitherto poorly organized and equipped, inadvertently helped to insure the political domination of the military. In these politically backward countries the new military elite produced some of the most striking examples of unprincipled and tyrannical rule in the history of Latin America.

The policy of intervention in the Caribbean and Central America can be explained and perhaps justified, historically, by the facts of geography, by the existence of chaotic conditions, by the threat of European intervention, and by the general practices of what was the "age of imperialism" all over the globe. From the strict viewpoint of the security interests of the United States in the area, the results of a failure to intervene might well have been worse than those of intervention. Yet there were strong factors working for the abandonment of the practice of military intervention, beyond those flowing from its obvious failure to produce stable constitutional government or to check irresponsible militarism. Chief among these was the reaction of other countries of Latin America, where the indignation over "Yankee imperialism" was both deep and vociferous. Concern for its relations with the whole of Latin America led the United States to the abandonment of intervention and to the adoption of what came to be known as the policy of "good neighbor." This change coincided with changes in world conditions which demonstrated that the vital security interests of the United States in the hemisphere were by no means confined to the Caribbean area.

World Wars and Hemisphere Defense

Despite the involvement of the United States in World War I, Latin America had failed to consider this conflict a matter for hemisphere-wide concern. Seven little republics in the Caribbean area and in Central America declared war on the central powers, but no republic in South America, save Brazil, did so. The lack of enthusiasm for a crusade against "Kaiserism" obviously disappointed the

United States. At that time, the concept of hemisphere defense did not even exist, let alone the machinery to implement it.

In the years which followed, as the United States relapsed into isolation, its concern with Latin America centered around matters of trade, loans, and investment. So far as South America was concerned, interest in military security was reflected only in the activities of United States naval missions in Brazil and Peru. The wartime emergency mission sent to Brazil in 1918 was set up on a permanent basis in 1922 after Congress had passed an act permitting "officers of the United States Navy to accept offices with compensation and emoluments from the governments of the republics of South America." Under this act a naval training-mission was sent also to Peru in 1920.[3] An act of May 19, 1926, authorized the United States army to send missions to Latin America, but the first army mission, to Colombia, was not sent until late 1938.

It was in the late 1930's that Washington first began to develop a policy aimed at the defense of the entire Western Hemisphere. Up to that time, with the immediate security interests of the United States largely confined to the Caribbean and the environs of the Panama Canal, inter-American cooperation was chiefly economic and cultural. With the rise of the Nazi-Fascist threat in Europe the emphasis changed, as the United States attempted to develop the inter-American system as a means of meeting it. Military defense suddenly assumed a new priority.

More than a year before World War II broke out in Europe, far-sighted Washington planners began mapping out Latin America's role in the impending world conflict. The Chief of Staff, the Chief of Naval Operations, and the Secretary of State set up a Standing Liaison Committee in

[3] U.S. Department of State, *Papers Relating to the Foreign Relations of the United States* (Washington: GPO, 3 v., 1936-1938), v. 3 (1920), p. 367 ff., and v. 1 (1922), p. 651 ff. Vargas, for reasons of "economy," terminated the activities of the United States naval mission in Brazil in 1930, then re-employed it in 1936.

April of 1938 to deal directly with this matter.[4] Realistic appraisal of the capabilities of the area's armed forces immediately ruled out the possibility that any nation in Latin America might make a major military contribution. Accordingly, the "good neighbors" were assigned in these plans what was primarily a limited, supporting role.

Objectives of United States policy included: (1) elimination of the threat of Nazi subversion in the Western Hemisphere; (2) maximum utilization of Latin America's limited military potential for primarily defensive roles; (3) use of naval and air-base sites on Latin American soil; (4) political stability of the region and its sympathetic attitude toward the aims of the United States; and (5) full access to Latin America's strategic raw materials.

The other American republics were by no means in full agreement with the United States' views concerning the developing world conflict. Although from 1938 to 1941 the United States attempted to convince them that the entire hemisphere was threatened, until Japan attacked at Pearl Harbor they displayed little sense of urgency. Ultimately, Latin America's role in the conflict came to fit in broadly with the strategy and war aims of the United States, but this was accomplished only gradually and belatedly, with varying degrees of participation; some of the republics cooperated fully, Argentina hardly at all.

Subversion was the immediate threat. Axis agents were active in nearly every country, aided in some cases by local German, Italian or Japanese minority elements, and all too often closely associated with domestic groups that wielded substantial political and economic power. Adding to Washington's uneasiness were German control of commercial airlines in Brazil and in Colombia (within easy reach of the Panama Canal), the activities of German and Italian military missions in South America, and shipments of arms from Axis powers to countries in the southern part of that continent.

[4] William L. Langer and S. Everett Gleason, *The Challenge to Isolation* (New York: Harper, for the Council on Foreign Relations, 1952), pp. 40-41.

The initial tasks of the Roosevelt administration were to expose the Axis threat, to convince the Latin Americans that they were underrating the Fascist menace, and to get their cooperation in defense against it. The principal medium for these efforts was the inter-American system. At the eighth Inter-American Conference held in Lima in December of 1938, although the United States failed to secure a convention pledging concerted action, it did obtain a joint declaration of continental solidarity and national resistance to foreign intervention. It was also agreed that in the event of a threat to the peace of the hemisphere, prompt inter-American consultation at the foreign ministers' level would take place.

The outbreak of World War II in Europe alarmed the other American republics to the extent that they were willing to support the United States-sponsored Declaration of Panama, which established a 300-mile wide neutrality zone around the shores of the entire hemisphere, leaving out Canada. Ten months later at Havana, in July 1940, they agreed to act cooperatively against possible Nazi control of the European colonies in the Caribbean. Thus one more step was taken toward full collaboration. But the practical task of cooperation for defense depended in large part on the developing relations between the U.S. armed forces and those of Latin America.

Replacing long-established German and Italian military missions with United States advisers did not prove difficult, although the United States was a late arrival in the competition for influence through missions. During the early 1920's, when United States naval advisory missions were employed by Brazil and Peru, the navies of other American republics had British, French, and German advisers. Until 1938 the training of South American armies was exclusively a European preserve,[5] with Axis missions predominating there. German and Italian officers were sup-

[5] Fritz T. Epstein, *European Military Influences in Latin America* (manuscript in possession of author in Library of Congress, 1941), pp. 250-263; Alfred Vagts, *Defense and Diplomacy* (New York: King's Crown Press, 1956), pp. 208-209.

plementing their professional military advice to the local officer corps with Nazi-Fascist political indoctrination.[6]

Primarily to counter this subversive threat, the United States started a military mission program in Latin America in 1938. In order to compete with the long-established Axis rivals, the State and War Departments agreed to underbid them, offering professional instruction at less than cost, if necessary.[7] In this manner rapid inroads were made. In February 1939, before the program had gained full momentum, the army already had twenty-two officers assigned to eight of the Latin American republics. Before the end of the year the sending of aviation missions began and the navy also prepared to expand its mission program. These programs were supplemented by the recruiting of promising Latin American officers to study at United States military academies and training-schools rather than in Germany and Italy.[8]

With the increasing threat to the hemisphere from the European conflagration during 1940, and the consequent strengthening of inter-American political solidarity, the position of Axis military advisers became untenable; by the time of Pearl Harbor all the missions had been eliminated. The United States then had military, air, or naval advisers in nearly all the republics. It had taken over the functions of the naval missions of Britain and France. The overseas training of Latin American officers was being conducted exclusively, and at an increasing tempo, at institutions in the United States.

Assumption of the task of advising and training involved the obligation to assist in the arming of forces heretofore European-equipped. This obligation became especially urgent when, with the outbreak of World War II, Latin America was suddenly cut off from imports of ammunition

6 Laurence Duggan, *The Americas: The Search for Hemisphere Security* (New York: Holt, 1949), p. 178.

7 Mark Skinner Watson, *Chief of Staff (Prewar Plans and Preparations)*, v. 7 of *United States Army in World War II* (Washington: GPO, 1950), pp. 89-91.

8 *New York Times*, February 15, 16, 1939; Epstein ms., cited, p. 295.

and spare parts from European suppliers. As early as March 1939, the U.S. War, Navy and State Departments had jointly supported a House resolution to "assist the governments of the American republics to increase their military and naval establishments" by making war matériel available to them at cost. The lower chamber promptly agreed to exempt Latin America from legislative restrictions prohibiting the sale of all but obsolete and surplus war goods, but the Senate, despite State and Navy pleas that arms for Latin America were essential for hemisphere defense, failed to act until May 1940.[9] That did not settle the matter, for the other American republics declared they could not possibly pay for the planes, ships, artillery and ammunition necessary for an effective contribution to hemisphere defense. Even if they had been able and willing to pay, the United States, which badly needed such items itself, was not until early 1942 in a position to begin supplying them. By this time the vexatious financing problem had been solved by the Lend-Lease Act, under which the United States was authorized to furnish Latin America $400 million worth of war goods.[10]

The United States-sponsored build-up of Latin America's armed forces was not undertaken for the sole purpose of providing the "good neighbors" with means to defend themselves against possible enemy attack from the outside. Equally important were arms for the maintenance of internal order and stability threatened by possible Axis attempts at internal subversion. Against this danger increasing cooperation from Latin American governments was forthcoming, notably through the Inter-American Commission for Political Defense, set up at Montevideo after the Rio Conference of 1942.

There were also good political reasons on both sides for

[9] Langer and Gleason, cited, pp. 275-276; *New York Times,* March 23, 1939, and May 29, 1940.

[10] William L. Langer and S. Everett Gleason, *The Undeclared War, 1940-1941* (New York: Harper, for the Council on Foreign Relations, 1953), pp. 162, 596-598.

the growing military cooperation. Half the Latin American countries were run by military strong-men, and in most of the others politically potent armies were demanding equipment. Under such conditions, the granting of at least minimum requests for matériel, whether militarily justified or not, was politically expedient. Grants of arms were deemed necessary in order to help ensure Latin America's cooperation in the fulfillment of United States strategic objectives. The political motive for military assistance to Paraguay, for example, was frankly admitted in a communication from General George C. Marshall to the Secretary of War in May 1941: "The State Department considers it politically desirable to assist Paraguay by financing improvements to its principal airfields." [11] The arms program was also used to coerce, or at least to set up protection against, uncooperative republics. In early 1944, Roosevelt sent additional arms and instructors to Brazil to enable that country to station "two or three divisions near the Argentine border" in order to impress "the present military gang in control of Argentina." [12]

The overriding reason for military assistance was to help the United States to obtain needed base facilities in Latin America. These Washington believed essential, for, despite some limited Latin American support in patrolling Caribbean shores and rooting out enemy subversives, it was obvious that in the event of an enemy attack the burden of defense would fall upon the United States. This became an especially serious concern during the summer of 1940, when Hitler, after his conquest of Western Europe, was rumored to be planning an invasion of the hump of Brazil. At the same time, Japan, which had just joined the Axis powers, loomed as a threat to the Pacific approaches to the Panama Canal.

Until the Japanese attack on Pearl Harbor brought the war to the Western Hemisphere, and until the United States was in a position to furnish military supplies as a

[11] Watson, cited, p. 96.

[12] Cordell Hull, *Memoirs* (New York: Macmillan, 1948), v. 2, p. 1390 ff.

quid pro quo, little progress was made in obtaining the badly needed bases. To the disappointment of United States military men, Latin America's officer corps tended to view the matter from the angle of advantages that might accrue to their own military establishments.[13] United States military bases on their soil, they argued, increased their vulnerability to enemy attack; therefore, they needed more arms and equipment for defense. The sovereignty issue complicated the problem, until Pearl Harbor and Lend Lease resolved it. In 1942 the desired facilities were secured from Brazil, Mexico, Cuba, Panama, and Ecuador.

In fact, soon after the United States entered World War II, its military program in Latin America fell rapidly into line with its strategic and policy objectives. At the conference held in January 1942 at Rio de Janeiro all the American republics except Argentina and Chile agreed to sever diplomatic and commercial relations with the Axis; all agreed to step up the production of strategic materials and feed them exclusively into the United States war machine, and all agreed "to consider any act of aggression on the part of a non-American state against any one of them as an act of aggression against all of them." [14]

Inasmuch as this declaration implied some sort of military cooperation, the Rio Conference approved a resolution providing for an Inter-American Defense Board, composed of military and naval technicians from each of the twenty-one republics, to study and recommend measures necessary for the defense of the hemisphere. Set up in March 1942, the Board was able to play no vital role in World War II largely because of the varying degrees of participation in the conflict. The Caribbean and Central American nations and Brazil actually declared war, but most of the South American states merely severed diplomatic and commercial relations; Chile was not even willing to go that far until later in the war, and Argentina was

[13] Langer and Gleason, *The Undeclared War,* cited, p. 152.

[14] Edward O. Guerrant, *Roosevelt's Good Neighbor Policy* (Albuquerque: University of New Mexico Press, 1950), pp. 173-185.

determined to remain neutral. Consequently, the United States found it expedient to conduct military cooperation in defense of the hemisphere on a bilateral basis. Joint United States-Mexican and United States-Brazilian defense boards were set up, and negotiations for bases and Lend-Lease arrangements were made bilaterally.[15]

Though Latin America made a significant contribution to the Allied cause in World War II by rooting out Axis subversives and supplying vital raw materials, its role in actual fighting was relatively minor. Two nations sent forces abroad, but both Brazil's infantry division in Italy and Mexico's small air squadron in the Philippines, which were sent late in the war, were in the nature of token contributions. Though there was a certain amount of useful cooperation, particularly in air and naval patrol work against Axis submarines, the primary burden of hemisphere defense fell upon the United States. More than 100,000 American troops were tied down in the Latin American area during the war.[16]

Because of their key political role, the armed forces in most Latin American countries largely determined the extent of their nation's support of the United States during World War II. Except in Argentina, their cooperation was generally forthcoming, spurred on by the granting of military assistance and the work of the military missions. In those few countries where the armed forces did not determine foreign policy, the problem of wartime cooperation was not a difficult one, save perhaps in the case of Chile. The support which Latin America provided to the war effort came from many sources, not least from those who felt that their liberties and their national independence were in danger. Yet the volume and effectiveness of that support was due in no small measure to its military men, who felt it to be in their interest, whether personal, professional, or national.

15 Same, pp. 185-191.

16 "Military Assistance to Latin America," U.S. Department of State, *Bulletin*, March 30, 1953, p. 466.

The Cold War

After World War II the United States was anxious to continue the cooperation with Latin America which had already served both so well, in order to meet whatever new challenges might arise to security and other common interests. To this end it took a leading part in placing the inter-American system on a more permanent treaty basis. But Latin America inevitably took a subordinate place in the newly developing global foreign policy of the United States, a fact which was only too obvious to the Latin Americans themselves. In fact, the United States did not find it easy to determine just where Latin America fitted into its strategy for the new situation, increasingly dominated by the cold war with the Soviet Union. And the Latin American nations, for their part, were quite naturally taking stock of their relationship to the United States, and looking at the problems of "hemisphere defense" in that context.

Though victories in Europe in late 1944 and early 1945 eliminated the Axis military threat to the Western Hemisphere, neither the United States nor many of the Latin American states were inclined to abandon the defense system they had so laboriously constructed since 1938. Accordingly, in February of 1945, a meeting in Mexico was called to plan the future of the inter-American system. That conference produced the Act of Chapultepec, the vital provision of which declared that an attack on an American state by any state, American or foreign, would be considered to be an attack against them all, and that collective measures would be taken to repel such aggression. This provision, formally embodied in a treaty signed at Rio de Janeiro on September 2, 1947, has become the cornerstone of the inter-American defense system. At this time the United States, in addition to its concern with the danger of aggression from without, was also disturbed over the threat to peace within the hemisphere. The Rio Pact was thus partly designed to check such would-be aggressors as Perón and his ilk.

At Chapultepec it was also decided to make the Inter-American Defense Board a permanent organization. Within a year, in October 1945, the IADB issued its first peacetime recommendations for insuring the military defense of the hemisphere. These included standardization of equipment, organization, and training[17]—goals long favored by the United States. Indeed, ever since 1938 it had expended considerable time, money, and effort to persuade the other American republics to adopt its methods and equipment. It was to protect this investment in national and hemispheric security that the Truman administration, accepting the recommendations of the IADB, requested Congress in May 1946 to approve a continuing program of inter-American military cooperation. In this program the United States would undertake to modernize the military establishments of the Latin American states, and to continue its wartime program of equipping their armed forces.[18] Congress, however, apparently unimpressed by the administration's proposal and perhaps also swayed by its critics, failed to act on the bill in 1946 and delayed action once more when it was presented in 1947.

The inaction was characteristic of the early postwar period in which little was done to maintain any minimum level of hemisphere defense. The U.S. military mission program continued, but after the end of Lend Lease it was hardly possible to maintain in Latin America even the existing defense posture. As the administration feared, the wartime program of standardization of matériel began to disintegrate, for now that Latin American governments had to pay for military equipment, they began to purchase where prices and terms were most favorable. All too often, in the opinion of the Pentagon, they turned to European suppliers.

World events, however, were taking a turn that soon

[17] *Encyclopaedia Britannica Yearbook* (1946), p. 395.
[18] *New York Times,* May 7, 1946.

served to reactivate a positive and vigorous United States security policy in Latin America. By 1947, the year of the Rio Pact, in the face of repeated aggressive moves by the U.S.S.R., the United States felt itself obliged to concentrate heavily on containment of the Communist threat, at first in Europe and then throughout the entire world. The Mutual Defense Assistance Act of 1949 inaugurated a comprehensive system of military aid to NATO countries. Then, when open war came in Korea, Washington was forced to the conclusion that defense against persistent and world-wide acts of Communist aggression could only be achieved by programs of military, economic, and technical assistance for many countries throughout the non-Communist world. Congressional authorization for such a program was provided in the Mutual Security Act of 1951, the objectives of which were:

> to maintain the security and promote the foreign policy of the United States by authorizing military, economic, and technical assistance to friendly countries, to strengthen the mutual security and individual and collective defense of the free world, to develop their resources in the interest of their security and the national interests of the United States, and to facilitate the effective participation of those countries in the United Nation's system for collective security.

This act authorized military assistance "to any nation whose increased ability to defend itself . . . [is] important to the security of the United States." Military equipment furnished under the act was to be used "solely to maintain the internal security and legitimate self-defense of the recipient nation, or to permit it to participate in the defense of its area or in collective arrangements and measures consistent with the Charter of the United Nations." Concerning Latin America, the act specified that "military assistance may be furnished to the other American republics only in accordance with defense plans which . . . require the recipient nations to participate in missions important to the defense of the Western Hemisphere." [19]

Even before the Mutual Security Act was passed, the Truman administration had already acted to secure the cooperation of Latin America in the hostilities which had broken out in Korea. At a consultative meeting of American foreign ministers, held in Washington in March and April of 1951, the President requested that the American republics support the war effort with their combined military strength, and that they plan a common program for resistance to the Communist threat. The response was a resolution recommending that the American republics

> orient their military preparation in such a way that through self-help and mutual aid . . . they can (a) increase those of their resources and strengthen those of their armed forces best adapted to the collective defense, and maintain those armed forces in such status that they can be promptly available for the defense of the continent; and (b) cooperate with each other, in military matters, in order to develop the collective strength of the continent necessary to combat aggression against any of them.[20]

To support this combined effort the Assistant Secretary of State for Latin American Affairs, Edward G. Miller, Jr., appearing before the House Foreign Affairs Committee in July 1951, requested $40 million of Mutual Security funds for a new program of military aid to Latin America. Such assistance, he asserted, would help overcome limitations on the ability of Latin America to contribute to hemisphere defense. In addition Mr. Miller requested, as an integral part of the over-all Mutual Security program for Latin America, $22 million for technical assistance.[21] The total of $62 million was comparatively modest, only three-fourths of one per cent of the total requested in the Mutual Security appropriations bill for 1951.

[19] *Public Law* no. 165, 82nd Cong., 1st sess. (October 10, 1951), "Mutual Security Act of 1951," sec. 105.

[20] U.S. Department of State, *Bulletin,* April 9, 1951, pp. 566-567.

[21] U.S. House Committee on Foreign Affairs, *The Mutual Security Program,* Hearings on H.R. 5020 and H.R. 5113, 82nd Cong., 1st sess. (Washington: GPO, 1951), pp. 1080-1082.

General Charles L. Bolte, chairman of the IADB, supported the request for military aid to Latin America, arguing that such assistance would relieve United States troops of the burden of defending the hemisphere in the event of war. He indicated that the IADB was planning specific tasks for each nation to assume in strategic areas. To help protect the critical Panama Canal area, for example, the IADB had recommended that the adjacent countries contribute an antiaircraft battalion. General Bolte indicated that, though the grant aid would help maintain modern standards in Latin America's armed forces, the United States expected that most of its military shipments to Latin America would continue, as in the past, to be on a reimbursable basis.[22] Secretary of Defense George C. Marshall, in his testimony, related the proposed military aid to the future availability of Latin America's strategic resources, as well as to the need to help the Latin American republics play a more active role in hemisphere defense.[23]

Congress having appropriated $38 million for Latin American military aid for 1951, negotiations were opened with eight countries—Mexico, Brazil, Chile, Uruguay, Ecuador, Peru, Colombia, and Cuba. In preliminary discussions Brazil, Chile, Mexico, and Uruguay balked at United States insistence upon limitation of trade in strategic materials with the Soviet bloc. They were unwilling to grant the United States exclusive access to their strategic resources. Ultimately, however, seven countries, all except Mexico, made formal requests for military aid from the United States.[24] With U.S. advice the estimated needs of each country were then calculated with reference to its potential contribution to hemisphere defense, its ability to supply part of its own requirements, and its capacity for

22 Same, pp. 1084-1089.

23 U.S. Senate Committees on Foreign Relations and Armed Services, *Mutual Security Act of 1951*, Hearings on S. 1762, 82nd Cong., 1st sess. (Washington: GPO, 1951), p. 38.

24 Richard P. Stebbins, *The United States in World Affairs, 1952* (New York: Harper, for the Council on Foreign Relations, 1953), p. 2.

effectively utilizing and maintaining various types of military equipment. The programs were then subjected to review by the Defense Department, the State Department, and representatives of Congress prior to formal signing of the agreements.[25]

The first Mutual Defense Assistance Agreement with a Latin American country was concluded with Ecuador on January 20, 1952. Under its terms the United States government agreed "to make available . . . equipment, materials, services, and other military assistance designed to promote the defense and maintain the peace of the Western Hemisphere." In return, Ecuador promised to make effective and exclusive use of this assistance for implementing defense plans, to build up and maintain its own defensive capacities, "to facilitate the production and transfer . . . of . . . strategic materials required by the United States," and to cooperate with the United States in limiting its trade with the Soviet bloc.[26] Before the year was out similar pacts had been signed with Cuba, Colombia, Peru, and Chile.

To expand the program, Congress, in support of the Mutual Security Act for 1952, appropriated an additional $65 million for Latin American military aid. The continuing program resulted in MDA pacts with Brazil, the Dominican Republic, and Uruguay during 1953, with Nicaragua and Honduras during 1954, and with Haiti and Guatemala during 1955.[27] By the end of fiscal 1959, the twelve countries included in the program had received about $317 million in grants for military aid. In addition, these twelve American republics and seven others obtained

25 "Military Aid Programs," a study prepared by the Systems Analysis Corporation, in U. S. Senate Special Committee to Study the Foreign Aid Program, *The Military Assistance Program of the United States,* 85th Cong., 1st sess., Committee print no. 10 (Washington: GPO, 1957), pp. 100-102.

26 U.S. Department of State, *Bulletin,* March 3, 1952, pp. 336-338.

27 For the texts of the U.S. agreements with Nicaragua and Honduras, see Appendix A and Appendix B respectively.

about $140 million worth of military equipment under the reimbursable aid provisions of the Mutual Security Act.[28]

28 U. S. House Committee on Foreign Affairs, *Staff Memorandum on Background Material on the Mutual Security Program for Fiscal Year 1960,* 86th Cong., 1st sess. (Washington: GPO, 1959), p. 27; U. S. President, *The Mutual Security Program for Fiscal Year 1960: A Summary Presentation* (Washington: GPO, 1959), p. 132; U. S. Senate Committee on Foreign Relations, Subcommittee on Disarmament, *Control and Reduction of Armaments: Disarmament and Security in Latin America,* 85th Cong., 1st sess., Staff Study no. 7 (Washington: GPO, 1957), p. 15. The shipments by fiscal years were as follows:

Military Assistance Program Shipments to Latin America

(Fiscal Years—Figures in $ Millions)

Year		Amount	Year		Amount
1952	—	.2	1956	—	21.2
1953	—	65.2	1957	—	32.0
1954	—	37.9	1958	—	56.8
1955	—	36.9	1959	—	67.0

Chapter 8

ANALYSIS OF U.S. POLICY

The Military Rationale

UNITED STATES SECURITY policy in Latin America is based generally on the purpose of obtaining and maintaining the cooperation of all the American republics in meeting any threat to the independence or security of any one of them. The policies adopted in furtherance of this purpose may be primarily political or economic in character. We are concerned here with the more strictly military aspects, and especially those which directly involve the role of the Latin American armed forces. From this standpoint, U.S. policy has been stated to rest upon three fundamental assumptions:

(1) That the hemisphere is threatened by Communist aggression both from within and without.

(2) That the security of strategic areas in the hemisphere and of inter-American lines of communication is vital to the security of every American republic.

(3) That the protection of these strategic areas and communications is a common responsibility.[1]

Ostensibly to meet the threat of Communist aggression, an elaborate collective-security system has been built up over the past decade. Its foundation is a military alliance—the Inter-American Treaty of Reciprocal Assistance, signed at Rio de Janeiro in 1947, which unequivocably declares that an attack against any nation in the hemisphere will be

[1] U.S. Department of State, *Bulletin,* March 30, 1954, pp. 463-464.

considered an attack against all, and that in the event of such aggression each will assist in meeting it; they will consult on the measures of a collective character that should be taken. Inherent in United States policy, in support of this collective obligation, is the principle that the armed forces of any one American republic will contribute most to the common purpose if combined in a strategy of defense with those of the others.

Accordingly, planning for the mutual defense of the hemisphere has proceeded through the medium of the Inter-American Defense Board, composed of upper-echelon officers representing each of the American republics. Since the United States is by a wide margin the strongest military power in this hemisphere and is far in advance of Latin America in arms production, military methods, and technology, it obviously must provide the leadership. And, since its wealth is so much greater than that of its Latin American allies, it must also assume the lion's share of the costs of the collective-defense program. These facts have been understood both by the United States and by the Latin American governments.

Military aid to Latin America's armed forces, a corollary to the principle of collective defense, is designed not only to add to their limited military capabilities, but also to stimulate their governments to help themselves. In exchange for grant aid, a recipient country is obligated "to make . . . the full contribution permitted by its manpower, resources, facilities and general economic conditions to the development of its own defensive strength . . . and to take all reasonable measures which may be needed to develop its defense capacities." [2] The official objective is to make Latin America's armed forces strong enough so that the United States, in case of war, need not divert its own limited manpower to the defenses of Latin America, and particularly to deter sudden enemy submarine and bomber

[2] Same, March 3, 1952, p. 338.

attacks, which "would destroy, by blockade and isolation, the economy of every American republic." [3]

The United States encourages the exclusive use of U.S. equipment, largely in order to simplify maintenance and to avoid the shortages of spare parts that rendered so much of Latin America's European equipment useless after the outbreak of World War II. For this reason the United States opposes the sale of British and French as well as Soviet armaments to Latin America. For a number of years standardization of arms was seriously hampered by our own peculiar pricing and selling policies. Until 1956 the Mutual Security Act provided that United States military equipment sold to foreign countries be priced at its acquisition or replacement cost, no allowance being made for depreciation through use or aging. Another difficulty was the absence of funds to finance sales on credit.[4] The result was that between 1951 and 1956 the Latin American republics purchased seventy-four ships, hundreds of airplanes, and a large variety of army equipment from European and Asian suppliers. Another impediment to standardization was the capacity of some Latin American countries to manufacture much of their own military equipment, including planes in Brazil and Argentina.[5] In spite of these handicaps, progress in standardization has recently been speeded through the reimbursable arms aid program, which has put the United States in a favorable position in competitive pricing, and by a Congressional appropriation which has made credit sales possible. However, European suppliers are by no means out of the picture.

No such difficulties plague progress toward "standardized" training, tactics, and methods, for here the United

[3] Same, March 30, 1954, p. 466.

[4] U.S. House Committee on Foreign Affairs, *Mutual Security Act of 1957*, Hearings, 85th Cong., 1st sess. (Washington: GPO, 1957), pt. 5, p. 905.

[5] U.S. Senate Committee on Foreign Relations, Subcommittee on Disarmament, *Control and Reduction of Armaments: Disarmament and Security in Latin America*, 85th Cong., 1st sess., Staff Study no. 7 (Washington: GPO, 1957), pp. 15-16.

States, by virtue of the mission system, does indeed have a monopoly. This system, introduced into Latin America during World War II, is a key component of United States military planning in the Western Hemisphere. Though some of the missions were recalled with the return of peace in 1945, the Korean emergency restored the system to a virtual wartime footing. At present some 500 to 600 United States officers and men are providing Latin America's armed forces with assistance and advice in military organization, training, and use of modern equipment. In 1957 there was a total of 40 missions (14 army, 11 navy, and 15 air force); every country but Mexico had at least one. Their strength ranged from a single army officer in Panama to 80 officers and men assigned to army, navy, and air force missions in Venezuela.[6]

The missions, in the view of the United States, perform an important military function. They help to strengthen collective defense and to unify operations in accord with United States standards. The very fact of training of their officers by advanced professional military men cannot help but improve the military capacities of the Latin American nations. Finally, not the least of the missions' accomplishments is encouragement of the exclusive use of United States equipment.

An important outgrowth of the work of missions, and contributing to the same ends, has been the sending of Latin American officers to United States military schools for advanced training. The army program, for example, provides openings for Latin American cadets at West Point and for Latin American majors and colonels at the Command and General Staff College at Fort Leavenworth, Kansas.[7] The navy conducts similar programs at Annapolis and Newport. In addition, Latin American soldiers, both officers and men, receive special training at military schools in the Canal Zone. For example, in 1956, 250 Latin Amer-

[6] *Mutual Security Act of 1957*, cited, p. 927.

[7] Alfred Vagts, *Defense and Diplomacy* (New York: King's Crown Press, 1956), p. 213.

ican students were attending the air force Albrook base training-school there.[8] Today, the officers who reach the top rungs of the Latin American military ladder generally display on their service records a tour of duty at some advanced military-training institution in the United States rather than in Germany, Italy, or France, as in the past.

Under the military assistance program, and the special bilateral Mutual Defense Assistance Pacts concluded with twelve Latin American republics, the United States provides military equipment, which the recipient country pledges to use to further the defense of the hemisphere. In each of these countries a United States Military Assistance Advisory Group (MAAG) has the task of supervising the use of the equipment furnished.[9] In contrast to the training-missions, which are employed by contract with each country concerned, the MAAG's are in Latin America by virtue of the requirements of United States legislation and the terms of the agreements with the countries receiving aid. The MAAG's work closely with the missions and lend valuable assistance in furthering their objectives; in some countries the two are consolidated.

Precisely what military contribution to collective defense the MDAP countries are expected to make is stated in secret articles of the agreements. Presumably the purposes are those which guide the planning of the Inter-American Defense Board: maintaining internal order, protecting strategic installations, and preparing against the possibility of outside invasion. The transfer of naval equipment appears to indicate that the recipient country's defense tasks include, as in World War II, defense of its own shores and coastal waters.

The United States expects that recipients of reimbursable military aid, which include all twenty of the Latin American republics, will cooperate in meeting the Com-

[8] U.S. Senate Subcommittee on Appropriations, *Department of Defense Appropriations for 1956,* Hearings on H.R. 6042, 84th Cong., 1st sess. (Washington: GPO, 1955), pp. 1191-1192.

[9] George Fielding Eliot, "The Defense of Latin America," *American Mercury,* October 1954, p. 105.

munist threat. The assumption is that this aid, like grant aid, should be used for defense against aggression and for strengthening the forces of law and order against subversion.

Finally, it is assumed that the provision of military assistance will help insure the accessibility of Latin America's strategic raw materials. The twelve MDA Pact signatories have all agreed, presumably in exchange for military aid, "to facilitate the production and transfer to the government of the United States" of such materials.[10]

Military Realities

This, then, is the military side of United States security policy in Latin America today. This is how the program is presented to the public by the State and Defense Departments in their press releases and official bulletins.[11] This is how it is presented by the Pentagon to the United States Congress, from which appropriations for the program must come. For example, in reply to a Senatorial query about the philosophy underlying our military aid policies in Latin America, General Bolte, chairman of the Inter-American Defense Board, replied that "the philosophy is that they [i.e., the Latin Americans] are contributing to the common purpose of defense against aggression. . . ."[12] Official statements emphasize also that the Latin American governments which participate in the collective defense program are convinced that U.S. military policy in that area is inherently sound.

The policy, however, rests on the questionable assumption that Latin America "is threatened by Communist aggression both from within and without." No serious observer believes that Soviet armies are about to invade the Western Hemisphere. Between Russia and Latin America

10 U.S. Department of State, *Bulletin,* March 13, 1952, p. 337.

11 E.g., same, March 30, 1954, pp. 463-467.

12 U.S. Senate Committees on Foreign Relations and Armed Services, *Mutual Security Act of 1951,* Hearings on S. 1762, 82nd Cong., 1st sess. (Washington: GPO, 1951), p. 402.

stand the NATO powers in Western Europe, the Atlantic Ocean, and the United States navy and air force. The western side of the area is even more firmly shielded by the vast expanses of the Pacific and by United States control over the approaches to the hemisphere. With such natural geographic shields and such powerful anti-Communist allies, the idea of a threat of Communist aggression from without is very remote.[13] In the event of general war, of course, the Soviet Union might conceivably direct a small part of its attention to Latin America, whose great cities are vulnerable to missile attacks from submarines, but the main objects of attack would surely be the United States, its European allies, and its base system. The fact is that, in military terms, Latin America is more isolated than any other major area in the world from the East-West struggle. It would be hard to imagine a more unlikely target for an armed Soviet assault.

Whatever the assumptions of United States policy, the Latin Americans themselves seem quite convinced that there is no prospect of external invasion today. So remote do they feel, moreover, that they have been moved by little or no sense of obligation to resist Communist aggression before it reaches the Western Hemisphere. Although the provisions of the Rio Treaty did not specifically cover the Communist attack in Korea, Latin America's apparent general acceptance of the principle of collective security led the United States to expect its military cooperation in fighting the Communists in Korea. Only Colombia responded, however. Despite the provisions of the bilateral MDA agreements under which the countries receiving military aid are pledged to participate in missions important to the defense of the hemisphere, eleven of the twelve Latin American signatories chose not to join in the fighting abroad. The Brazilian government cooperated with the United Nations Expeditionary Forces in police-type duties in the Suez Canal area after 1956, but in mid-1958 Brazil, apparently fearing involvement in Near East fighting,

[13] Eliot, cited, p. 102.

made it clear that it would not participate if additional United Nations forces were organized to maintain stability in Lebanon.[14] Clearly, all Latin America gives "hemisphere defense" a narrow interpretation, not going beyond the letter of the Rio Treaty. The MDAP signatories see their obligations as limited to defense of their homeland and nearby waters, where no Communist military threat need be feared.

Highly pertinent to the question of the contribution that Latin America might make to the security of the hemisphere is the strength and capability of its armed forces. As of 1955, the numerical strength was reported as follows: [15]

Country	Total Armed Forces Strength	Army	Navy	Air Force
Argentina	147,500	107,000	21,500	19,000
Bolivia	12,000	10,000*	*None*	2,000
Brazil	107,200	90,000	8,000	9,200
Chile	41,500	20,500	8,000	13,000
Colombia	16,700	15,000*	1,500	200
Costa Rica	*None*	*None*	*None*	*None*
Cuba	23,400	19,000	2,000	2,400
Dominican Republic	18,500	13,500	3,000	2,000
Ecuador	19,800	13,000*	3,700*	3,100
Guatemala	8,400	8,000*	*None*	400
Haiti	4,953	4,553	*None*	400
Honduras	3,700	2,500	*None*	1,200
Mexico	47,800	41,800	2,500	3,500
Nicaragua	11,300	10,000	*None*	1,300
Panama	3,500	3,500	*None*	*None*
Paraguay	7,300	5,800	1,000*	500*
Peru	37,500	30,000	2,500	5,000
El Salvador	6,900	6,000	400	500
Uruguay	6,450	3,000	1,450	2,000
Venezuela	17,240	10,000	2,240	5,000
Total	541,643	413,153	57,790	70,700

[14] *New York Times,* July 18, 1958.

[15] Figures marked with asterisk taken from *Statesman's Yearbook, 1956.* All others from *Control and Reduction of Armaments,* cited, p. 14.

Thus Latin America, with only a little over half a million men in uniform out of a total population of 180 million, less than one-third of one per cent, is anything but a heavily armed area. Because of their distance from the scenes of conflict in Europe and Asia, the twenty republics have not been interested in building up their armed forces for the purpose of resisting a major invasion or in fighting in force abroad. Nor, despite their local rivalries and arms races, have they prepared on a large scale for local wars. In the twentieth century the only real war that occurred within the hemisphere was between Paraguay and Bolivia in the 1930's. Aside from this, only boundary squabbles in Central America and northwestern South America disturbed the peace from time to time.

The actual military power and war-making potential of the Latin American states count for practically nothing when compared with the major powers of the world. Their little armies are equipped generally with yesterday's weapons, hand-me-downs from the world's first-rank military powers. Dependence upon outside suppliers, mainly the United States, means that the Latin American armed forces are neither independent nor self-sufficient. Their effectiveness is even further reduced by factionalism within and among the services, by perversion of the military function, and by the squandering of capabilities in domestic political adventures. The inadequate training and skills of the enlisted personnel is another limiting factor, for the men in the ranks are generally handicapped by poor health and illiteracy, and most are anything but enthusiastic soldiers.

Judged by United States standards, Latin American armies are ill equipped and badly trained, despite the work of military missions and the aid programs. They lack adequate transport. No Latin American state has a significant air force; only three (Argentina, Brazil, and Chile) have even marginal navies. United States military strategists are well aware of these facts; consequently, they do not count on Latin American forces to provide any significant assistance in operations outside the hemisphere, either in a general or in a limited war. Even for military tasks closely related to hemisphere defense, such as keeping the Atlantic, Pacific, and Caribbean sea lanes open and defending the Panama Canal, all but the most peripheral must be assumed by the United States.

United States military planners in these circumstances do not really want large-scale Latin American participation in extra-hemisphere operations. The incorporation of Brazilian troops with United States forces in Italy during World War II proved difficult because of both their limited capabilities and the language barrier. Similarly, the main reason for wanting Latin American forces in Korea was political, to demonstrate the collective character of the operations. Thus, both the United States and its southern neighbors appear to have arrived at a tacit understanding that the armed forces of practically all the Latin American countries will fight only at home, if at all.

Since in fact neither the United States nor the Latin American countries are convinced that the latter have any real role to play in meeting the external Communist threat, the only practical military justification for providing them with military training and aid is to enable them to combat the internal Communist menace. The Latin American governments have been generally willing to accept the official United States assumption that a serious Communist "threat from within" exists. Mexico, in resisting the signing of an MDA agreement that might obligate it to send troops to Korea, maintained that for it the Communist threat from within was much greater than for the United States, and that Mexican forces consequently should be kept at home. Brazil also takes the position that its internal Communist menace is so serious that to combat it large quantities of United States arms are needed. The last point provides some key to the motivation for the official view on the extent of the danger, which seems often to depend on the political purpose uppermost at the time. In Mexico's case, judging from the Mexican delegation's attitude at the 1954 Caracas Conference, there was no agreement with the United States that a Communist threat existed in Guatemala.

Actually, the Communist "threat from within" is not serious as a military problem. In no Latin American country do the Communists have anything approaching the strength they had in Guatemala under Arbenz (1950-1954). While their capacities for subversion through penetration, propaganda, and influence in such organizations as trade-unions do represent a serious threat in some countries, this is not a military problem. They do not possess the military capabilities to challenge successfully any Latin American government. Yet it is ostensibly to deal with the Communist threat from within that countries receiving MDAP aid are expected to strengthen their armed forces. Their military capability is assumed to be so limited that it needs strengthening in order to maintain internal order. But such is not the case. Latin America's forces may be incapable of effective action in the event of a major invasion or war, but few military experts in the area would question that they were perfectly capable of maintaining internal order before they began receiving United States aid, and that even without it they would have been able to continue to perform this function indefinitely. Besides, in most of the countries of the area the task of preserving internal order against Communist subversion is well handled by the police forces. Considering that the Communist party is outlawed in most countries and party membership is relatively small, the minor threat that exists from within is primarily a problem for the police. It seems that if the United States military planners are primarily concerned about the internal Communist threat, they should channel aid to the police rather than to the armies.

If enabling Latin America to meet the Communist threat from within and from without affords no sound military basis for U.S. assistance, there is even less reason for it as a means of preparing Latin American countries to defend themselves against each other. The need for this type of defensive assistance is clearly greatly reduced by the existence of the Organization of American States, whose charter provides for the peaceful settlement of disputes. Repeatedly the OAS has proven itself effective in preventing aggression within Latin America, as, for example, in the conflicts between Costa Rica and Nicaragua, and between Ecuador and Peru, in 1955.

On all counts, therefore, it is difficult to avoid the conclusion that as a purely military proposition the concept of collective planning and defense has little, if any, practical application. Even if the need should arise, the anemic armed forces of the various Latin American states probably could not be combined for effective military use. Military planning on a regional basis with provision for joint operations on anything comparable to the NATO system is impracticable and unnecessary. Furthermore, the differences among the Latin American governments over the extent of military participation, their unwillingness to cooperate in defense tasks outside their own boundaries, their reluctance to make hemisphere-wide agreements with respect to such matters as base rights and access to strategic raw materials, their national rivalries—all these difficulties have forced the United States to employ bilateral rather than multilateral agreements for practical military cooperation. This is why Mutual Defense Assistance Pacts have been arranged individually with each of twelve Latin-American republics and why a joint Brazil-United States Military Command and a joint Mexico-United States Defense Board continue to function independently of the Inter-American Defense Board.

The latter organization has thus inevitably become primarily a piece of window dressing. After sixteen years of semimonthly meetings it is still trying to come up with a comprehensive hemisphere defense plan. The Board achieves little because its members do not choose to give it real authority. No Latin American nation is anxious to give up any sizable measure of control over its armed forces. Besides, genuine military planning is hampered by the secrecy surrounding the classified clauses of the bilateral MDA Pacts. Since no nation except the United States really knows exactly what contribution twelve of the twenty countries are expected to make toward hemisphere defense, the Board can plan only in very general terms. Understandably, the United States, with its ultramodern weapons and its defense commitments elsewhere, is reluctant to reveal fully its own plans for hemisphere defense. Though both the United States and Latin America appreciate the impracticability of undertaking joint military efforts, they seem to believe that maintenance of the collective-defense façade warrants the indefinite continuance of the rather pointless IADB discussions. Small wonder that Latin America's high-ranking military representatives on the Board are not generally appointed with a view to serious military planning; indeed, this Washington assignment is often given to generals with political claims to a sinecure, or to those considered too ambitious and dangerous by the government of the day to be allowed to remain at home.

The mission system has no genuine military objective. The training it provides is not extensive enough and the amount of equipment supplied is not large enough to improve significantly Latin America's capabilities for contributing military assistance to the United States in operations elsewhere in the world. The Latin American officers are being taught the elements of modern tactics and methods, both by the missions and at United States schools, but it is difficult to see where and when they will ever put them to military use, except perhaps in their own countries in dealing with purely internal situations.

Nor is the standardization program geared to the prospect of Latin America's having to engage in modern warfare. Much of the arms and equipment supplied consists of obsolete, discontinued items, useful for short-term training purposes perhaps, but destined to become useless once the spare parts and ammunition no longer are manufactured in the United States. The most modern weapons the United States needs itself, and accordingly discourages

Latin America from requesting them. When such requests are made anyhow, and are denied, Latin America shops elsewhere, to the detriment of standardization. Thus the Ecuadoran and Venezuelan air forces, for example, are equipped today with British-made Meteor jet fighters and Canberra jet bombers.

It follows from these facts that the United States military planners have no desire, since the basic requirements are missing, to prepare Latin American forces for a meaningful military role in the cold war, or in a hot one. This fact becomes even more evident when the military assistance figures are examined. Military aid to Latin America has been extremely modest, compared with that extended to other areas of the free world. Since the program began in 1951, only 1.3 per cent ($317 million) of MDA funds have gone to Latin America. The program over the past seven years has averaged about $65 million annually, some $45 million in MDA grants and $20 million in reimbursable aid. For fiscal 1960, the Eisenhower administration has requested $96 million in MDA assistance for Latin America, the substantially higher than average figure being largely accounted for by two special items, one a requested appropriation for credit sales and the other extraordinary additional military assistance grant to Brazil for use of Fernando de Noronha Island.[16] Altogether, the United States' contribution represents about 5 per cent of the $1.4 billion Latin America spends yearly to maintain its armed forces.[17]

Recently the military rationale for U.S. policy has been rendered even more dubious by statements of high U.S.

[16] U.S. House Committee on Foreign Affairs, *Mutual Security Act of 1959,* Hearings, 86th Cong., 1st sess. (Washington: GPO, 1959), p. 753.

[17] "Military Aid Programs," a study prepared by the Systems Analysis Corporation, in U.S. Senate Special Committee to Study the Foreign Aid Program, *The Military Assistance Program of the United States,* 85th Cong., 1st sess., Committee print no. 10 (Washington: GPO, 1957), pp. 89, 96; *Control and Reduction of Armaments,* cited, p. 15; U.S. House Committee on Foreign Affairs, *Staff Memorandum on Background Material on the Mutual Security Program for Fiscal Year 1960,* 86th Cong., 1st sess. (Washington, GPO, 1959), pp. 4, 27.

officials themselves. When the MDA program was inaugurated in late 1951, it was declared that Latin America's armed forces had to be strengthened and improved. Hence the donor's insistence on the clause obligating the recipient nation to "take all reasonable measures . . . to develop its defense capacities." Yet, the Eisenhower administration in recent years has been concerned lest excessive expenditures for armaments should weaken Latin American economies. The late Secretary of State John Foster Dulles, in testimony before a Senate committee, stated that the underdeveloped countries ought to maintain military establishments no larger than were required for internal security, and that unless they were in the vicinity of heavily armed Soviet areas there was no need for them to be active participants in the free world's military defense structure.[18] Similarly, at the Inter-American Economic Conference in Buenos Aires in August 1957, when the Latin Americans made a plea for aid in the form of "defense support," which none of them presently receives, to meet the economic burden of military defense, they were told by Secretary of the Treasury Robert B. Anderson to trim their military budgets to the minimum level for defense.[19] The unspoken fact was that, despite the size of their military budgets and after six years of the so-called military build-up program with U.S. aid, Latin America's armed forces possessed no meaningful defense capabilities.

It is doubtful, moreover, that the military aid programs have really improved access by the United States to Latin America's strategic raw materials. Protection against possible sabotage at the source of supply is a police function. The armies do not mine the ores or control the output; and the naval and air capabilities of the Latin American nations will not be sufficient in the foreseeable future, even

18 U.S. Senate Special Committee to Study the Foreign Aid Program, *The Foreign Aid Program*, Hearings, 85th Cong., 1st sess. (Washington: GPO, 1957), p. 413.

19 *New York Times*, August 19, 1957.

with much greater outside aid, to protect the transfer of strategic materials to the United States. The production of the principal strategic materials (e.g., copper, lead, zinc, petroleum) in most Latin American countries is in the hands of private companies, many of them armed and controlled by U.S. citizens. (Tin in Bolivia and oil in Mexico are exceptions.) It is true that a Latin American republic, like any sovereign state, can close down operations or embargo exports to the United States; but such action seems highly improbable, irrespective of the extension of U.S. military assistance. It cannot even be convincingly argued that such assistance would tend to make those Latin American governments in which the armed forces are influential more willing to make their strategic raw materials available to the United States. In peacetime, the United States is by far the best customer for raw materials of all kinds, and for reasons of economic self-interest they are anxious to sell all they possibly can in that market. In wartime the United States would be their only market.

Political Objectives

Since neither the official U.S. military objectives nor the means of attaining them make sense in terms of the real conditions in Latin America, some pointed questions might well be asked. Are the United States military authorities naïve or unwilling to recognize realities? Or, are they perhaps guilty of deliberately perpetrating a gigantic hoax upon the American public and on their Latin American allies? The answer to both questions is decidedly "no." There is a simple and logical explanation for the discrepancy between official policy statements and actual practice. It is that the objectives of United States military programs in Latin America are primarily political, although it has seemed wiser to express them in military than in political terms.

The 1947 Rio Treaty had been justified by the concept

of collective security and by the assumption of the threat of aggression. When NATO was created the following year, upon a similar concept and assumption, the United States began pouring military aid into Western European countries. That made it embarrassing for the United States to deny Latin American requests for similar aid. What grounds for outright refusal could possibly be given without admitting that for Latin America collective security was meaningless, thereby wrecking the structure of hemispheric cooperation? The United States took the decision to grant military assistance to Latin American countries, not primarily to strengthen their armed forces for military reasons, but to reinforce the inter-American political system.

Thus, even though sound military logic made it unavoidable that the United States assume the role of protector of the hemisphere, political considerations made it essential that the fact should be muted. Therefore the United States has created, and is deliberately preserving, a myth with respect to Latin America's military cooperation. In a recent analysis, Edgar S. Furniss, Jr., wrote:

> . . . If the United States should act as if there were no danger of hemisphere aggression or as though the other American republics had no contribution to make, the foundations of the Organization of American States would be endangered . . . for United States spokesmen have been fond of repeating that our common policy rests upon respect for the sovereignty and the juridical equality of all the American states.

And he added that, if the United States were to refuse to grant military assistance to Latin America,

> . . . twenty weak republics shut up in one hemisphere with one giant would have to take their comfort in juridical equality only. [However] their nationalistic pride requires that we support that most basic attribute of sovereignty, that is, a national army outfitted, equipped and commanded like others elsewhere in the world. . . . The fact that these armies have

little or nothing to do with international defense, or with national protection for that matter, is beside the point.[20]

The myth is maintained also to avoid the difficulties that might arise if the basic premises for military programs were openly admitted to be political. Each Latin American country is able to give the United States an endless number of reasons why, on political grounds, it should get more aid than a neighboring country. The necessity of making difficult choices is averted by requiring military justification for all projects strictly on the basis of hemisphere defense. Also, the military rationale corresponds to the legal basis of the aid program, for under the Mutual Security Act military assistance grants can be legally made only for purposes of hemisphere defense.

The State Department, in Congressional hearings on the MDA program, has occasionally acknowledged a political motivation for the military aid program. Assistant Secretary of State for Inter-American Affairs Roy R. Rubottom, Jr., speaking recently in support of the program before the House Foreign Affairs Committee, said:

On the political side, our objective is to do all we can to help develop the friendliest possible relationships between ourselves and our neighbors in Latin America, and to encourage and bring about support of United States policies both in this hemisphere and elsewhere in the world.[21]

The only logical reason, moreover, for including the smaller and militarily insignificant Latin American nations in the MDA program admittedly has been political. They get aid because their governments desire it. In 1954, the Assistant Secretary of State for Inter-American Affairs, Henry F. Holland, requested funds to include Haiti in the program because "she feels left out since the Dominican Republic is included." He added, rather as an afterthought, the military consideration that "Haiti has a fairly large army [4,000] and is strategically located on the Windward

20 *American Military Policy* (New Brunswick, N.J.: Rutgers University Press, 1957), p. 241.

21 *Mutual Security Act of 1957*, cited, p. 905.

Passage where many ships were sunk during World War II." [22]

Whether publicly admitted or not, the main objective of the United States has been to keep Latin America friendly and cooperative. Military aid and planning for the common defense are means of attaining that objective, in the hope that the return for assistance will be made in the form of political support.

The political orientation of Latin America in the cold war is of vital importance to the United States. In the United Nations the Latin American bloc, which possesses one-quarter of the total vote, often holds the balance on key issues in the East-West conflict. In Latin America itself the thwarting of Communist subversion depends far more on the political attitudes of Latin American governments than on the level of their armaments. Even in situations where the United States asks Latin America's military support for overseas operations, the reason is political. All that was wanted in Korea was token contributions, such as Colombia sent, so as to create the impression of solidarity on the part of the OAS and the United Nations vis-à-vis the Communist aggression. The key question is: what are the most suitable means for achieving the desired solidarity and cooperation?

The great importance attached to military assistance in securing Latin America's political cooperation flows in large measure from the political role of Latin America's armed forces and their continuing desire for more arms. The outstanding feature of the political life of most Latin American states, as our earlier analysis shows, is the influential role played by the armed forces. The army is practically a branch of politics. Where the officer corps dominates political parties and civilian leaders, or where countries are ruled directly by military strong-men, the United States has little choice but to do business with the military if it expects to do business at all. For the cold-war

22 U.S. Senate Committee on Foreign Relations, *Mutual Security Act of 1954*, Hearings, 83rd Cong., 2d sess. (Washington: GPO, 1954), pp. 348-349.

emergency has dictated, in the thinking of our policy-makers, full collaboration with friendly incumbent governments, regardless of their political coloration.[23]

Because of the key roles military personalities play in government and politics, the United States, through its military programs, makes a pointed effort to influence them. The mission program, for example, which as we have seen serves no important military purpose, is nevertheless most useful in providing opportunities for cementing political as well as professional relationships between the sending and the recipient government. Also, the practice of training Latin American officers in the United States helps to secure their political sympathies.

The political function of the missions carries over to the plans for standardization of arms, which the missions themselves do their utmost to promote. Standardization is primarily a political tool in the sense that if the United States succeeds in cornering the Latin American armaments market, it closes a potential avenue of Soviet penetration in this hemisphere. In addition, it brings the American republics closer together, at least in relations among their military establishments. The danger lies not so much in the acquisition of Soviet arms, but rather in the missions that might accompany them—missions that would have obvious political aims.[24]

A further benefit from cooperative political attitudes on the part of Latin American governments, induced at least in part by U.S. military programs, is the assurance, or expectation, that bases in Latin America may be available when the United States needs them. What *quid pro quos* for military aid may have been incorporated in the classified clauses of the MDA Pacts is a matter of conjecture. However, in the light of the experience of World War II and the contemporary importance attached to achieving

23 "Military Assistance and the Security of the United States," a study prepared by the Institute of War and Peace Studies, Columbia University, in *The Military Assistance Program of the United States,* cited, pp. 71-72.

24 Same, p. 65.

additional bases in the Latin America area in case of war, it would be reasonable to assume that, wherever possible, arrangements for wartime base rights probably have been made. At present the United States has only four military bases in the Latin American area. Use of the Guantánamo naval base in Cuba and possession of the Canal Zone in Panama date from the period when the United States helped to make these two nations independent around the turn of the century. The missile-tracking station in the Dominican Republic was apparently obtained in exchange for signing an MDA Pact with Trujillo, and the similar station on Fernando de Noronha Island in exchange for substantial additional military assistance to be granted Brazil under the existing MDA Pact beginning in fiscal 1959.[25]

An additional political objective of military assistance is the promotion of internal stability in Latin America. The mere provision of such aid by the world's leading power gives a certain psychological support that strengthens an incumbent regime. In addition, the weapons received improve the recipient government's ability to cope with internal disorder, as was apparent in the recent civil wars in Colombia and in Cuba, though they are no guarantee of ultimate success. Under the provisions of the Mutual Security Act, United States military assistance may be used only for hemisphere defense, but so long as the latter encompasses the notion of defense against internal subversion, the incumbent government has virtual license to use the equipment against any and all domestic opposition. It is not always easy to tell how much Communist inspiration or participation is present in antigovernment rebellions, nor is it certain that U.S. security interests will be threatened and Soviet interests served only when such rebellions are specifically Communist. Any violent social upheaval or an ultranationalist revolution could undermine a government friendly to the United States. Accordingly, the

[25] *New York Times,* February 10, 1957.

strengthening of the internal security forces of friendly governments is considered good insurance against damage to United States interests.[26]

Finally, the prevention of wars within the area is another legitimate political objective which military programs are designed to support.[27] It is always possible that national rivalries and jealousies in Latin America will sap the United States' energies, distract its attention from the main problems which lie outside the hemisphere, and provide golden opportunities for Soviet meddling. Accordingly, the collective-defense concept is used to encourage the Latin American countries to concentrate upon cooperative defense rather than upon the use of force against each other. To prevent an upset in the Latin American balance of power two things are done. First, the small amount of military aid is parceled out in a fairly balanced fashion among all the receiving countries. Secondly, through the OAS peace machinery, which collectively involves the twenty-one member states, the overwhelmingly powerful United States attempts to persuade the other American republics that disputes among them must be settled peacefully. The military missions, of course, also play an important role in this regard. Their mere presence reduces the chance of conspiratorial action by one Latin American nation against another.

To sum up, the real aim of United States military policy is to improve the United States security position by gaining the political collaboration of Latin America. The United States is not counting upon the Latin American states to make a military contribution to the defense of the free world. Its key concern is to keep the area friendly and cooperative, and to exclude Soviet influence. Military planning, the work of the missions, and military aid programs

26 "Military Assistance and the Security of the United States," cited, p. 52.

27 Furniss believes that the hemispheric collective-security program is designed primarily to insure pacification of the Latin American area; cited, p. 235.

are all aimed at the influencing of governments, the promotion of stability, and the assurance of strategic needs. The critique which follows will show how the policy works in practice and whether these purposes are actually being achieved.

Chapter 9

CRITIQUE OF U.S. POLICY

MUCH OF THE criticism of United States policy in the military field shows a lack of understanding of the principle that political objectives determine military policies. Those policies, as we have seen, are not designed to meet the military threat of communism, but rather to gain Latin America's friendship, to win its cooperation and support in the United Nations and the Organization of American States. The Rio military alliance, the MDA Pacts, the arms grants, the reimbursable aid, the work of the IADB and of the military missions—all of these have no great military significance. They are designed, above all, to draw the Latin American officer corps, which exercise great influence over the political scene in most of the republics, closer to the United States, in the hope that they will exclude Soviet influence, give the United States their support, maintain political stability, ensure continued access to strategic raw materials, and provide rights to the use of bases.

The Political Attitudes of Latin America's Armed Forces

Any meaningful critique of U.S. policy must begin, therefore, not with sterile attacks upon its failure to achieve announced military objectives, but with an examination of its political results. Such results, of course, are impossible to measure, for the relationship of cause and effect is never clear. But the evidence does not provide much support for the contention that our military measures have produced marked political success. For example, in the United Nations the Latin American states, except for Argentina and Guatemala during the early 1950's, have generally shown steady support for the United States in the voting on key political issues in the East-West controversy. Yet this support is more readily explained by Latin America's political and economic stake in the United States position than as recompense for military aid. Political cooperation has come just as readily from countries that did not receive aid, like Mexico and Costa Rica, as from those that did. The influence of the military has even tended to be negative. When it came to the hard decision, for example, on whether to fight in Korea in cooperation with the United States, a decision in which the armed forces' voice was decisive in most Latin American countries, all except Colombia decided not to take part.

In the Organization of American States, although all continue to give lip service to the myth of collective defense, the Latin American states have shown little enthusiasm for collective action except in dealing with quarrels within the hemisphere. They have not been convinced of the merits of a cooperative program to meet the alleged Communist threat from within, although certain governments have cited it as a reason for requesting more military aid. When it came to a concrete case, at the tenth Inter-American Conference at Caracas in 1954, there was very little agreement that a real Communist threat existed. At that conference a resolution outlawing communism, which many countries failed to implement effectively, was obtained only in exchange for United States promises to give more attention to Latin America's economic needs.

United States military programs, it is true, make this country's influence stronger than that of other nations among Latin America's armed forces. So long as the programs continue, they should contribute to excluding Soviet influence and minimizing that of other European states. It is sometimes questionable, however, how much this advantage actually enhances the security position of the United States, for the Latin American armed forces cannot be assumed to have the same political objectives as the United States. Such military dictatorships as exist in the Dominican Republic and Paraguay, whose primary enemy is internal civilian opposition rather than world-wide communism, can hardly be depended upon to follow any but the most opportunistic course in time of crisis. They may label all opposition as "Communist," thereby hoping to increase their eligibility for United States military aid, but any true identity between such a regime's strategic interests and those of the United States is purely accidental. Their "cooperation" generally costs them nothing, and in the process they reap tangible rewards in the form of military equipment. Sometimes military dictators, such as Batista in Cuba and Pérez Jiménez in Venezuela, even cooperated with local Communists in fighting the civilian opposition. Demosthenes' dictum that "close alliances with despots are never safe for free states" is as pertinent today as it was in 345 B.C.

While it can be argued that military ties will guarantee political support in those nations where the military are influential in politics, the United States still runs the risk that today's military elite, with whom the ties have been made, may be out of power tomorrow. Rebellious young officers gaining political power may not respect pacts and understandings concluded by their seniors, as happened in Argentina and Bolivia in the latter years of World War II. There is always the danger that a faction coming to power will use arms provided by the United States to support a government unfriendly to the United States.

The availability or hoped-for use of bases is a justification for continued U.S. military programs not lightly to be discounted. Apparently in exchange for MDAP aid, missile-tracking stations have already been obtained in the Dominican Republic and Brazil. Commitments for the use of bases in wartime may be similarly obtainable. Such bases might be of real strategic importance to the United

States, although developments in nuclear weapons which seem daily to decrease the likelihood of general warfare of long duration may cast doubt on that point. In any case, the most solid guarantee of their availability lies more in the continuing favorable disposition of the Latin American nations in question than on a paper guarantee from an ephemeral military regime.

Perverted Use of Military Aid

If the ultimate justification of U.S. military relations with Latin America, and especially of the aid program, is political, the actual political effects in those countries are worth careful scrutiny. In the first place, it seems incontrovertible that the aid program exacerbates endemic rivalries and mutual suspicions among the Latin American republics and gives rise to arms races. Since World War II, beginning with the $400 million worth of Lend-Lease military aid, the grants and sales of arms by the United States have helped to raise appreciably the level of armaments in Latin America. Unintentionally and despite its efforts to keep the aid balanced as between the various receiving countries, the United States may be helping to arm Latin America against Latin America. Whether for reasons of prestige or fear, the acquisitions of one country are generally duplicated by its watchful, ever-suspicious neighbors. If one nation is given, or buys, one type of jet aircraft, its neighbor is likely to demand one just like it. In 1951 Brazil wished to purchase two light cruisers from the United States. The impending sale provoked demands from Argentina for similar vessels so as to maintain the balance with Brazil, a request which gave rise to a purchase order from Chile, anxious to keep up with Argentina. In the end each of the three nations obtained two cruisers.

That kind of military aid fails to raise Latin America's capabilities sufficiently to defend itself against an outside threat, but it does provide the military in some countries with the wherewithal to provoke or intensify feuding within the hemisphere. Certainly Trujillo's saber-rattling in the Caribbean and Somoza's massing of tanks and armored cars along the troubled Costa Rican border were made possible by our sales and grants of military equipment to those regimes. Also, the roughly equivalent amounts of military aid, both reimbursable and in grants, provided to Peru and Ecuador make it likely that if their long-standing border dispute should again break out into open warfare, that war will be more destructive than it would otherwise have been.

Another particularly relevant question is whether U.S. military aid tends to provoke militarism inside individual countries by encouraging the armed forces to play politics. In a situation where the energies of the armed forces of Latin America are mainly devoted to the sphere of internal politics, military equipment and support from the United States may be converted into political power. The quantity of arms provided is probably less important than the psychological effect. Where the civilian and military elements are vying for power, United States military aid could unwittingly tip the balance in favor of the armed forces. Where the latter are already in control, it might well contribute to perpetuating their dominance.

The continued stress which the United States lays on Latin America's role in hemisphere defense also inclines the officer corps toward politics, increasing their power and inflating their ambition to play a decisive role in time of crisis. United States military planners, deliberately or unconsciously, transfer to Latin American officers their own sense of crisis. The preoccupation with the imminent Communist threat, the drive for collective hemispheric security, the prominence of military factors and of military men in United States foreign policy—all these, plus the arms aid, give encouragement to those elements always present within Latin America's armies that seek political power.

In Brazil, for example, following the receipt of nearly $300 million in Lend-Lease equipment and the sending of a token expeditionary force to Italy during World War II, the armed forces assumed the right to depose President Vargas when the war was over. According to Laurence Duggan, the United States equipment and experience in European fighting built up the role of the officer corps in the country's politics; thenceforth they began making and breaking governments.[1] Again in 1954, following receipt of more military aid and the assumption of a new defense-of-the-hemisphere role with the signing of the 1953 MDA Pact, they arrogated to themselves the right to depose Vargas again, although this time he had been freely elected to the presidency.

In Colombia, prior to the military coup of 1953, the army had been receiving both grant and reimbursable aid from the United States. The officer corps, its confidence bolstered both by its fighting role in the Korean War and by its assumption of the task of "preserving order" during the civil war, could not resist the temptation to seize power. United States military aid must certainly be considered as one contributing factor that helped to tip the balance, bringing the Colombian army back into politics after a half-century of civilian rule.

The parallel with the past is striking. Just as militarism was encouraged and made more efficient by the build-up of armed forces in the Caribbean and Central American area earlier in this century under the guidance of the United States, so the concentration upon the external military threat to the hemisphere, and on the collective-defense program to meet it, must be considered as one factor contributing to the general resurgence of militarism in Latin America after 1948. The strengthening of the armed forces, for defense or for preserving internal order, seems only to give encouragement to the Latin American officer corps to convert themselves into even more highly political instruments than they are already. The intentions of the donor are, as in the past, perverted by the recipients.

[1] *The Americas: The Search for Hemisphere Security* (New York: Holt, 1949), p. 180.

Military Assistance and Democracy

The most significant, and the most controversial, question of all concerns the relation of U.S. policies to the political evolution of Latin America. Are those policies, intentionally or unintentionally, strengthening the forces of dictatorship and thwarting the progress of democracy? Three points are involved. First, is there in fact a trend toward responsible democratic government and not just a continuing series of ups and downs, revolutions and counterrevolutions, with dictatorship, especially military dictatorship, a natural and more or less permanent part of the Latin American scene? Second, do U.S. policies, more particularly those involving association with or assistance to Latin America's armed forces, have any bearing on the struggle for power and for political self-expression? Third, would modification of those policies serve the United States in its long-run relationships with Latin America?

It can hardly be denied that most countries of Latin America have been moving toward greater democracy. Despite halts and setbacks, the nature of politics and the character of some of its new civilian governments do register some change from the pattern of the past. The civilian regimes of the late 1950's are more securely grounded in popular support and in responsible practice than were those which appeared in the late 1940's only to be overthrown before many years had passed. Recent events in Colombia, Argentina, Venezuela, and Cuba seem to show, moreover, that the movements which have unseated dictatorial regimes in those countries represent a widespread popular striving toward the ideal of stable, democratic government. And the fact is that the fallen dictators were all military men.

These events have shown also that, insofar as the military aid programs have increased the political influence of the armed forces, the prospects for democracy have suffered. For the military, far more often than not, resort to nondemocratic procedures to achieve the internal order and stability which both they and the United States, for quite different reasons, so ardently desire.

These considerations raise other pertinent questions. Is the military threat to the security of the United States and of the hemisphere really so urgent that concern for the future growth of democracy and freedom must be sacrificed? Do the political and security advantages that accrue to the United States from its military aid programs in Latin America outweigh the political, moral, and psychological disadvantages? Does a net security gain result from a program that gives doubtful protection against an unlikely authoritarian menace from the outside in exchange for the encouragement or consolidation of military authoritarianism within?

It may not be easy to strike the proper balance. But one element in the picture is clear enough: the disillusionment and distrust felt by democratic leaders in Latin America when the United States, leader of the "free" world, provides aid which is so frequently put to internal political use, and thereby underwrites antidemocratic forces. From this viewpoint it matters little whether United States military policies are actually the determining factor in helping military men to seize or to retain power. The point is that the Latin American advocates of freedom and enemies of despotism believe this to be true. If they do in fact represent the general sentiments of the peoples of Latin America, then the satisfaction of the alleged security requirements of the United States, upon which the military programs are based, must be paid for in severe injury to its moral and psychological position. The real reason for these programs, we have seen, is political. It comes down, then, to a choice whether the political advantage of trying to win the cooperation of military leaders is worth the risk of losing the good will and support of those who oppose them.

The United States lays itself open to the charge that its insistence upon maintaining political stability as a defense against the Communist menace leads it into a policy of coddling dictators. Obviously, the United States has no such deliberate policy. Rather, it feels that it has to deal with any and all governments, in order to get maximum security in the hemisphere. Since some of these governments are dictatorial, this policy inevitably means that that type of government is strengthened. Not only does military aid increase the capacity for repression, but also, by identifying the dictator with the United States, it equips him with a psychological and propaganda tool to reinforce his despotism. The mere presence of newly provided United States military equipment in the country tends to persuade the people that the United States is underwriting the tyranny under which they suffer.[2] The rancor of the victorious forces of Fidel Castro in Cuba against the U.S. military mission and the arms aid program, on the ground that they helped to maintain Batista's tyranny, provides a clear illustration.

Under the Truman administration the question of support for undemocratic regimes was not so clearly posed. At this early period in the cold war at least lip service was paid to democracy. Following the overthrow by military officers of the popularly elected Acción Democrática government in Venezuela in 1948, President Truman wrote to the ousted President Gallegos:

> I believe that the use of force to effect political change is not only deplorable, but also contrary to the ideals of the American peoples. The government of the United States proposes to do everything possible, in accordance with its international obligations, to fortify the democratic forces in this hemisphere.[3]

A State Department press release of December 21, 1948,

[2] "Military Assistance and the Security of the United States," a study prepared by the Institute of War and Peace Studies, Columbia University, in U.S. Senate Special Committee to study the Foreign Aid Program, *The Military Assistance Program of the United States,* 85th Cong., 1st sess., Committee print no. 10 (Washington: GPO, 1957), pp. 71-73.

[3] *Bohemia* (Havana), February 13, 1949.

referring to military coups in Peru and Venezuela, warned that "if this use of force continues, it cannot fail to become a sufficiently serious issue to engage the American republics as a whole." Secretary of State Dean Acheson, in the following year, underscored this line of policy by publicly proclaiming that "we deplore the action of any group in substituting its judgment for that of the electorate."[4] And yet the Truman administration, by the policies it inaugurated in Latin America soon after the outbreak of the Korean War, gave encouragement to just such groups, even going out of its way to give aid and comfort to General Trujillo. Ambassador Ralph H. Ackerman, expressing his appreciation for the guided-missile-tracking base facilities the United States had just received from the Dominican government, said to the people of the Dominican Republic on June 9, 1952:

All western nations today are striving . . . for the amelioration of mankind. Governments are taking interest in the welfare of peoples. . . . Your own illustrious president . . . Trujillo . . . gave illustration of this trend when, in a speech he made only a few days ago, he reiterated an aspiration he has often voiced before, to raise the standard of living of the Dominican Republic so that his people may benefit from a fuller life. No one can gainsay the great benefits he has already succeeded in bringing about.[5]

The Eisenhower administration, in carrying on the military program, has gone further in manifestations of open support for authoritarian military regimes. Soon after assuming office it undertook a *rapprochement* with the Perón regime in Argentina and granted a loan. In November 1954 President Eisenhower presented Legion of Merit citations to Presidents Odría and Pérez Jiménez, the very men who six years previously had seized power, forcefully overthrowing freely elected, popular, civilian governments.

[4] "United States Leadership in the Americas," reprint from U.S. Department of State, *Bulletin*, Inter-American Series no. 39 (Washington, February 1950), p. 463.

[5] U.S. Department of State, *Bulletin*, July 14, 1952.

It should have occasioned no surprise when, on the recent collapse of those dictatorships, resurgent popular elements demonstrated their resentment against Vice-President Nixon during his visits to Peru and Venezuela. In these cases the strategic and political advantages obtained by United States military policies were temporary only. They were quickly undone, and in the process the psychological and moral position of the United States suffered severely.

There is no evidence that United States military programs in Latin America are genuinely supported by people other than the military officers, a minute fraction of the total population. That the great majority of civilians, whose experience leads them to fear their own armed forces far more than they do the Russians, are opposed to these programs becomes apparent when one samples the mountain of criticism heaped upon the United States military policies by respected civilian political leaders.

This is no new issue. Civilian opposition to United States arms aid was apparent before World War II. A typical view was that expressed by Eduardo Santos, leader of the Liberal party in Colombia. When, in 1937, Under Secretary of State Sumner Welles suggested the possibility of lending warships to certain Latin American nations, Santos replied,

> Don't do this evil to us. The use of armaments is like the vice of morphine. Once begun, the cure is almost impossible. You will ruin us with cruisers and create for us new problems . . . because there is always someone with the desire to try out the armaments and obtain from them some advantage.[6]

Similarly, after the war, great apprehension was expressed by Latin American civilian leaders when the Inter-American Military Cooperation Bill was submitted to the U.S. Congress in 1946. Many of them feared militarism; they feared that armaments would encourage political ad-

[6] Eduardo Santos "Mis conferencias con el Presidente Roosevelt y los planes de organización militar interamericana," *Revista de América* (Bogotá), April 1947, p. 10.

venturism by the military. Others, like President-elect González Videla of Chile, opposed an arms build-up for economic reasons. "I don't like any idea that means an increase in our spending on armaments," he said, ". . . [for] almost one-quarter of our budget now goes for national defense. . . . We're too poor to bear the load and need the money to raise the public standard of living." [7]

The split between military and civilian elements over United States military policies was made glaringly apparent when the MDA program was launched in 1952. Countries like Cuba and Peru, where military regimes were in power, signed military aid agreements promptly, but where the civilian element dominated politics the negotiations ran into difficulties. With Mexico no agreement at all could be signed, and in the case of Uruguay ratification was delayed considerably.[8] In Chile, presidential candidate Carlos Ibáñez successfully exploited civilian antagonism toward the MDA Pact to help him win the 1952 elections.

Probably the most damning criticism of the whole United States military program again came from Santos, who had seen his warnings ignored and his dire predictions come true in his own country. Speaking in exile in the United States in 1955 before a Columbia University forum, he made the following pointed criticisms:

> Against whom are we Latin Americans arming ourselves? Why are our countries ruining themselves buying arms which they will never use? . . .
>
> Have we perhaps a military role to play in the great international world conflicts? . . . In this day of the atom bomb, with the new arms whose cost is fabulous, with technical systems involving thousands of millions, what are our poor countries about, bankrupting themselves upon armaments which in the event of an international conflict would spell absolutely nothing? Then, what we are doing is building up armies which weigh nothing in the international scale but which are

[7] Duggan, cited, p. 185; *New York Times,* November 3, 1946.

[8] William G. Carleton, *The Revolution in American Foreign Policy* (Garden City, N.Y.: Doubleday, 1954), p. 88.

Juggernauts for the internal life of each country. Each country is being occupied by its own army. . . .

If in Latin America, the dictators prevail, if they continue to discredit freedom and law, a fertile field for Communist harvest will be provided. Why? Because our resistance will be gone. We are poor nations who have no investments or great fortunes to defend. What we would defend against Communism would be our freedoms; but if we have already been stripped of them, we have nothing left to defend. It is thus that the gateway for the Communist invasion is thrown open by the anti-Communists.[9]

The mere fact of popular opposition, although it cannot be lightly disregarded, does not necessarily mean that United States military programs are mistaken. The issue of democracy versus dictatorship is not always the vital one in Latin American society. The issues of social change and reform, and the role of the military in relation to them, may be equally or more important, as earlier chapters have shown. United States policies must therefore be judged also by the way in which their impact on a society in flux affects our long-term interests in Latin America.

Military Programs and the Social Problem

The Latin American environment is dynamic. United States policies which emphasize stability in order that Latin American governments will be friendly and peaceful, and will provide military bases and other facilities when we need them, either fail to recognize that a social revolution is in progress in Latin America or assume that it can be delayed while the cold war lasts. A strategy of buttressing with military aid all governments-in-being can hardly be effective for more than a brief period. In World War II, it is true, a policy of freezing incumbent regimes in power was remarkably successful: no Latin American government

[9] "The Defense of Freedom in Latin America," in Angel del Río, ed., *Responsible Freedom in the Americas,* Columbia University Bicentennial Conference Series (Garden City, N.Y.: Doubleday, 1955), pp. 219-221.

was overthrown from the time of Pearl Harbor until the crisis in the war began to ease in the summer of 1943. The consequence of the freeze, however, was a rapid, unsettling thaw between 1943 and 1945 as the suppressed popular nationalistic and social forces took power by revolution in Argentina, Bolivia, Ecuador, Guatemala, Cuba, Venezuela, and Peru.

The danger in the present military program with its emphasis upon stability lies in the fact that, whereas the World War II emergency in the hemisphere lasted only a couple of years, the cold war has lasted already for over a decade and shows no sign of letting up. The critical question is: Is the United States, in pursuing its supposed hemisphere security goals, interfering with the normal social evolution of the Latin American peoples, and, if so, how long can it continue to do so? The armed forces which in many countries are sitting atop the social boiler cannot control indefinitely the inexorable build-up of popular pressures for change.

What makes the problem doubly explosive is that the United States entered the picture just at that juncture when the old order of society was at the point of breakdown. The old oligarchy, as well as the military allied with it, quite understandably exploit what the United States conceives to be its security needs in order to save themselves. Their solicitude for hemisphere defense springs from the use they hope to make of it, not to stop Soviet aggression, but rather to stop social change. The result is that the opposing social forces, which comprise the majority of the population, rightly or wrongly tend to hold the United States at least partially responsible for preserving the order they felt they were well on the way toward destroying over a decade ago when the cold war began.

It is because of the pressing Latin American social problem, that of finding new political and social institutions which will satisfy the demands of new groups and provide outlets for their energies without dissolving society in chaos, that United States anti-Communist military programs may be playing directly into the hands of the enemy against whom they are directed. Robert J. Alexander's recent study of communism in Latin America demonstrates that where the effect of military aid has been to underwrite backward societies and stifle reforms, as for example in Paraguay, the Dominican Republic, Nicaragua, Peru, and Venezuela, United States policies have unwittingly helped "to break down the barriers between the genuine advocates of the Latin American social revolution and the Communists." [10] This is because these policies provide the Communists, who are well aware of the potential of popular discontent, with the opportunity to cooperate and make common cause with civilian resistance to militarism. The danger is that our policies will unwittingly improve the Communist capabilities. Admiral Arthur W. Radford, after a tour of South America, recognized this threat. The main problem, he said, is not communism itself, but "economic security [for the people], to prevent Communism from seizing any opportunity to penetrate local situations." [11]

For the great majority of Latin Americans, who see no great danger of aggression from outside, the United States military program compounds their internal problems, interferes with the process of social change, and hinders progress in economic development. The reimbursable aid program, the evils of which are magnified by the new credit policies, gives license to the armed forces to squander money on flashy military "toys." And, as already indicated, the provision of U.S. arms to military regimes often stymies the popular urge to political freedom. The short-run basis of our policies, which is one of expediency, seems to ignore these considerations. The long-range view of Latin America which they represent is pessimistic as well as static, for it does not count upon the developing popular forces.

10 *Communism in Latin America* (New Brunswick, N.J.: Rutgers University Press, 1957), p. 89.

11 *Washington Post and Times Herald,* May 20, 1957.

U.S. military planners, while methodically pursuing their programs in Latin America, regard it as a low-priority area. They realize that it can play no important direct military role in the struggle against communism. They wish to keep it quiet, stable, and pacified, providing strategic materials and bases and other facilities as needed. According to a shrewd American observer, they want Latin America to behave like a docile and contented milk cow.[12] And the way to attain that ideal, in their view, is to propagate the myth of collective military defense and to grant arms and support to the governments of the day. Small wonder that, as Louis J. Halle recently stated, "the inter-American system is degenerating into a mere market place in which our neighbors, no longer conscious of making common cause with us, trade with us for such bounty as they can get in exchange for their votes." [13]

What does it really mean, in terms of the present world conflict, for the United States to have Latin America "on its side" in this way? Militarily, it is recognized that Latin America counts for little. Politically, the support of the governments has been generally obtained, but political cooperation lacks roots if it is dependent on the temporary good will of military leaders primarily interested in arms and other favors and is not tied to a joint effort to cope with Latin America's real problems, which are internal rather than external. As a State Department official testified before Congress, "most of the people do not live in circumstances that enable them to recognize that they have a stake in the present struggle." [14] And the concept of a hemisphere-wide fight for freedom against authoritarianism is rendered somewhat meaningless by the existence inside the hemisphere of too many governments that hold

12 Edgar S. Furniss, Jr., *American Military Policy* (New Brunswick, N.J.: Rutgers University Press, 1957), p. 235.

13 "Why We Are Losing Latin America," *Harper's,* April 1955, p. 49.

14 U.S. House Committee on Foreign Affairs, *Mutual Security Act Extension,* Hearings on H.R. 5710, 83rd Cong., 1st sess. (Washington: GPO, 1953), p. 855.

power, with military support, against the will of the vast majority of their own people.

The Voice of the Pentagon

The "cold war" policy of the United States in Latin America quite naturally has reflected the greatly increased influence of the Department of Defense and the expansion of the role of military men in the formation and execution of American foreign policy. More fundamentally, since national survival was at stake in the face of the Communist threat, the requirements of security became all-important. These requirements included military alliances, arms aid programs, bases on the territory of other nations, and a general military build-up in the free world.[15]

This military definition of the crisis had great plausibility when applied to most areas of the world. But it clearly did not apply to Latin America. Consequently, before the military view prevailed, a bitter dispute took place within the U.S. government. It was opened when the Pentagon insisted, early in 1947, that United States arms be transferred to Latin America. Assistant Secretary of State Spruille Braden opposed the idea, contending that more arms would only exacerbate national rivalries and encourage militarism. Under Secretary of State Dean Acheson, in a memorandum of March 19, 1947, to the War and Navy Departments, wrote that if the United States were to rearm Latin America, it would encourage needless military overspending and thus would run counter to its own policies aimed at encouraging economic development and rising living standards in that area. But Secretary of War Robert Patterson argued that Latin America needed and wanted arms to defend itself, and that if it did not get them from the United States it would get them elsewhere, in which event the U.S. missions would lose their monop-

[15] See Burton M. Sapin and Richard C. Snyder, *The Role of the Military in American Foreign Policy* (Garden City, N.Y.: Doubleday, 1954).

oly position.[16] Secretary of State Marshall resolved the issue by siding with the Pentagon.

Thenceforth, as the cold war became hotter, military and strategic considerations were increasingly emphasized in United States foreign policy in Latin America, as well as elsewhere. Yet application of the same criteria of military urgency to Latin America and to Europe and Asia becomes each day more untenable. Neither our military policies in Latin America nor Latin America's responses to these policies fit meaningfully into the United States' world strategy or correspond to its long-term interests.

It is open to question, moreover, whether the United States military programs now being carried out in many of the Latin American countries, particularly the uses to which the arms are put, are in conformity with the legislation on which they are based. The eligibility of some of the recipients for continued aid is at least doubtful, for the Mutual Security Act specifically states that

> No [military] assistance shall be furnished to any nation unless such nation shall have agreed to—
> (1) join in promoting international understanding and good will, and maintaining world peace;
> (2) take such action as may be mutually agreed upon to eliminate causes of international tension;
> (3) fulfill the military obligations, if any, which it has assumed under multilateral agreements or treaties to which the United States is a party.[17]

The recipient states agreed to those conditions. But how well have they carried them out?

Trujillo's threats in the Caribbean area in the early 1950's and continued wrangling by Peru and Ecuador over their boundary clearly have not promoted international understanding and peace. All except Colombia stuck to a narrow interpretation of their military obligations under the Rio Pact when they refused to send troops to Korea.

16 *New York Times,* May 23, June 24, 1947.

17 *Public Law* no. 665, 83rd Cong., 2d sess. (August 26, 1954), "Mutual Security Act of 1954," sec. 142.

Also, contrary to the spirit of the Mutual Security Act,[18] several Latin American recipients of military aid unquestionably have used it for other purposes than the common defense of the hemisphere. In 1957 the Ibáñez government used MDAP tanks in the streets of Santiago to break a strike. In that same year Rojas Pinilla in Colombia and Batista in Cuba were using MDAP equipment to quell internal opposition that could hardly be defined as a Communist threat from within. Reimbursable aid has likewise been put to questionable use. One of the two cruisers sold to Argentina in 1951 for purposes of hemisphere defense was effectively used by Admiral Isaac Rojas and the Argentine navy in the successful revolt against the Perón regime in 1955. In a particular case we may be pleased by the outcome. But the fact is that military aid is used by the Latin American recipients as they see fit, regardless of whether such use is in line with the conditions laid down by the donor. And the donor, in many cases, does not seem to bother to scrutinize the uses to which his aid is put.

Such considerations, added to the others which have been cited, cast the gravest doubts on whether the military emphasis in United States policy toward Latin America is not seriously out of line with our political and economic objectives and long-term interests. This inconsistency contains the real danger that, unless some major changes of approach are made, our entire foreign policy in Latin America may be destined for frustration and failure.

[18] Same, secs. 101, 105(b)(4).

Chapter 10

POLICY FOR THE FUTURE

The Shape of the Future

FOR THE POLICY-MAKER to deal intelligently with Latin America, he must gear his decisions to probable future developments in the area. With respect to the military programs, the particular focus of this study, policies should be considered primarily in their political context; and they should proceed primarily from the best estimate that can be made of the future of militarism in Latin America.

Spectacular though the current antimilitaristic trend is —as we have seen, it has reduced the number of military presidents from a total of thirteen to four since 1955—there is no guarantee that it will not be reversed in the future as similar trends have been reversed in the past. The future of militarism will depend partly upon the growth of professionalism in the armed forces, but above all upon the ways in which Latin American society develops. Critical in this connection will be the intensity of the social conflict, the degree of political instability, and the nature and magnitude of the economic problems in the area. Only against a background of such fundamental considerations can the United States find the most appropriate form and content for its foreign policy in general, and for its military programs in particular.

Latin America is an area of very rapid growth. Its population is increasing at a faster rate than any other area in the world today (over 2½ per cent net gain per year). Already the area contains over 180 million people. By the year 2000 its population is expected to exceed half a billion.

The Latin American economy is expanding rapidly. Since it has room to develop and untapped resources to exploit, its relative importance in the world will rise. The economic growth of the area over the next twenty years may well be double the extraordinary development that has occurred during the past twenty.

Latin America's role in world affairs will increase in significance. It will speak with greater authority in international organizations. The political and strategic value of its friendship and cooperation will grow as its material and manpower resources make their weight felt in the world balance, especially if the cold war continues indefinitely. There may even be some increase in its military potential, but this can hardly be of any great significance when weighed against economic and political factors.

The overwhelming problem in Latin America today and for the foreseeable future is the social revolution. It is a problem for the Latin Americans themselves, but also for any outside power that hopes to have an influence there. The entire area is in the throes of a painful process of social, economic, and political transformation. Only a few countries are yet in advanced stages of the ordeal. Most of them are just beginning.

The symptoms are obvious. Over half the people of Latin America are undernourished; nearly half are illiterate. The great majority are virtually propertyless, for in most countries both land and natural resources are still concentrated in the hands of the few. Over half the working population lives and toils under conditions that retard health, welfare, and education. This situation is not new. It is people's desires, attitudes, and ambitions that have changed. Those growing numbers who, over the past generation, have begun to escape their miseries, to resist exploitation, to read, and to enjoy the benefits of improved health, are pointing the way to their less fortunate brethren. Emancipation from semifeudal working conditions on the land through economic opportunities in booming cities, an end to political apathy through realization of the potential power of organization and political pressure, the taste of a better life at home and the knowledge of living conditions far better abroad—all these are making irrepressible the force of Latin America's restless masses. Demographic pressures will add to that force, and economic development will probably accelerate the social revolution before it serves to temper it.

The revolutionary process will be long and drawn out. How to meet the rising dissatisfaction of the masses will be the imperative task confronting Latin American governments for the remainder of the present century. The transitional period will be far from smooth. Until a new and more broadly based equilibrium is achieved, Latin America will remain an area of turmoil. Demagogues will spring up to exploit popular discontent and aspirations—neo-Peróns or neo-Nassers may rise to power. Exaggerated nationalism will reappear. Traditional ruling groups, as they have before, are likely to compound the difficulties by calling on the armed forces to preserve the passing order. Violent social upheavals and civil wars are not improbable. Political instability will vary from one country to another in relation to the extremism of the competing new and old forces, as well as to the extent to which civilian demagogues, Communist conspirators, or military adventurers attempt to exploit the struggle for their own advantage.

As inevitable as the process of social change, and intimately related to it, is the drive for political emancipation. While the social struggle rages, attempts at authoritarian political solutions, either of the left or of the right, will be common. It will appear at times that Latin America is adopting a system of less, rather than more, freedom and democracy. But authoritarian regimes can be but temporary. The long-term trend is likely to be against dictatorship and in favor of responsible representative government if the social problems are progressively resolved, for the conditions that gave rise to despotism will then tend to disappear.

In these circumstances the political role of the armed forces in the long term is almost certain to decline. The emerging new balance of social forces as embodied in labor organizations and the middle groups will offer increasingly effective resistance to the political preponderance of the military. Militarism is likely to be a strong political factor as long as the social crisis continues and government is not firmly rooted in a broad representative base, but ultimately the political control by the military must wane. Neither political holding operations against social change nor predatory militarism can last long beyond the point where the people become aware of their "rights" and their ability to assert them. And the wave of popular pressure, already evident in a number of countries, will be reinforced by the growth of professionalism within the armed forces themselves.

The dynamic processes of growth and change under way in contemporary Latin America pose real challenges to the United States, for the role that Latin America will play in world affairs, and especially in the cold-war struggle, will be largely determined by the approaches to its developing problems taken by the two major world powers. Speaking in terms of general trends—for the pattern may not be uniform in all the republics and the facts of geography will continue to be important—Latin America can take one of three possible courses. It can ally with the United States, cooperate with the Russians, or remain neutral. At present it follows the first course, but not without some doubts and uncertainty whether this is the final answer in Latin America's own best interest. If it appears that both major antagonists in the cold war are merely exploiting the area for their respective advantage, Latin America's peoples, feeling that they have no stake in the international conflict, are likely to assume a neutral position. To the Communists will belong the future if they succeed in capturing control of popular nationalist revolutions. The United States could help them to do so by insufficient foresight and vigilance or by a too close identification with an outworn order.

There is little doubt that the social revolution now in progress in Latin America will provide new opportunities for the Communists to exploit. We must assume that the Soviet Union will devote increased energies to the effort, promoting both neutralism and communism as the tactical situation demands. The tasks for the United States are to prevent Soviet penetration and use of the area against us and to find an improved basis for stable and mutually beneficial relations with Latin America. These two aims, of course, are intertwined.

Policies for the Short Run

"Military expenditures by their very nature act as a brake on rising living standards and for that reason they should be held to a level that will provide an adequate posture of defense," cautioned the United States Secretary of the Treasury, Robert B. Anderson, at the Inter-American Economic Conference held in Buenos Aires in 1957. The time has now come for the United States government to promote vigorously this suggestion that Latin America curtail its military expenditures. A program of arms limitation in Latin America, sponsored by the United States and by some Latin American governments, would provide a simple method by which some of the inconsistencies in our current foreign policy could be removed. It would be welcomed by the Latin American public, relieve the United States of much of the onus of supporting unpopular governments, and allow the savings on arms to be plowed into economically productive endeavors.

The logic in support of a limitation of armament appears militarily irrefutable. The level of armament in Latin America is now many times that of the pre-World War II period. Yet the actual need for armament has, if anything, decreased: first because of the effectiveness of the OAS in acting to prevent intra-hemispheric warfare, at least between smaller countries; and, second because no external military threat exists against which Latin America's own arms could really be useful.

It may not be easy to convince Latin American governments that they should seek agreement on a limitation or reduction of their armaments. All governments are understandably cautious on anything affecting their capacity for self-defense. Considerations of pride and prestige are mixed with real concern over the maintenance of national sovereignty and independence. Obviously the United States, which does not propose to disarm itself, may not find it easy to persuade others to do so. Yet this fact need not be an insuperable obstacle; the United States is already so powerful militarily in comparison to Latin America that the reduction of the latter's level of armament would not basically affect that disparity. Actually, the United States may be in a favorable position to promote disarmament in Latin America.

Washington can create a climate favorable to such an effort, first of all, by de-emphasizing the military aspects of its policy toward Latin America. This does not mean sudden abandonment of the whole complex of military programs in the area. We are already committed to programs of military assistance from which the probable consequences of immediate withdrawal would be foolhardy to risk. In some countries they represent a sizable military investment, without political liabilities, which it would be wise to protect. It also remains necessary to exclude Soviet military advisers and equipment. If the United States summarily withdrew from the provision of arms, before any agreement on arms limitation were reached, Latin America would shop elsewhere, first for equipment, after which the politically important missions would be likely to follow. Therefore, much of the military mission work and certain aspects of the arms program must be continued. Present military programs, however, can and should be curtailed and the points of emphasis changed.

A firm guiding principle should be the discouragement of any further arms build-up. To this end, the United States should gradually reduce its military aid, in general to the minimum amount necessary to keep the Latin American governments from seeking aid elsewhere. This precise point may not be easy to ascertain or to reach, for much will depend on the attitudes and policies of those governments, but the important thing is to begin moving in that direction. The grant aid problem can be handled, at first, by expanding neither the MDAP program itself nor the defense "missions" that the signatory countries are pledged to carry out under the pacts. In order to forestall new demands for military aid, the MDAP requirement that the recipient country do all it can to improve its defense posture should be soft-pedaled. Then, appropriations under the MDA legislation should be reduced annually with a view to eliminating all grant military aid within a few years.

The reimbursable aid program presents much tougher problems, for it involves many individual decisions on what quantities and upon what terms military equipment is to be sold for cash or credit. The utmost should be done to discourage waste of scarce Latin American resources on prestige items. If Latin America's governments and armed forces cannot be convinced that the purchase of certain items is unwise, they should be told that the equipment cannot be spared. They might then turn to European suppliers, in spite of less favorable prices and tighter credit policies; but so long as this does not jeopardize the position of our military missions, little harm is done to United States security interests by limited Latin American purchases elsewhere in the free world, even of such expensive items as jet planes and aircraft carriers.

It should be possible to cut down on Latin American military expenditures by controlling credit. The United States, for example, might restrict the amount of credit extended for military purposes by setting up a revolving fund of perhaps $100 million for the entire area. This would look impressive as a total sum, but would not be enough, when divided among twenty countries, to do much harm in any one country.

The United States cannot for a moment ignore ill-advised Latin American purchases for either cash or credit, especially when the purchasing nation is already unable to pay for vitally needed social and economic improvements. Accordingly, every military aid request from Latin America must be scrutinized with extreme care.

A policy aimed at promoting lower levels of armament by cutting back military aid and encouraging Latin America to disarm will, of course, involve shelving the collective-defense "myth." The idea that all American republics must be concerned with threats to the security of any of them and should cooperate in meeting them can and should be preserved but not the pretense that they all have a significant *military* role in this regard. The United States need not worry about exposing this myth, for Latin Americans are well aware that the United States, in the final analysis, must assume unilaterally the task of defending the hemisphere. A more realistic concept of collective defense will also give the United States greater flexibility in dealing with the different situations in individual countries. Obviously a program for the reduction of armaments will meet resistance in those countries where the armed forces are politically entrenched. And in all countries such a policy must be conducted in such a way that the issue of sovereignty, for which the armed forces still offer at least symbolic protection, does not arise.

Even the role of the missions, the most useful and justifiable facet of our military programs, should be limited. Officers serving in them should concentrate their energies on the encouragement of greater professionalism. The missions should be promptly withdrawn from those countries where they have become symbols of United States support for unpopular military regimes. The example of Cuba, where the mission remained beyond that point to our political detriment, is a lesson for the future.

By thus abandoning the use of military programs as a means to win the political support of the military, the United States would dissipate much of the ill will engendered in Latin America by its overemphasis upon military thinking and military policies. It would soon become apparent that the risks of possible alienation of the armed forces of a few countries are outweighed by the political advantage of growing support from the mass of the people.

Though encouraging Latin America to reduce its armaments, the United States itself must remain militarily strong. This is not a question of selfishness or of discrimination, but purely one of common sense on both sides. Latin America needs the assurance that it can rely on the power of the United States for protection and for keeping the peace. We must give Latin America that assurance by the facts of power as well as by words if we are to ensure continuation of the area's political support. An imminent danger is the Soviet threat to the United States in the field of modern weaponry. If the Latin Americans begin to fear that the United States is not keeping up in this competition, that it is no longer possible for them to count on the United States for military protection, they will drift toward neutralism. To counter such tendencies, the United States must, by its accomplishments and its conduct, present to Latin America the best possible image of its military capability to deter war and to safeguard the security of this hemisphere.

By de-emphasizing the military aspects of its policy, the United States can help Latin America to attack its economic problems. As one minor contribution to this end, the United States ought to encourage the Latin American nations to make greater use of their armed forces directly in the process of economic development and social improvement. In many countries military officers, as a result of their training and experience, possess valuable technical skills that could be of great benefit to their respective countries if used productively. Establishment of engineering corps, for example, as has been done in Bolivia and Mexico, will enable qualified men in uniform to play an honorable and constructive role in the progress of their country. More important is the opportunity for the United States to help by compensating Latin American countries for reductions in military aid through comparable increases in economic assistance, which is of far more benefit to them. In the likely event that a mere shift in emphasis in existing aid programs should prove insufficient, greater attention should be given to the widely expressed Latin American desires for still greater economic cooperation. The political reasons for so doing are compelling, whether or not such measures are wholly in line with what the United States has regarded as sound economic policy. It is here that the current policy considerations merge into those of longer range.

Policies for the Long Run

The foregoing recommendations, important though they are for the immediate future, shrink in importance before the long-range policies the United States must follow if it hopes to create the kind of relations with Latin America that will best serve the interests of both sides, including the vital interest in security. The grand long-range strategy must be to build for Latin America a greater stake in its own and in the free world's future. Pursuit of this goal in itself holds the promise of a more positive role for Latin America in the struggle against the Communist menace.

This does not mean that the United States should now embark upon long-range plans to develop the military potential of Latin America. The most likely result of such an effort would be a growing fear that the United States was planning to involve the Latin American states in war to serve only its own purposes. Technological developments are going so fast, with Latin America falling further and further behind the lightning advances in nuclear and missile weaponry, that its prospects for becoming a military factor in a future war are becoming each day more remote. Consequently, it would not be useful to build a policy upon the assumption that the military power of Latin America, in weapons or in trained men, will become important in the future. There should be plenty of time to consider this matter later, if necessary, after more fundamental long-range policies are developed.

We cannot, however, avoid difficult decisions if Latin America's demands for arms and military power, instead of contracting, continue to grow. A particularly delicate question may arise if Latin America's armed forces begin demanding nuclear and missile weaponry. As tactical nuclear missiles become "conventional," it may be very difficult to resist Latin American demands for them, especially if the alternative is to see them supplied from some other source. This prospective dilemma points up all the more sharply the need for a previously agreed limitation of armaments in Latin America, particularly if a general international agreement on control of nuclear weapons proves unattainable.

The United States' basic aim for the future must be a sound, prosperous, and stable Latin America, one that will contribute to the strength and solidarity of the Western world and will advance the security of the entire hemisphere. If Communist imperialism is the greatest threat to that security, it is apparent that Latin America's positive contribution to opposing that threat will be proportionate to the stake its people feel that they have in the struggle. To have a stake in it men must be properly nourished, healthy, literate and possessed of a degree of individual independence and dignity. In most of the Latin American area, where illiteracy is high, nourishment inadequate, disease widespread, and material poverty the rule, the ideological fight against communism is meaningless. The Latin American masses are disturbingly neutral today. In a recent poll, even the people in the more enlightened larger cities voted overwhelmingly in favor of a neutral position in preference to taking sides.[1] They feel they have nothing to gain and much to lose from being sucked into the conflicts of the great powers, in which they will only be exploited. Only if Latin Americans feel that they have something worth fighting for will this isolationism give way to a feeling of identity and equality with the United States in the struggle for a free world.

Present military policies ostensibly directed against the Communist menace can do almost nothing to improve Latin America's present narrowly based cooperation with the United States. It is hard for the Latin American peoples to understand why the United States focuses upon what they consider a minor threat and pays so little attention to the basic problem of improving their lot. The attitude is not unlike that of the newly independent nations of Asia and Africa. The United States must pay far more attention to these desires before it can hope to derive from other nations solid popular support against communism. As Chester Bowles so wisely recommended,

> the political objectives of the United States aid program . . . [must be] to develop indigenous political and economic strength among the nations of the free world so they can survive as free people. . . . As they succeed in meeting the needs of their people, their confidence in democratic methods will grow, and with it their determination to defend their achievements against all adversaries, either from within or without. With such nations, the United States can form a free and dynamic partnership which over the years will erase the threat of Communist aggression. . . .[2]

The great danger is that the Communists will capture control of Latin America's social revolution. The struggle for Latin America really narrows down to a long-term competitive battle between communism and democracy, each endeavoring to secure the allegiance of the Latin American peoples. Which side ultimately wins will depend

[1] International Research Associates, *A Survey of Latin American Public Opinion* (New York: Time, Inc., 1958), pp. 46-47.

[2] "Partners in Freedom," *Atlantic Monthly*, December 1954, p. 51.

upon the attitude each takes toward the revolutionary process. The present United States Ambassador to Brazil, John Moors Cabot, showed a deep appreciation of this vital issue when, as Assistant Secretary for Latin American Affairs in 1954, he stated,

Social reform is coming. It may come by evolution or revolution. There are reactionary elements in every country in the hemisphere which do not want social reform. They are willing to tie down the safety valve and wait for the boiler to burst. In many countries, liberal elements, confronted by such intransigent opposition, have more and more fallen under Communist influence. To my mind there is nothing more dangerous from the viewpoint of long-range American policy than to let the Communists, with their phoney slogans, seize the leadership of social reform. We simply cannot afford to identify ourselves with the elements which would tie down the social safety valve. That wouldn't protect our national interest; it wouldn't even for long protect our investments.[3]

The potential Communist threat renders it particularly urgent that the United States promptly develop a comprehensive policy that will associate it more closely with the aspirations of the Latin American people. There need be no fear about the choice of sides the latter will make if there is a clear democratic alternative. It is only when the Communists are the only significant group pointing the way to social and economic reform that there is danger of their ultimate success. Once the United States demonstrates sincere, enlightened leadership in assisting the Latin Americans through their difficult process of social revolution, it will take the edge off the Communist drive for domination of the area.

If the United States is to achieve its basic aims in Latin America, economic policies will assume an ever-increasing importance. The deterioration in United States-Latin American relations, according to Dr. William Manger, retiring assistant secretary-general of the OAS "is due to the

[3] *Toward Our Common American Destiny* (Medford, Mass.: Fletcher School of Law and Diplomacy, Tufts University, 1955), p. 21.

lack of progress in the solution of the economic problem." [4] Basic to mutually beneficial economic ties will be the further expansion of the already high levels of trade. To this end, the United States will have to take into account, more fully than it has in the past, Latin America's dependence upon exports of foodstuffs and minerals. The other main issue concerns the pace of Latin America's economic development and the contribution the United States makes to it.

It is not the purpose here, in a book devoted to the military element in foreign policy, to take up in detail such thorny questions as U.S. import restrictions on raw materials, commodity agreements, stabilization of prices for basic Latin American exports, the volume of future U.S. investment in Latin America, and the proper division between private investment and public loans or grants. It is the purpose, however, to stress the need for economic policies that are not just the bare minimum with which we can get by from year to year, or that hew narrowly to certain general axioms which condition our economic thinking but are simply not convincing to Latin Americans. Policies must be judged by their results and by the response they elicit in Latin America, and the fact is that those pursued hitherto have not been adequate on either count.

At present, the United States government has no large-scale assistance programs to promote the economic development of Latin America. It makes no grants of economic aid except continuing minor emergency assistance to Guatemala, Bolivia, and Haiti, and technical assistance, which amounted to only $35 million for all twenty countries for fiscal 1958. In addition, there have been loans (mostly by the Export-Import Bank) averaging about $70 million to Latin America annually over the past decade.

In the total U.S. foreign-aid program Latin America's share is quite small, less than 2 per cent, although this comparison does not give an accurate picture because it

[4] *New York Times,* March 6, 1958.

ignores the substantial flow of private capital into Latin America which brings many benefits with it. On the other hand, many basic projects necessary for development do not attract private capital, and for them an effective program must be worked out. There is, of course, no iron law by which Latin America must receive public loans and grants on the same scale as underdeveloped countries elsewhere in the world, but the fact of Latin America's dissatisfaction with its low-priority status is surely one of the factors to be taken into account. That the United States is at least doing more in the way of assisting Latin America economically than before World War II is significant but not the decisive answer, for Latin America's socio-eonomic problems have become more critical, and a large measure of responsibility for their resolution, rightly or wrongly, is placed squarely upon the shoulders of the United States. Fortunately, the United States government seems finally to be moving in this direction by its participation in the newly established Inter-American Development Bank.

There is no certainty, of course, that economic aid will buy political loyalty. In fact, it is likely that in some countries a concomitant of the area's economic development will be exaggerated nationalism, which might take the form of attacks upon U.S. public policies or private American corporations. If and when these attacks occur, we should avoid blind opposition. Instead we should try to sympathize with the other nation's sense of inferiority, to show understanding while holding to policies we regard as right, so that the excesses of nationalism do not bring ruin both to those countries and to United States interests, and so that they do not turn, in their desperation, to the U.S.S.R.

Since economic aid is intimately related to the problem of militarism, great care ought to be taken to provide it in such a way that militarism is discouraged. This means, particularly, that no aid should be granted to military regimes bent on preserving an outworn order. In fact, the United States should be wary of granting assistance to any military regime in Latin America, for the experience of the past has demonstrated that even when men in uniform have assumed leadership of the social revolution, they have shown little capacity for resolving their nations' problems in an orderly, progressive fashion. The best way to insure that economic aid becomes a counterpoise to militarism is to show preference in supplying such aid to broadly based civilian governments. Over the long term, militarism will be discouraged to the extent that United States economic assistance is wisely used to relieve some of the pressures that exist among large groups of discontented people in the recipient nation.

Militarism, Dictatorship and Democracy

The foregoing argument is not meant to suggest that nonintervention should not remain a guiding principle of United States policy. It does imply, however, that the United States ought to make some distinction between highhanded military dictatorship and struggling civilian democracy, for the former, by retarding the normal evolution of Latin America, hampers realization of its potential and thus adversely affects the long-range security interests of the United States. For every despotism inevitably must come a day of reckoning, for itself and for those allied with it. The popular demonstrations against Vice-President Nixon in Peru and Venezuela, following the downfall of dictators supported and decorated by the United States, illustrates the unhappy consequences of close association with dictatorial regimes. The man in the street cannot agree with the apparent reasoning that the Communist threat is of sufficient magnitude to justify countenancing the brutal practices so characteristic of those regimes.

In both its aid policies and its general attitude, the United States must take into consideration the character of the governments with which we deal, the degree of democracy or of dictatorship. Difficult as it is to establish criteria for such distinctions, since we have no slide rule for measuring progress in democracy, distinctions nevertheless can and should be made, as Dr. Milton Eisenhower has recently recommended.[5] This does not mean that we should have nothing to do with dictatorial regimes. Rather, an attitude neither of friendship nor of antagonism, but one which is still correct, should be displayed, with relations restricted to the level of polite, inoffensive diplomatic intercourse. In this manner the United States may subtly persuade people living under military dictatorships that it has no confidence in their oppressors; and such an attitude should hasten, or at least not retard, the demise of the retrogressive despotism. It might be well to recall Theodore Roosevelt's remark concerning Panama, one which is applicable to almost all the unrepresentative regimes the United States has supported: "You don't have to foment a revolution, all you have to do is take your foot off and one will occur." Conversely, to those regimes that by acceptable democratic processes are making progress in the development of their resources, more positive encouragement and economic assistance should be given.

Although the United States, more than any other outside power, has an opportunity to influence the future destinies of Latin American nations, our policies can have only a limited effect upon Latin America's evolution. The destiny of the area cannot be molded by our policies. It has to find its own way. The United States can, however, provide constructive help, so that Latin America's way does not conflict with our own. It can avoid fostering militarism and dictatorship, and thus increase the chances that governments will rest upon a representative base.

Military questions, of course, form but a segment of our total policy. Certainly, changes that are made in our military programs, no matter how sweeping, will not be decisive in United States-Latin American relations. But their effectiveness can be compounded if they are related to changes in the other aspects of our general policy. Above

5 "Report to the President on United States-Latin American Relations," U.S. Department of State, *Bulletin*, January 19, 1959, p. 15.

all, a reduction of the current emphasis upon military considerations and programs can be particularly helpful to our long-range security interests if it contributes, as it should, to a decline of militarism in Latin America, to steady economic growth, and to the creation among the Latin American peoples of a more favorable image of the United States.

Chapter 11

CASTRO'S CUBA AND HEMISPHERE SECURITY, 1959-1961

Triumph of the Rebel Army

THE SPECTACULAR VICTORY of Fidel Castro's "26th-of-July" guerrilla fighters over Fulgencio Batista's 30,000-man, seasoned, modern-equipped regulars was a military feat unprecedented in the hemisphere's history. True, guerrilla bands had been able to hold out almost indefinitely against the armed forces of Brazil in the late 1920's and against those of Colombia in the decade 1948-1957, but never before Castro had they even seriously threatened, let alone overwhelmed, a regime which until the final stages of the revolt retained the loyalty of the army. Prior to this time, at least in the twentieth century since Latin American armies became modernized and professionally organized, substantial army defection was a necessary concomitant to the overthrow of a government.

On July 26, 1953, Fidel Castro learned something about the wrong way to destroy a military dictatorship. That was the date when he led two hundred anti-Batista underground rebels in the famous assault on Fort Moncada barracks just outside Santiago. He had hoped to take the fortress by surprise, then appeal to the Cuban people to revolt against the dictatorship. Instead, most of the rebels were cut down by machine-gun fire; Fidel and his brother Raúl escaped into the nearby Sierra Maestra, but they were captured shortly by an army patrol and sentenced to long prison terms on the Isle of Pines.

Following his mid-1955 pardon by the then confident and well-entrenched Batista, Fidel Castro went into exile to gather support for an invasion force. In Miami and New York his appeals to Cuban exiles reportedly netted fifty thousand dollars, which he later used to purchase arms and a yacht. A residence in Mexico City became his headquarters, around which gathered eighty-one followers, most of them Cubans associated with the "26th-of-July" movement. One important exception was Dr. Ernesto "Ché" Guevara, a Communist-oriented, Argentine-born physician, who had been banished by Juan Perón and who later lent his revolutionary zeal and talents to the government of Jacobo Arbenz in Guatemala.

Early in 1956, Castro and his little band of followers began intensive training in guerrilla fighting at a ranch just outside Mexico City. The master hired to teach harassment tactics, hit-and-run maneuvers, sabotage operations, bomb making, and jungle survival, as well as use of firearms, was Colonel Aberto Bayo, a veteran guerrilla fighter of the Spanish Civil War. On November 20, 1956, the eighty-two-man invasion force sailed for eastern Cuba aboard the "Gramna," a sixty-foot yacht of doubtful seaworthiness. Less than a week after landing, seventy had been either cut down by Batista's troops or captured and imprisoned. Only twelve (including Fidel, Raúl, and Guevara) managed to reach their destination—the Sierra Maestra. And yet these twelve became the nucleus of an amateur, civilian revolutionary army which in just two years time developed sufficient military capacity to overcome the allegedly invincible Batista army.

Castro's army was recruited primarily from the peasantry. The long-exploited *guajiros* gained new hope from Fidel's promise of land, and many became adept students of guerrilla warfare. To the Sierra Maestra also came a number of urban, middle-class refugees from the Batista tyranny. A rebel underground began to supply arms and conduct sabotage. Financial aid came from tyrannized middle-group elements, who looked to Fidel, long associated with the democratic Ortodoxo party, as their leader in the fight for restoration of civil rights and political freedoms. Cuban exiles in Miami sent vital material help by parachute. Additional arms and ammunition were secured by frequent ambush of Batista's army patrols.

Unequal to the guerrillas in isolated mountain skirmishes, Batista's army began mass assaults, but with equally frustrating results. It was not long before the regulars began to lose stomach for the dangerous business of pursuing the guerrillas. Finally, in May of 1958, Batista launched an all-out onslaught with 13,000 troops against Fidel's guerrillas, then estimated to number less than five hundred. But despite the twenty-five to one odds, the offensive failed. By August, the increasingly confident rebels had opened a second front in the Escambray Mountains in the center of the island. Meanwhile, Batista's armed forces began to become worried and restless. Batista had to crush a navy rebellion in Cienfuegos during 1957, and in late 1958 air force pilots refused to follow his orders to bomb rebel-held towns. Meanwhile, mounting opposition from urban middle-class elements steadily sapped the strength of the regime. The final rebel drive occurred in late December as the guerrillas, now eight thousand strong and overwhelmingly supported by the civilian populace, descended from their mountain fastnesses and attacked the cities of Santiago in the east and Santa Clara in the center. When the latter fell, Batista's generals forced his resignation. On New Year's Day 1959, Major Fidel Castro, age thirty-two, became the new ruler of Cuba.[1]

Castro Consolidates His Military Power

Inasmuch as Batista's army, though beaten, still loomed as a potential threat, Castro, during his first six months in power, destroyed the entire organization. Batista and the top military officers had fled, but hundreds of middle-rank

[1] For a vivid description of the rebel campaigns see Ruby Hart Phillips, *Cuba, Island of Paradox* (New York: McGraw-Hill, 1960).

officers were promptly taken into custody and brought to trial for "war crimes." Sitting in judgment at the court-martial were three newly appointed young majors of the "26th-of-July" movement. When Castro first called a halt to these military trials on May 7, nearly five hundred officers had died before the firing squad. When one tribunal acquitted forty-three Batista airmen, Castro ordered a retrial, after which all were convicted and executed.[2]

Those Batista officers fortunate enough not to be brought to trial, most of them captains and lieutenants, were summarily dismissed from the service, and the new officer corps soon consisted of nothing but "26th-of-July" partisans.

Concomitantly, there occurred a complete purge of the rank and file. As quickly as they could be replaced by loyal Castro supporters, all 25,000 soldiers who had served under Batista, whether voluntarily or not, were returned to civilian life. The whole process was completed by mid-1959.

In part, Castro's annihilation of the Batista armed forces represented a move to consolidate his victory, but equally important was his determination, at least in the first months of power, to rid Cuba of the long curse of militarism. Fidel's antimilitary bent was clearly evident in his revolutionary declarations and writings, and soon after he came to power he began to implement the civilian thesis upon which his "26th-of-July" movement was based.[3] As commander in chief of the armed forces of the revolutionary government, he promptly decreed a thorough reorganization. He announced that he was going to cut the traditional size of Cuba's army by one-half (from 30,000 to 15,000) as soon as practicable, and that ultimately the army would be disbanded completely and the police would then assume the task of preserving internal order.[4] Symbolically, Camp Columbia (just outside Havana), where many coups

[2] *New York Times*, March 4, 1959.

[3] See Jules du Bois, *Fidel Castro: Rebel—Liberator or Dictator?* (Indianapolis: New Bobbs-Merrill, 1959).

[4] *New York Times*, January 13 and February 4, 1959.

and attempted coups had been nurtured against duly elected Cuban governments of the past, was turned into a school. Major Castro, when he visited the United States in the spring of 1959, declared: "The last thing I am is a military man. . . . I have no medals. I don't like armaments. Ours is a country . . . without generals and colonels." [5]

And yet, within a year following the elimination of Batista's army Cuba had become a thoroughly militarized state, with more men under arms than in any other Latin American country. Why? It was primarily because Castro, from mid-1959 onward, began to fear his regime was in jeopardy from a growing assortment of enemies of the revolution. Accordingly, he came to see ever larger military defense measures as essential to his survival.

During the first half of 1959, Castro's troubles were principally with his Caribbean and Central American neighbors, and they stemmed primarily from his apparent willingness to permit revolutionary Cuba to become both a haven of refuge and a base of operations for numerous exile groups. At the end of April 1959, a mixed Cuban-Panamanian rebel force of ninety sailed from Cuba and launched an abortive attack against the ruling conservative government in Panama. In an uprising against the Nicaraguan government which took place in the following month, Fidel Castro was accused—though the charge was not conclusively proved to the satisfaction of the commission of the OAS sent to investigate—of aiding the rebels. In June, a group of Dominican exiles set sail from Cuba, but they were all massacred when they attempted to invade their homeland.[6] This series of adventures had the result of raising temperatures and tensions in the Caribbean and of causing governments to look to their military defenses.

[5] Same, April 21, 1959.

[6] See "Post-World War II Political Developments in Latin America," Appendix I, a study prepared by the School of Inter-American Affairs, University of New Mexico, in U.S. Senate Committee on Foreign Relations, Subcommittee on American Republics Affairs, *United States-Latin American Relations: Compilation of Studies,* 86th Cong., 2d sess. (Washington: GPO, 1960), pp. 75-76.

Thus, just about the time Castro had destroyed the Batista army and had begun to demilitarize Cuba, he had to consider threats of vengeance from Trujillo of the Dominican Republic and the Somozas of Nicaragua. Then too, he rather seems naïvely to have assumed that he could achieve a revolutionary transformation of Cuba without provoking armed resistance at home. How wrong he was became apparent in August when a major conspiracy against his government was only quelled by the arrest of thousands of former Batista soldiers. That same month anti-Castro elements from the Dominican Republic led an unsuccessful invasion attempt.[7]

In addition, as the revolution itself deepened and took on a more radical and totalitarian character after mid-1959, Castro began to lose the support of many of his moderate followers. Defections of prominent leaders of the "26th-of-July" movement, such as Major Pedro Díaz Lanz, chief of the air force, and Major Hubert Matos, became more and more frequent during the latter half of 1959. By April of 1960 more than two thousand anti-Castro rebels were estimated to be operating against the government in the Sierra Maestra, and the following month a second front against the regime was opened in the Escambray Mountains.

It was this mounting foreign and domestic threat to the regime that provoked the military build-up that began in earnest in October of 1959, when Major Raúl Castro became minister of the armed forces with instructions to enlarge and strengthen all three branches of the service (then totaling about 30,000 men) immediately. At the same time, Fidel Castro announced the formation of an armed workers' and peasants' militia.[8] Military tribunals were re-established, and the execution of opposition leaders began again.

This semimobilization produced an urgent need for arms. Heretofore, Castro had been getting along on the accumulated war matériel in Batista's arsenals, so that the U.S. arms embargo in the troubled Caribbean (in effect

[7] Same, p. 76.

[8] *New York Times,* October 18, 24, 25, and 30, 1959.

since March 1959) had not hindered him. Nor did it now, for the United States' NATO allies initially posed few impediments to indiscriminate arms sales to all Caribbean purchasers. True, the United States, by applying pressure upon the British government, was able to stop the sales to Cuba of fifteen jet fighters, but Italian, French, and particularly Belgian companies supplied Castro with as much light equipment and ammunition as he was able to pay for. By March of 1960, for example, Castro had already purchased 100,000 Belgian automatic rifles.[9]

The equipment was put into the hands of Castro's burgeoning militia, which in five months time (by March of 1960) had grown to over 50,000. Peasant, worker, and student branches drilled for two hours at the end of each day and longer on week ends. At Matanzas, over five hundred cadets were enrolled at a special militia officers' training school. Meanwhile the army went into combat as Castro, during April of 1960, personally led five thousand troops against Captain Manolo Beatón's rebels in the Sierra Maestra.

In the spring of 1960, Castro's European sources of military supply began to dry up. Partly, this change was due to increasing pressures exerted by the United States on its NATO allies as Cuban-U.S. relations deteriorated badly. But more important was the fact that Cuba, in serious financial straits, could no longer pay. Castro began appealing to the people in March of 1960 for donations for arms and planes, and, when this proved insufficient, he decreed payroll deductions for arms. Wary West European arms firms began demanding payment in advance, terms with which after May 1960 Castro could no longer comply.

It was at this juncture, in the last half of 1960, that Russia, Poland, and Czechoslovakia took advantage of an obvious opportunity and entered the Cuban military picture. Major Raúl Castro, on his trip behind the iron curtain in July, had found the Czech and Russian governments willing to supply MIG fighters, heavy Stalin tanks,

[9] Same, March 10, 1960.

antitank guns, antiaircraft guns, artillery pieces, plus great quantities of light arms and ammunition on very liberal, long-term credit arrangements. In addition, they volunteered to supply military technicians to train the Cubans.

The day-by-day exacerbation in Cuban-U.S. relations and the increasing military ties that the regime was making with the Communist nations convinced Castro that he would ultimately have to face a U.S.-backed invasion. In anticipation of it he stepped up arms purchases from the Soviet bloc and mobilized the nation. By mid-August of 1960 there were 45,000 men in the armed forces and nearly 200,000 in the militia. By the end of the year, Soviet freighters had delivered an estimated 28,000 tons of military equipment. With her 55 tanks (40 of them Soviet), 60 antitank guns, 80 antiaircraft guns, jet and propeller-type aircraft, and ample guns and ammunition for a military establishment numbering a quarter-million men, Cuba, by the end of 1960 had indeed become a major military power in the Latin American area.[10]

Totalitarian Techniques

Ever since the triumph of January 1, 1959, the government of Cuba was under the control of the revolutionary army. Virtually absolute political power was vested in one man—Major Fidel Castro. A triumvirate, consisting of Fidel, his brother Major Raúl Castro as minister of the armed forces, and economic czar Major Ernesto Guevara, made policy. The real lines of power ran through military governors with the rank of major in the provinces, captain and lieutenant at the district and municipal levels. The means of violence were entirely in the hands of the revolutionary army and of the so-called peasants' and workers' militia.

[10] This narrative of the build-up of Soviet arms in Cuba is based principally on dispatches to the *New York Times*, particularly July 10, August 1, 4, 7, 12 and 24, September 23, October 29 and 31, and November 6, 14, 19, and 25, 1960.

The unmistakable trend was toward an increasingly totalitarian political structure, toward outright military dictatorship. Such has been an inevitable consequence of Castro's determination to transform hastily and completely Cuba's economy and society. Dictatorship was simply a *sine qua non* for a fundamental social revolution which practically destroyed the former upper and middle classes.

Great had been the optimism, in the immediate aftermath of the revolutionary triumph, among those who backed Castro in his heralded fight for political freedom. Initially, well-known believers in democracy were given cabinet posts, and Castro promised that elections would be held and normal constitutional processes restored within two years. Batista's dictatorial structure was speedily dismantled as the new government restored independence to labor and the universities, freed the press, destroyed Batista's police and spy apparatus, and declared war on dishonesty in government.

However, the disillusionment of the partisans of political liberty, most of them middle-group moderates, was not long in coming. It started with Castro's assault on private property. This began with the March 1, 1959, seizures of property of all Batista collaborators. Within a month there followed decrees reducing rents by 30 to 50 per cent and interest rates (customarily 8 to 12 per cent) to 4 per cent. In addition, during April, businessmen became extremely uneasy over the government's sympathetic response to the unprecedented demands of organized labor, while large landholders were equally upset over the government's absence of action against property seizures by the peasantry.

The May 1959 Agrarian Reform Law and the ways in which it was immediately put into effect by an all-powerful National Institute for Agrarian Reform headed by a dedicated Marxist precipitated a break between the moderates and the left and turned the revolution, at least in part, into a class struggle between the proletariat and the people with property. During June-July 1959, the moderates, including President Manuel Urrutia and five middle-group cabinet officers, were forced out of the government and replaced by radical leftists.

As expected, there followed during the latter half of 1959 a series of defections, conspiracies, terrorist acts, and counterrevolutionary movements on the part of the moderates. These Castro met with arrests, imprisonments, executions, the creation of a military intelligence and spy organization, and, as already mentioned, the building up of a people's militia.

Democratic freedoms were eliminated step by step. During 1960 political activity was banned; Castro made it clear he was planning no elections; the opposition press was first censored, then seized by the workers; the courts were purged of bourgeois judges; the churches were attacked for alleged counterrevolutionary statements and activities. Many who had been Castro's supporters lost their jobs or liberty as control of labor and the universities was also assumed by the government. By the end of 1960 Cuba had become a full-fledged police state.

Meanwhile the regime began a drive for state control of the entire economy. The National Institute for Agrarian Reform, directed and manned by the revolutionary army, instead of redistributing expropriated land to the peasantry as promised, set up hundreds of government-owned sugar, cattle, and food-raising cooperatives. In addition, the Institute established over two thousand "people's stores" where a variety of foods and consumer goods items were sold at such low profit margins that small merchants were forced into bankruptcy. The troops of the Institute also seized from both foreign and domestic owners manufacturing, mining, and utility enterprises. During the latter part of 1960 and early 1961 private business rapidly vanished and, along with it, Cuba's middle and upper classes, nearly 200,000 of whom went into exile in the United States. Indeed, so deep and complete had the social revolution become that Castro could proudly declare on May Day 1961 that Cuba had now become "a Socialist state" and that there would be no more elections.

Cuba, of course, had her economic difficulties. First there was the job of reconstruction after Batista's flight. Then there was the costliness of the revolutionary reforms, in the absence of taxes formerly received from private enterprise and in the presence of mismanagement on the part of the government operators. Financial crisis was chronic due to the arms build-up, elimination of the sugar quota by the United States, and the curtailment of credits by the Western nations. However, as the economic "fat" from confiscation was used up during 1960, the Soviet bloc came increasingly into the breach and helped, through trade and credits, to keep the Cuban economy afloat.

Another important aspect of Castro's revolution is an ambitious government-sponsored industrialization program (scheduled to begin in 1962), which includes plans for steel production, mineral and petroleum development, electric-power expansion, and textile manufacturing. In addition, Castro has also been overhauling Cuba's outmoded educational system in order to eliminate illiteracy and to train—and indoctrinate politically—mechanics, engineers, and skilled technicians to run the nation's newly emerging agricultural and industrial complex. Also, the state is making ambitious plans, though somewhat questionable progress, toward solving the tremendous housing and health problems of its subjects.

Drift from the Western to the Soviet Camp

Throughout the two-year period of his valiant fight against Batista, Castro had the sympathy and support of the American press and public opinion. Washington aided and supported the Batista dictatorship longer than it perhaps should have, but once it was apparent in March of 1958 that Castro's revolution had a chance of succeeding, an embargo was placed on all military aid to Cuba. Just five days after the triumph of the rebels, on January 6, 1959, the United States recognized the new regime. All America welcomed into the Western Hemisphere community of nations a government that promised to restore political freedom, to honor international obligations, and to protect foreign investments in Cuba.

This vast reservoir of good will was squandered by Castro in less than six months time. The record clearly shows that the United States made every reasonable effort to get along with Cuba, but exercise of the utmost patience and forbearance by the Eisenhower administration proved fruitless. The Castro regime, for reasons best known to its leaders, was apparently determined to alienate itself from the United States and to make anti-Yankeeism the rallying-cry of its appeals to the Cuban people and to the rest of Latin America.

The trouble began less than a week after recognition when Castro announced his intention of executing several hundred Batista "war criminals." When the American press and several congressmen protested against what they believed to be an unnecessary and inhumane "blood bath" without due process of law, Castro lashed out that he would slaughter "200,000 gringos" if the United States should attempt to intervene in Cuba. The U.S. government responded that it intended to hew to a "hands-off" policy, and on January 19 it appointed a most tactful, experienced, and patient ambassador, Philip Bonsal, to soften and repair the distasteful legacy of the United States' long and close association with Batista.

Castro, however, showed little disposition to forget the past. Instead, he made domestic political capital by repeatedly condemning "fifty years of U.S. intervention." Extremely sensitive to criticism, he frequently accused the American press and congressmen of distorting the facts about his revolution and labeled such critics "Batista sympathizers." His pledge to honor existing international agreements became suspect as he forced the withdrawal of U.S. army, navy and air force missions—which he had a right to do under the agreement—and announced on April 4, 1959, that in the event of war between the Soviet Union and the United States, Cuba would remain neutral—which was clearly a repudiation of Cuba's commitments under the Rio Treaty of Reciprocal Assistance. In addition, Castro's promises to protect foreign investments were broken early and repeatedly. In June he announced that he was opposed to foreign investments in Cuba, and the new Agrarian Reform Law not only expropriated 1,667,000 acres of Cuban land held by American individuals and firms, but also provided for only fractional and delayed compensation. When the U.S. government protested mildly the inadequate compensation, Castro roundly condemned U.S. interference.

During the latter half of 1959, the tempo of Castro's verbal attacks against the United States increased. During August he charged that certain groups in the United States were conspiring with Trujillo to oust him and criticized the Eisenhower administration for permitting his enemies to organize a counterrevolution on U.S. soil. At huge rallies organized in Havana in October and November he railed against the United States and held it responsible for a leaflet bombing of Havana and for several incendiary bombings of cane fields by planes which had obviously taken off from Florida. At the end of the year he began calling on Cubans to gird themselves against an imminent Yankee invasion. Meanwhile, confiscations of U.S. cattle ranches, sugar lands, mineral concessions, and even hotels and industries went on apace without authorization, inventory, receipt, or the issuance of bonds as provided by the Agrarian Reform Law.

In the face of such provocation, the record convincingly demonstrates that the Eisenhower administration exercised great moderation, fairness, and forbearance in dealing with the Cuban problem. Ambassador Bonsal persisted in his efforts to negotiate for nearly three months (from June 9 to September 9, 1959) before Castro even agreed to speak to him. In response to the charges of bombing, the United States acted promptly and vigorously to police the many Florida air strips and prevent unauthorized flights to Cuba by Castro's foes. On December 19, 1959, the U.S. Department of Agriculture raised Cuba's 1960 quota by 60,000 tons to a total of 3,120,475 tons, and a week later President Eisenhower urged Congress not to cut the quota despite the unwillingness of the Castro government even to discuss the compensation issue.

The U.S. government was frankly puzzled over Castro's behavior. While it tried to defend the legitimate interests of its nationals, it expressed at the same time sympathy with the reforms, the aims, and goals of the revolution. To American policy makers, Castro seemed not only determined to destroy Cuba's long friendship with the United States, but also to undermine his own regime. He needed foreign capital badly, yet he confiscated U.S. holdings; he badly needed tourist dollars to alleviate the exchange shortage, yet he ruined this lucrative business by his anti-U.S. harangues; he needed to sell sugar in the American market, yet he apparently did his best not only to alienate the U.S. press and public, but also the congressmen who voted on quotas.

What explains the perplexing—from the American point of view—anti-U.S. policies and behavior of the Castro regime? The simplest explanation—sinister Communist influence—is not borne out by the record. During the first six months of the Castro regime little trace of communism was detectable in the revolutionary coalition. Ernesto Guevara had well-known Marxist inclinations, but known Communists had no official posts in either the primary or secondary echelons of government. "Twenty-sixth-of-July" leaders and sympathizers controlled not only political power, both at Havana and at provincial and local levels, but also organized labor, both urban and rural.

Thus, two other explanations for Castro's anti-Yankeeism at the early stages seem more plausible. First, from January to June 1959, he used deliberate exacerbation and exploitation of discord with the United States in order to distract attention from serious domestic difficulties and to stir up popular enthusiasm for the revolution. Second, from July 1959 onward, he had a genuine fear and personal conviction, after he became aware that American public opinion had turned against him, that the United States, both business circles and government, was bent on bringing about his overthrow. Once this latter stage had been reached, both domestic Communists and the Soviet Union were presented with an opportunity which they did not hesitate to exploit.

The Cuban Communist party, outlawed by Batista, had been rebuffed by Castro in 1956 in its bid to collaborate in a united opposition front. Conversely, the Communists failed to support Castro's April 1958 appeal for a general strike against the Batista dictatorship. They preferred at that stage to maintain their informal collaboration with Batista. However, in January of 1959, underground, imprisoned, and exiled Communist leaders promptly took advantage of the new political freedom and began to reorganize the Popular Socialist (Communist) party. In addition, there soon appeared the Communist newspaper *Hoy,* which, along with Communist radio and television commentators, lauded Castro's policies—his executions of counterrevolutionaries, his sweeping agrarian reform decrees, and especially his confiscations of foreign business and his fulminations against the United States.

Initially, Castro neither publicly accepted nor rejected this Communist support, but his "26th-of-July" followers were apprehensive quite early over the Communists' aggressive attempts to influence Fidel. They had to wage a fierce struggle to prevent an early Communist take-over of the newly formed Cuban Confederation of Labor, and when *Revolución,* the "26th-of-July" newspaper, publicly condemned the Communists' aggressive tactics, *Hoy* responded with high praise for Fidel and all his policies.

The opportunity for Communist penetration of the revolutionary government came when the "26th-of-July" movement split over the Agrarian Reform Law. As defections increased, as middle-class influence was eliminated, and as armed opposition to the regime broke out, it was then that Castro needed all the domestic support he could get, and the Communists, the only well-organized political party in Cuba, came forward to save him. Captain Antonio Núñez Jiménez, a confirmed Marxist, was placed in charge of the National Institute for Agrarian Reform and brought into the policy-making echelons of this all-powerful economic organization both Cuban and foreign Communists. Also, after July 1959, Communist officials began to appear in the communications industry, the education ministry, and the army. The influence of Guevara rose rapidly in November of 1959 when his appointment as president of the National Bank made him economic czar of all Cuba. By this time the top Cuban Communists, Juan Marinello (head of the party), Carlos Rafael Rodríguez (editor of *Hoy*), Blas Roca, and Lázaro Peña, had worked their way into the inner councils of the Castro government.

In their drive to control labor, the Communists fought their toughest battle and, before they could win, needed the intervention of Castro himself. Beginning in January 1959, "26th-of-July" leaders clashed head-on with the Communists for control of local unions. This struggle went on all through 1959 with "26th-of-July" leaders maintaining the upper hand. By the time of the labor congress in November they controlled twenty-nine of the thirty-three federations, and in the elections for the executive committee to the Cuban Confederation of Labor they succeeded in voting in a 100 per cent non-Communist slate. It was at this juncture that Fidel Castro, presumably pressured by the Communists then in his government, came before the convention and demanded unity, which meant that Secretary-General David Salvador was forced to appoint several known Communist sympathizers to the executive committee and to allow Jesús Soto, a Communist, to assume the number-two post in the Confederation, namely that of organizing secretary. Thereupon, Communist delegates sponsored two resolutions which made their drive to power a routine matter. One was a move to withdraw from the anti-Communist ORIT, which was branded an "agency of Yankee imperialism," and the second, and more important, device was a motion to purge all those officials associated with the Batista regime. Communist investigators then came forth with a multitude of charges tying "26th-of-July" leaders in with labor activities, however innocent, during the Batista era. Soto, aided by close associates in the Ministry of Labor, led the relentless purge of all anti-Communists, and in the spring of 1960, when David Salvador himself was forced to resign, the Communist victory was complete.

Meanwhile, the Soviet Union, in the immediate wake of the successes of the local Communists and the growing estrangement between Castro and the United States, took advantage of its best opportunity since Guatemala under Arbenz to make political inroads into the Western Hemisphere. In August 1959 the Soviet government agreed to purchase 170,000 tons of Cuban sugar; in October, 330,000 tons more. The following month this economic assistance was coupled with some of the political variety as Moscow supported Castro's leaflet-bombing charges against the United States.[11] During February 1960, First Deputy Premier Anastas Mikoyan visited Cuba to conclude a trade pact under which the Soviet Union guaranteed to purchase five million tons of Cuban sugar over a period of five years and to supply the hard-pressed Castro regime with petroleum, iron and steel, machinery (along with Soviet technicians to train Cubans in its operation), and $100 million in credits. Thus the Castro regime, no longer able to get loans from West European bankers to carry on its revolutionary reform programs, had found an economic savior. However, the political price came high, for, after the February 1960 trade pact, Castro became increasingly dependent upon the Soviet Union for his survival.

Following his assurance of backing from the Soviet Union—perhaps it was in exchange for such backing—the

11 Peking also echoed these charges, for which support the Cuban UN delegation demonstrated its gratitude by abstaining on the vote to admit Communist China to the United Nations. See the *New York Times*, November 12, 29, 1959.

Castro regime unleashed a series of attacks upon the United States of unprecedented bitterness and fury. On March 3, Guevara labeled the $150 million annual subsidy the United States extended for Cuban sugar "a form of economic enslavement." On March 6, Castro blamed the United States for the explosion of the French ammunition ship "Le Couvre" in Havana harbor. On March 9-10, $100 million more in U.S. properties and investments were seized. On March 23, Castro questioned the United States' jurisdictional rights over the Guantánamo Bay naval base. More of the same occurred during April, May, and June. All the while, Cuban ties with the Soviet bloc were being cemented. A trade pact with Poland was signed in April. On May 7, Cuba resumed diplomatic relations with the U.S.S.R. By late June, Raúl Castro began reporting success in his arms-purchasing mission behind the iron curtain.

News of Soviet arms sales to Cuba was the last straw. It brought to an end the eighteen-month policy of patience of the Eisenhower administration. The repeated offers (twenty-five of them) to negotiate all outstanding differences with Cuba had gotten nowhere. This fact, coupled with the apparently willing drift of the Castro regime into the Soviet camp, obviously called for a drastic change of policy.

It took another six months before the break between Cuba and the United States was complete, but the trend toward rupture was unmistakable in the summer of 1960. Highlights of a month-long crisis were: (1) June 22—President Eisenhower's request to Congress for authority to cut the Cuban sugar quota; (2) June 23—Castro's warning that he would retaliate by seizing all remaining U.S. holdings; (3) June 29—U.S. denunciation of Cuban slander before the OAS Peace Committee; (4) July 1—seizure of Standard Oil of New Jersey's Cuba refinery; (5) July 5—U.S. suspension of all Cuban sugar imports; (6) July 9—Khrushchev's declaration that the U.S.S.R. would use rockets to halt U.S. military intervention in Cuba; (7) July 10—Eisenhower's statement that he would not tolerate a regime dominated by international communism in the Western Hemisphere; (8) July 12—Khrushchev's pronouncement that the Monroe Doctrine "is dead"; (9) July 13—Communist China's trade-pact negotiations with Cuba; (10) July 18—Cuba's charge of U.S. invasion plans before the United Nations; (11) July 21—new Soviet pledges of military and economic support for Cuba.

By August, the schism between Washington and Havana was so deep and the Cuban commitments to the Soviet bloc so broad that there could be no turning back. Charges and countercharges were exchanged before the United Nations in August and before the OAS in September. On October 19, the United States imposed an embargo on all exports to Cuba save food and medicine. By the end of the year Castro was hurriedly mobilizing the country in an anticipation of an invasion. On January 3, 1961, following Castro's demand that the United States reduce its embassy staff in Havana to eleven, the Eisenhower administration severed diplomatic relations.

By this time, Cuba had gone nearly all the way in the process of conversion into a Soviet satellite state, not subject to the same degree of ultimate control that Moscow held over the satellites of Eastern Europe, but nevertheless following the Soviet line in both domestic and foreign policy. Trade pacts had been made with nine Soviet-bloc nations. The island was swarming with Soviet technicians. Soviet arms (including tanks and planes) had made Cuba, though no direct threat to the United States, a military power to be reckoned with in Latin America.

Cuba now possessed nearly all the features that characterized Communist states everywhere: a small, tightly organized group ruling in the name of the "dictatorship of the proletariat" with complete absence of civil liberties and political freedom; state control and operation of commerce and industry and of workers' organizations; and an anti-American, pro-Soviet line in foreign policy. By the end of 1960 the last Cuban stronghold of opposition to communism, the Roman Catholic Church, was relentlessly and systematicaly being silenced.

The Cuban Problem and Hemisphere Security

It was the sudden and quite unexpected threat to hemisphere security posed by the Cuban problem that prompted the U.S. government first to reappraise anew its Latin American policy and then to begin a drastic overhaul of that policy. The low priority of the area, the insistence on conservative bankers' criteria in responding to pleas for economic aid, the refusal to come to grips with the mounting social crisis—all these facets of U.S. policy toward Latin America now demanded prompt re-examination.

The danger that loomed for the United States came from the fact that Cuba was both a model for other Castro-style, Communist-oriented revolutions and also a base from which they could be launched. As already mentioned, Castro had engaged in or at least tolerated military adventures in the Caribbean area during 1959, permitting exiles from Panama, Haiti, the Dominican Republic, and probably Nicaragua to use Cuba as a base of operations. Aside from any concrete efforts on his part to export revolution and subvert other governments, it was quite apparent that among the depressed and oppressed classes throughout Latin America the Cuban social revolution was gaining rapidly in its appeal—and not only in Central America and the Caribbean. In Venezuela, President Rómulo Betancourt's liberal democratic administration was repeatedly harassed by pro-Castro, leftist extremists impatient with the pace of orderly reform, and in northeastern Brazil Castro rapidly became an idol to millions of poverty-stricken peasants, organized into leagues which demanded sweeping social reforms.[12] Strong Fidelista currents appeared in the ruling revolutionary parties in Bolivia and Mexico and inside the strong APRA party in Peru. In addition, pro-Cas-

[12] Tad Szulc, "Castro Tries to Export 'Fidelism,'" *New York Times Magazine*, November 27, 1960, p. 10.

tro Communist propaganda increased notably in Chile, Colombia, and Ecuador.[13] Moscow added its blessing as Khrushchev himself, on July 26, 1960, hailed the Cuban revolution as the precursor and foundation of an all-Latin American national-liberation movement that would soon bring an end to U.S. dominance and exploitation in the area.[14]

Contributing to the general Latin American pressures for a Cuban-type violent social revolution were the area's deepening economic woes. The trend, which began in 1955, toward declining production and income quickened. During 1959 the per capita supply of goods and services dropped 1.9 per cent while the gross per capita growth in 1960 was the lowest for any year in a decade (except 1959). During both years market conditions for Latin America's exports remained unfavorable, foreign investment declined, and population growth outpaced agricultural output to such an extent that 8 per cent more food had to be imported during 1960 than in 1959.[15] In addition, most governments were saddled with serious financial problems.

The United States had to attempt to check the unfavorable trend or face the possibility of disaster. It had to give a new emphasis and priority to Latin American affairs and to revise its relatively static policies. President Eisenhower's trip to South America early in 1960 was a sign of the new mood. Thereupon, following several months of high-level discussions and the concomitant Cuban alignment with the Soviet bloc, the Eisenhower administration came to the conclusion that to head off new Castro-type upheavals it would be necessary to assist Latin American governments in alleviating the social crisis. In obvious response to the new Soviet threat to the Western Hemisphere, President Eisenhower in July of 1960 asked Congress for $500 million to be used for land reform, health programs, housing projects, and educational facilities.

13 *Time* (Latin American edition), December 5, 1960, p. 22.

14 *New York Times*, July 27, 1960.

15 United Nations, Economic Commission for Latin America, *Economic Survey of Latin America, 1960* (New York, 1961).

Meanwhile, as planning for the new social welfare programs went forward, the United States tried to move against Castro on the diplomatic front. At the Consultative Meeting of Foreign Ministers held in San José in August, Secretary of State Herter warned that Communist guerrilla fighters were being trained in Cuba for operations against various Latin American governments and urged that the necessary collective measures be taken. However, the Latin American governments showed considerably less concern than the United States over the Communist threat. Also, most of the foreign ministers had to be wary of the broad popular support Castro enjoyed in their own countries. Consequently, in the Declaration of San José, which embodied the agreement reached at the conference, the United States had to settle for a condemnation of Soviet intervention in the Western Hemisphere without specific mention of Cuba.[16]

Though somewhat disappointed in its efforts to obtain stronger collective political action against Cuba, the Eisenhower administration went forward at the Inter-American Economic Conference held in Bogotá the following month with its new socio-economic policy. The U.S. loan offer was $500 million, with more to come, for "social overhead" projects. The Latin American recipients of this assistance pledged to provide for a more equitable distribution of land, to sponsor low-cost housing projects, to fight illiteracy and provide technical training, to attack disease and infant mortality, and to revise their tax structures and improve collection procedures.[17] Thus the Act of Bogotá set forth a common policy for reducing the causes of popular discontent that made conditions ripe for future Communist gains.

However, the practical problem of dealing with an existing Communist-oriented state remained, and, in the ab-

[16] For proceedings of the conference, see Richard P. Stebbins, ed., *Documents on American Foreign Relations, 1960* (New York: Harper, for the Council on Foreign Relations, 1961), pp. 516-518.

[17] See text of Act of Bogotá in same, pp. 539-546.

sence of effective collective action against it, the United States began to act on its own. On November 16, 1960, without consulting the OAS, President Eisenhower sent naval units to patrol the coasts of Nicaragua and Guatemala against a rumored invasion from Cuba. The patrols were maintained until December 7, 1960, when the "emergency" ended.

Meanwhile American agencies had begun to support clandestinely, in collusion with the governments of Guatemala and Nicaragua, the training and equipping of Cuban exile groups in preparation of a projected assault on the Castro regime. When the Kennedy administration assumed office in January of 1961, it continued the preparations for an armed landing of anti-Castro forces in Cuba, ruling out any participation by U.S. forces in the fighting.

In the third week of April the invasion took place on the southern coast of Cuba. In a very few days the invaders, about fifteen hundred strong, were utterly crushed by Castro's far superior military might. Some twelve hundred of them were taken prisoner. The anticipated mass defections against the regime did not occur as thousands of opposition suspects were jailed. It appears that the invasion forces failed to coordinate their movement with the Cuban underground. Not only was the whole operation an incredible military fiasco, but it was also a flagrant violation of the nonintervention principle to which the United States had repeatedly subscribed in various inter-American declarations and treaties.[18] The participation of the United States was too limited to assure success but quite significant

[18] For example, under Article 15 of the OAS Charter, "no State or group of States has the right to intervene, directly or indirectly, for any reason whatever, in the internal or external affairs of any other State. The foregoing principle prohibits not only armed force but also any other form of interference or attempted threat against the personality of the State or against its political, economic and cultural elements." See Raymond Dennett and Robert K. Turner, eds., *Documents on American Foreign Relations,* v. 10: January 1-December 31, 1948 (Princeton: Princeton University Press, for the World Peace Foundation, 1950), p. 487. The full text of the Charter, signed at Bogotá on April 30, 1948, appears on pp. 484-502.

enough to make it impossible to refute the charge of intervention.

In the aftermath of the Cuban invasion debacle, the Kennedy administration saw an opportunity to salvage something following Castro's speech of May 1, 1961, declaring Cuba a "Socialist state" and indicating elections would not be held. Here, according to Washington, was ample proof that Cuba was a Communist state. Public reaction in the Latin American nations seemed to increase the chances of an OAS "quarantine" of Cuba, of collective action to sever diplomatic relations and to impose economic sanctions against the Castro regime. But inasmuch as Latin America's two largest nations, Brazil and Mexico, and Ecuador as well, made it clear that they were not willing to go along, the United States was not yet in a position to mobilize the hemisphere against Castro. President Jânio Quadros' administration in unequivocal language declared:

> . . . the Brazilian Government . . . defends the determination of the Cuban people [and] . . . is opposed to any foreign intervention, be it direct or indirect, aiming at the imposition upon Cuba of some particular form of government, and considers that economic measures and ideological activities, as well as military action, undertaken with that end in view constitute indirect intervention. . . .[19]

President Kennedy also began to carry through and expand, with somewhat happier results, the new economic program embodied in the Act of Bogotá. In March he had formally proposed a hemispheric Alliance for Progress the basis of which was to be U.S. sponsorship of a ten-year aid program in support of Latin American economic and social development. In addition to the land use, education, housing, and health reforms agreed on at Bogotá, President Kennedy added a pledge of support for economic in-

[19] Brazilian Embassy (Washington), *Statement by Brazil's Foreign Minister on Continental Problems,* Press Release, May 1961.

tegration, sympathy for commodity marketing problems, emergency grants of food, and more cultural exchange.[20]

The next step was the Inter-American Conference which opened on August 5, 1961, at Montevideo to establish the ways and means of translating the new program into practical action.

Militarism and Disarmament in Latin America

Though it was not at all clear by mid-1961 what Kennedy's political program for Latin America, especially with respect to Cuba, would be, nor what difficulties he might encounter in launching the new economic programs, it was clear that two integral and related components of the overall Latin American problem, namely militarism and the growth of armaments, were being ignored—this despite the obvious exacerbation of both these problems in many Latin American countries during the past two years.

The most notorious case of militarism was in Argentina, where the military repeatedly forced President Arturo Frondizi to bow to their whims and wishes. The difficulties, which had their roots in the strong position taken and held by the military since the fall of Perón, entered an acute stage in early 1959 when the administration, in the face of bitter Peronist-Communist labor resistance, inaugurated an austerity program designed to restore a semblance of economic health to the nation. The determined President, operating under a state of siege, kept the workers in line by repeated use of military force, but in so doing inevitably made himself dependent upon the armed forces for his survival.

By May of 1959 a large number of bitterly anti-Peronist officers (the so-called "gorillas") were demanding rewards for their services in the form not only of a purge of Peronista labor officials, but also of all high officials in the Frondizi administration suspected of being willing to com-

[20] John F. Kennedy, *Alianza para Progreso,* address delivered at the White House, March 13, 1961 (Washington: GPO, 1961).

promise with labor. As a result, Frondizi was forced to remove five cabinet officials and his principal economic adviser.[21] At the same time, the military forced relaxation of austerity controls to the extent that funds were provided for the army to build a steel mill, for the navy to purchase an aircraft carrier and two submarines, and for the air force to purchase twenty-eight jet fighters.

During June and July the "gorillas" steadily pressured the President into ousting all high military officials suspected of being insufficiently anti-Peronist in their sympathies (the so-called "Green Dragon" group). The result was the dismissal of the Minister of War, General Hector Solanos Pacheco, who had tried in vain to curb the political activities of all officers, and a number of "Green Dragon" officers.

This persistent pressure upon the government came principally from the conservative Córdoba garrison where the army Commander in Chief, General Carlos Toranzo Montero, had his headquarters. In September of 1959, he forced still another humiliating presidential surrender as he threatened a coup unless his close friend and associate in the "gorilla" group, General Rodolfo Larcher, was appointed war minister. During the remainder of the year the entrenched "gorillas," without apparent presidential authorization or support, ruthlessly pursued and persecuted suspected Peronists.

During 1960 continued austerity and the use of military force to curb labor led to several new crises. In June, against the President's wishes, the army forced the resignation of the Governor of Córdoba, then intervened to hunt down Peronist terrorists in the province. In October, General Toranzo and the "gorillas" forced the dismissal of General Larcher, who they suspected was becoming too loyal to the President. When Frondizi denounced the "army plot," sixteen generals demanded that he apologize.

By March of 1961, the new War Minister, General Rosendo Fraga, had achieved broad enough support to

21 *Hispanic American Report,* January, April, and May 1959.

oust the troublesome General Toranzo from his command of the army. However, the armed forces demonstrated on April 25, 1961, that they were still the nation's ultimate political arbiters, as they forced the President to dismiss his capable Economic Minister, Alvaro Alsogaray, because they resented his attempts to dismantle the army's coveted industrial complex.

Thus the Argentine armed forces, despite their promises to restore constitutional government following the fall of Perón, and despite some progress in this direction during the years 1957-1958, in the following years could hardly be classed as defenders of political freedom, democratic processes, or civilian government. For, as of mid-1961, they still displayed a marked reluctance to allow duly elected civilian authorities a free hand in making political decisions, particularly those involving the Peronistas and the vested and organizational interests of the armed forces. President Frondizi, of course, approved of the Peronistas no more than did the military, but he felt a responsibility, while working to establish a viable economy, to restore civil rights and orderly constitutional processes. However, as already noted, the arbitrary hands of the politically inclined generals and admirals made his already burdensome tasks more troublesome and complex.

Another freely elected government that was frequently subjected to the interference of the military was that of Villeda Morales in Honduras. As a price for restoring civilian government to the nation, the army, under the 1957 constitution, insisted upon complete autonomy. During early 1959, four successive coup attempts against the administration were made, and in October of that year, when three civilians were involved in the shooting of an officer, the army, ignoring the civil courts, meted out its own justice by sending two of the three before a firing squad. To curb such autonomous power, President Villeda Morales began building a civil guard as a counterpoise, but by mid-1961 the army still refused to take orders from the chief of state and remained the nation's ultimate political arbiter.

In neighboring El Salvador, where the army had excluded civilian participation at the top level in government since 1931, the increasingly unpopular and tyrannical President, Colonel José María Lemus, was overthrown on October 26, 1960, by a reform-minded army clique, which set up a military-civilian *junta* and pledged prompt elections and restoration of democratic freedom. In just three months, on January 25, 1961, the *junta* was in turn deposed by a rightist army faction, which pledged to defend the country against the Communist and Castro influences which it asserted were present in the deposed *junta*. The new *junta* was initially composed of three civilians (all of them from the oligarchy) and two colonels (Julio Rivera and Aníbal Porillo). Within three months the army had reduced the *junta* to three by forcing out two of the civilians. Thus the traditional pattern of exclusive military domination of the nation's politics was restored in El Salvador.

While Castro was establishing his dictatorship in Cuba, the Duvalier government in neighboring Haiti also evolved toward an out-and-out military dictatorship, and in the whole process enjoyed the unwitting cooperation of the U.S. government. The latter, ignoring the obvious and repeated lessons of the history of such operations, agreed early in 1959 to send in a sixty-man U.S. marine corps mission to train and modernize Haiti's five-thousand-man army. The naïve assumption was that the strengthened army would restore order and ultimately divorce itself from politics, whereupon President Duvalier, who had been operating under martial law ever since late 1957, would presumably restore political freedom and constitutional government. Just as in the 1916-1934 period, however, the net effect of the work of the U.S. marines in building a more efficient army in Haiti was to insure absolute military sway over the nation's politics. During the next two years, ostensibly in response to the Cuban threat,

Duvalier made use of the army to expel opposition congressmen, to terrorize all civilian opponents, and to muzzle his critics in the Catholic Church. The "elections" of May 7, 1961, in which there was only one slate of candidates for the National Assembly (all of them personally selected by the President) and in which Duvalier forced the populace to vote on an extension of his own term for the period 1963-1967, made the military dictatorship in Haiti virtually complete.

On May 30, 1961, Generalissimo Rafael Trujillo, dictator of the Dominican Republic for thirty-one years, was assassinated by a group of disgruntled generals. In the immediate aftermath of this event, following the pattern set in Nicaragua after General Anastasio Somoza was killed in 1956, the familial and political heirs of the victim remained in control. The dictator's thirty-two-year-old son, General Rafael Trujillo, Jr., promptly assumed his father's mantle in a bold attempt to make sure that the Trujillo dynasty would continue to run the Dominican Republic. Whatever the outcome of the political struggle for power, the chances that the country could escape from militarism did not look bright.

In the two years preceding his death, General Trujillo continued, as usual, to exacerbate the problems of the troubled Caribbean. To deal with the threat from Castro, he reportedly purchased during 1959 $50 million of military equipment in Europe and called an additional six thousand men into the army. In April 1960 he was implicated in an abortive coup against the Venezuelan government. When the latter, during May and June, brought charges of intervention and flagrant violation of human rights against the Dominican Republic, Trujillo responded by sending his agents to Venezuela to assassinate President Rómulo Betancourt. This maneuver very nearly succeeded, as Betancourt was severely burned in a bomb incident. At the Foreign Ministers Conference held in San José all the other American nations agreed to sever diplomatic relations with the Dominican Republic, and some applied other sanctions. The domestic opposition, particularly the church, momentarily stepped up its activities, as the regime's foreign complications increased. However, Trujillo was able to throttle this opposition by increasing terror. Also, in response to the hemispheric ostracism, he arrived at a modus vivendi with Castro, who was also being increasingly isolated, at least in the Caribbean. At mid-1961 it was too early to determine whether or how the Dominican Republic's relations with the OAS or with Cuba might be altered as a result of the assassination of the dictator.

Two other Latin American dictatorships—of the Somozas in Nicaragua and of Stroessner in Paraguay—had growing troubles but survived. During 1959 and 1960, the Somozas found it necessary to quell at least a half-dozen small invasions by exile groups and to deal brutally with rising student opposition. However, by mid-1961, their control over the country as their family fief remained intact. Similarly, in Paraguay, there were several abortive attempts by opposition exiles to invade the country, and periodically rioting students were kept in line by beatings and arrests. Political parties and the church increasingly criticized the regime and pleaded for relaxation of the long-term, predatory military dictatorship, but General Stroessner and his army colleagues were more than equal to the challenge.

Latin America's other remaining military president, General Miguel Ydígoras Fuentes of Guatemala, moved toward the right and took sterner measures against his domestic opposition. This political tightening-up was primarily in response to the Castro threat, for Cuba was the scene of much activity on the part of Guatemalan exiles, including Jacobo Arbenz. As already indicated, the U.S. navy, in late 1960, shielded General Ydígoras' regime against a possible invasion attempt, and he in turn offered Guatemalan bases for U.S. training of an anti-Castro invasion force.

There were changes of government in three other countries in the 1959-1961 period (in addition to Cuba, the Dominican Republic, and El Salvador). In Panama the inauguration of Roberto F. Chiari in October 1960 merely meant that one oligarch had replaced another in the presidential palace. In Ecuador the perennial president, José María Velasco Ibarra, assumed office for the fourth time in September 1960 and promptly proceeded to exacerbate the long-standing border dispute with Peru. In October, for the third successive presidential election, Brazilian voters rejected a military candidate, General Henrique Teixeira Lott, in favor of his civilian opponent, Jânio Quadros.

The general problem of disarmament in Latin America was discussed more frequently during the past two years than before, but got nowhere as the arms race was actually stepped up. When Argentina purchased an aircraft carrier, plus two submarines and some jet fighters, the armed forces of Brazil also secured a carrier from Great Britain and persuaded the United States, in exchange for missile-tracking station facilities, to deliver additional equipment of all kinds under the MDAP agreements. To mollify its admirals, the Peruvian government purchased two cruisers from Great Britain, a move which prompted the Chilean navy to put pressure upon President Alessandri to redress the naval balance of power in the South Pacific. As Ecuador purchased assorted armaments to counter the alleged Peruvian threat, Peru's generals (both air force and army) moved to maintain the existing armaments disparity over its weaker rival. In Venezuela, President Rómulo Betancourt, in return for the continued loyalty of the army, was obliged to continue the highly inflated military expenditures that characterized the Pérez Jiménez dictatorship. As already indicated, the arms build-up in the troubled Caribbean area was one of unprecedented proportions. Only one nation, tiny Costa Rica, moved in the opposite direction as it exchanged two thousand surplus rifles for six new tractors.

While the arms race flourished, many Latin American

presidents, clearly seeing the relationship between growing military expenditures and their deepening economic woes, joined President Jorge Alessandri of Chile in his pleas for a hemisphere-wide disarmament conference. It was ultimately agreed to place a disarmament item on the agenda at the eleventh Inter-American Conference scheduled to meet in Quito, but this conference was postponed in 1960 due to the Peru-Ecuador border problem and again in 1961 because of the Cuban affair.

Although nothing apparently could be achieved to halt the surge of indiscriminate arms purchases by Latin American governments, acting at the insistence of their armed forces, grant military aid from the United States under the Mutual Defense Assistance program was effectively curtailed. The limitation on Latin American arms aid resulted from the Congressional reaction to the Eisenhower administration's annual requests for increases in the program. From a low of $21 million in arms supplied in fiscal year 1956, U.S. military aid shipments had risen steadily to $67 million in fiscal year 1959. In the Mutual Security Act hearings for 1960, the administration requested a Latin American military aid item of $96.5 million.[22] This request did not represent a deliberate attempt to encourage an arms build-up in Latin America, for the administration had publicly supported the disarmament proposals of President Alessandri. Rather, the United States was obliged, in exchange for use of an island missile-tracking station, to supply the Brazilian armed forces with additional equipment. Also, $25 million of the additional request was meant to finance credit to all Latin American nations to purchase military equipment from the United States, the object being to meet European competition and thus promote hemisphere-wide arms standardization.

Whatever the motives of the Eisenhower administration, Congress was convinced that an increase in arms for Latin America was not a good thing, and it turned down the re-

[22] U.S. House Committee on Foreign Affairs, *Mutual Security Act of 1959,* Hearings, 86th Cong., 1st sess. (Washington: GPO, 1959), p. 746.

quest. Instead, it ordered that Latin American military assistance for fiscal year 1960 not exceed that of 1959 (i.e., $67 million), and that beginning with fiscal year 1961 the maximum should be $55 million annually.[23]

Castro's successful guerrilla operation and his subsequent drift into the Soviet camp has already given rise to discussions, both within and outside the United States government, on the advisability of sending Latin American governments certain special types of arms with which they might better combat Communist or proto-Communist guerrilla operations. Such arms shipments would require a fundamental revision of the Latin American section of the Mutual Security Act which now restricts military aid to that intended for external defense of the hemisphere. At this juncture, such a shift in policy would be ill-advised, for anti-guerrilla-type arms shipments would likely involve the United States in internal security problems in Latin America that have nothing to do with communism. The basic problem for the United States is to prevent the Communists from exploiting indigenous guerrilla movements, and this remains a social and ideological problem rather than a military one. Gradual reduction of the entire arms aid program should continue to be an essential ingredient of our over-all military policy for Latin America.

The Problems Ahead

The author sees no reason to alter the conclusions and recommendations on U.S. policy offered two years ago in the first edition of this book (see Chapter 10). Some of them have been or are currently being carried out. In view of the rapid movement of events following the coming to power Fidel Castro in Cuba, however, a few additional comments may be in order.

It was obvious in mid-1961 that an effective political pro-

[23] See the following amendments to the Mutual Security Act of 1954: *Public Law* no. 108, 86th Cong., 1st sess. (July 24, 1959), sec. 105 (b); *Public Law* no. 472, 86th Cong., 2d sess. (May 14, 1960), sec. 103.

gram to deal with the potential threat to hemisphere security posed by the Communist beachhead in Cuba was yet to be developed. Either because of the United States' overestimation of that threat or because of Latin America's underestimation of it, effective collective action against Cuba was out of the question for the time being. It was also clear from recent experience that indirect intervention on the part of the United States was a woefully ineffective means for bringing Castro down. Direct unilateral military intervention seemed to be the only remaining means for the United States to achieve at an early date its immediate end in Cuba, but that course had been ruled out by President Kennedy except as a last resort clearly necessary to preserve the security of the United States.

Under present conditions, direct intervention, though advocated by some who feel Latin Americans would in their hearts applaud it even if they did not do so publicly, so long as it were done quickly and successfully, would in fact be laden with dangerous and wholly unnecessary risks. Even discounting possible Sino-Soviet countermoves in the Eastern Hemisphere and the general world reaction, reappearance of the old specter of Yankee military intervention would probably create a lasting climate of fear and distrust in Latin America that would be far harder to deal with than Castro's Cuba.

In dealing with Cuba, patience should be our watchword. We should be prepared, of course, to use military force to meet military force, such as a Cuban assault upon the Guantánamo naval base or a Cuban invasion of some Central American or Caribbean republic. If there is no such provocation, however, the United States should confine itself to a policy of political containment of *Fidelismo* and of creating conditions which will check and defeat it throughout the hemisphere. We should continue, without any attempt at coercion, to persuade Brazil, Mexico, Ecuador and others of the wisdom of our policy, and move with the important Latin American nations, when the time is ripe, in collective action against Cuba. The battlefield is all of Latin America, and, if the Communist push is defeated on the broader front, Castro will wither on the vine in Cuba.

The immediate struggle between the United States and the U.S.S.R. in connection with the Cuba-Latin America problem is primarily political. The Soviet Union is obviously investing a good deal of money in Cuba in order to obtain political dividends in all of Latin America. Our policy should be to take every reasonable, intelligent, nonviolent action to prevent Communist inroads elsewhere in the hemisphere. If such a policy of containment can be made effective, it is likely that the Soviet leaders, over the long term, will begin to lose interest in an unprofitable venture. With the redirection or withdrawal of Soviet support the internal collapse of the Castro regime would be only a matter of time.

It does not seem that the United States would gain anything by cutting off all contacts with Cuba. The thesis that "communism is not negotiable in this hemisphere," the official reaction to Cuba's offer to negotiate differences with the United States shortly after the invasion fiasco, is basically sound but need not rule out all communication. While it is true that no basis for negotiation of fundamental differences exists, it is not beyond the realm of possibility that opportunities for at least limited discussions and accommodations might arise in the future. We should not forget that the Soviet successes in Cuba came about only after a long period of waiting for an opportunity to exploit.

With respect to our new long-range economic program to fight communism and to prevent violent social upheavals by assisting social transformation in Latin America, Americans should be neither impatient nor too optimistic. Noble and idealistic as is the idea of collaboration between the United States and the propertied or middle-class elements of Latin America in a grand scheme to alleviate the miseries of the masses, there is good reason to doubt that the end can be achieved by nonviolent, evolutionary, and democratic means.

One serious problem will be getting the U.S. taxpayers to pay for a scheme of this magnitude. In relation to the area's needs, the initial installment of $500 million does not even take care of the area's present annual balance of payments deficits. To make a substantial dent in the massive housing, education, and health problems, to say nothing of the cost of modernizing agriculture and developing industry, will take many billions of dollars.

And even if the U.S. taxpayer would be willing to make substantial sacrifices, it is still more doubtful that Latin America's middle and upper classes will give the cooperation that is necessary. Incumbent Latin American governments may be expected to put laws on their books to redistribute the tax burdens, but it is simply too much to expect, for some time, that collection procedures will suddenly become effective. Also, in view of the centuries-long traditions and tenacity of the landlord class, it seems unreasonable to expect that they will passively capitulate to the demands for land from the peasantry. For the history of Latin America has shown that effective agrarian reform has only come when preceded or accompanied by violent social upheaval.

All this does not mean that deep pessimism should prevail or that the United States should write off Latin America as a lost area. Rather, we should gird ourselves to deal with crises and violent upheavals for some time to come. Indeed such revolutions will in all likelihood be the United States' major policy headache in Latin America for the next generation.

Finally, action to meet the related problems of militarism and disarmament must become an integral part (as they are not, at present) of both our economic and political programs, lest our entire effort in Latin America fail.

APPENDIX A

MILITARY MISSION TO NICARAGUA

Agreement between the
UNITED STATES OF AMERICA
and NICARAGUA

Signed at Managua November 19, 1953

Entered into force November 19, 1953

Agreement between the Government of the United States of America and the Government of the Republic of Nicaragua

In conformity with the request of the Government of the Republic of Nicaragua to the Government of the United States of America, the President of the United States of America has authorized the appointment of officers and non-commissioned officers to constitute a United States Army Mission, hereinafter referred to as Mission, to the Republic of Nicaragua under the conditions specified below:

TITLE I

Purpose and Duration

ARTICLE 1. The purpose of this Mission is to cooperate with the Ministry of War, Navy and Aviation of the Republic of Nicaragua and officials of the Nicaraguan National Guard, and to enhance the efficiency of the Nicaraguan National Guard in matters of training, organisation and administration. The members of the Mission are, in the exercise of their functions, obliged to use the Spanish language.

ARTICLE 2. This Agreement shall enter into effect on the date of signing thereof by the accredited representatives of the

Government of the United States of America and the Government of the Republic of Nicaragua.

ARTICLE 3. This Agreement may be terminated in the following manner:

(a) By either of the Governments, subject to three months' written notice to the other Government;

(b) By recall of the entire personnel of the Mission by the Government of the United States of America or at the request of the Government of the Republic of Nicaragua, in the public interest of either country, without necessity of compliance with provision (a) of this Article.

ARTICLE 4. This Agreement is subject to cancellation upon the initiative of either the Government of the United States of America or the Government of the Republic of Nicaragua in case either country becomes involved in foreign or domestic hostilities.

TITLE II

Composition and Personnel

ARTICLE 5. This Mission shall consist of a Chief of Mission and such other personnel of the United States Army as may be agreed upon by the Department of the Army of the United States of America and by the Ministry of War, Navy and Aviation of the Republic of Nicaragua. The individuals to be assigned to the Mission shall be those agreed upon by the Ministry of War, Navy and Aviation of the Republic of Nicaragua or its authorized representative and by the Department of the Army of the United States of America or its authorized representative.

ARTICLE 6. Any member of the Mission may be recalled at any time by the Government of the United States of America provided a replacement with equivalent qualifications is furnished unless it is mutually agreed between the Department of the Army of the United States of America and the Ministry of War, Navy and Aviation of the Republic of Nicaragua that no replacement is required.

TITLE III

Duties, Rank and Precedence

ARTICLE 7. The personnel of the Mission shall perform such duties as may be agreed upon between the Minister of War,

Navy and Aviation of the Republic of Nicaragua and the Chief of Mission, except they shall not have command functions.

ARTICLE 8. In carrying out their duties, the members of the Mission shall be responsible to the Minister of War, Navy and Aviation of the Republic of Nicaragua and this responsibility shall be enforced through the Chief of Mission.

ARTICLE 9. Each member of the Mission shall serve on the Mission in the rank he holds in the United States Army, and shall wear the uniform and insignia of the United States Army, but shall have precedence over all Nicaraguan officers of the same rank, except the Commander of the Nicaraguan National Guard.

ARTICLE 10. Each member of the Mission shall be entitled to all benefits and privileges which the laws and regulations of the Nicaraguan National Guard provide for Nicaraguan officers and noncommissioned officers of corresponding rank.

TITLE IV

Privileges and Immunities

ARTICLE 11. Members of the Mission and their dependents, while stationed in Nicaragua, shall have the right to import, export, possess and use the currency of the United States of America and to possess and use the currency of the Republic of Nicaragua.

ARTICLE 12. Mission members shall be immune from the civil jurisdiction of Nicaraguan courts for acts or omissions arising out of the performance of their official duties. Claims of residents of the Republic of Nicaragua arising out of acts or omissions of members of the Mission shall be submitted to the Chief of Mission for appropriate disposition. Settlements of such claims by the Government of the United States of America shall operate as a complete release to both the Government of the United States of America and the Mission member concerned from liability for damages arising out of such acts or omissions. Determination as to whether an act or omission arose out of the performance of official duties shall be made by the Chief of Mission.

ARTICLE 13. The personnel of the Mission and the members of their families shall be governed by the disciplinary regulations of the United States Army.

ARTICLE 14. Mission members, whether they be accredited or nonaccredited, or on temporary duty, shall not be subject to any tax or assessments now or hereafter in effect, of the Government of the Republic of Nicaragua or of any of its political or administrative subdivisions.

TITLE V

Compensation and Perquisites

ARTICLE 15. The members of the Mission shall receive from the Government of the Republic of Nicaragua such net annual compensation, expressed in United States currency, as may be established by agreement between the Government of the United States of America and the Government of the Republic of Nicaragua for each member of the Mission.

This compensation shall be paid in twelve (12) equal monthly installments, payable within the first five days of the month following the day it is due. Payments may be made in Nicaraguan national currency and when so made shall be computed at the rate of exchange in Managua most favorable to the Mission member on the date on which due.

The compensation provided herein, and any which the members of the Mission may receive from the Government of the United States of America, shall not be subject to any tax, now or hereafter in effect, of the Government of the Republic of Nicaragua or of any of its political or administrative subdivisions. Should there, however, at present or while this Agreement is in effect, be any taxes that might affect this compensation, such taxes shall be borne by the Government of the Republic of Nicaragua in order to comply with the provision of this Article that the compensation shall be net.

ARTICLE 16. The compensation agreed upon as indicated in the preceding Article shall commence upon the date of departure from the United States of America of each member of the Mission and, except as otherwise expressly provided in this Agreement, shall continue, following the termination of duty with the Mission, for the return trip to the United States of America. Compensation shall be paid for unused accrued leave at time of termination of duty and prior to departure from Nicaragua.

ARTICLE 17. The compensation due for the period of the return trip shall be paid to a detached member of the Mission before his departure from the Republic of Nicaragua and such payment shall be computed for travel by the shortest usually travelled route, regardless of the route and method of travel used by the member of the Mission.

ARTICLE 18. Each member of the Mission and his family shall be furnished by the Government of the Republic of Nicaragua with first class accommodations for travel, via the shortest usually travelled route, required and performed under this Agreement, between the port of embarkation in the United States of America and his official residence in Nicaragua, both for the outward and for the return trip. The Government of the Republic of Nicaragua shall also pay all expenses of shipment of household goods, baggage and automobile of each member of the Mission between the port of embarkation in the United States of America and his official residence in Nicaragua as well as all expenses incidental to the transportation of such household goods, baggage and automobile from Nicaragua to the port of entry in the United States of America. Transportation of such household goods, baggage and automobile shall be effected in one shipment, and all subsequent shipments shall be at the expense of the respective member of the Mission, except as otherwise provided in this Agreement or when such shipments are necessitated by circumstances beyond his control. Payment of expenses for the transportation of families, household goods and automobiles in the case of personnel who may join the Mission for temporary duty at the request of the Minister of War, Navy and Aviation of the Republic of Nicaragua shall be determined by negotiations between the Department of the Army of the United States of America, or its authorized representative, and the Ministry of War, Navy and Aviation of the Republic of Nicaragua or its authorized representative, at such time as the detail of personnel for such temporary duty may be agreed upon.

ARTICLE 19. Should the services of any member of the Mission be terminated by the Government of the United States of America for any reason whatsoever prior to completion of two years of service as a member of the Mission, the cost of the return to the United States of America of such member, his family, baggage, household goods and automobile shall not be borne by the Government of the Republic of Nicaragua, nor shall the expenses connected with transporting the replacing member to his station in Nicaragua, except the cost of shipment of his automobile, be borne by the Government of the Republic of Nicaragua.

ARTICLE 20. The personal and household goods, baggage and automobiles of members of the Mission, as well as articles imported by the members of the mission for their personal use and for the use of members of their families or for official use of the Mission, shall be exempt from import taxes, custom duties, inspections and restrictions of any kind by the Government of the Republic of Nicaragua and allowed free entry and egress upon request of the Chief of Mission. This provision is applicable to all personnel of the Mission whether they be accredited or non-accredited members, or on temporary duty. The rights and privileges accorded under this Article shall in general be the same as those accorded diplomatic personnel of the United States Embassy in Nicaragua.

ARTICLE 21. Compensation for transportation and travel expenses incurred during travel performed on official business of the Government of the Republic of Nicaragua shall be provided by the Government of the Republic of Nicaragua.

ARTICLE 22. The Ministry of War, Navy and Aviation of the Republic of Nicaragua shall provide the Chief of Mission with a suitable automobile, with chauffeur, for use on official business. Suitable motor transportation, with chauffeur, shall, on call of the Chief of Mission, be made available by the Government of the Republic of Nicaragua for use by the members of the Mission for the conduct of the official business of the Mission.

ARTICLE 23. The Ministry of War, Navy and Aviation of the Republic of Nicaragua shall provide suitable office space and facilities for the use of the members of the Mission.

ARTICLE 24. If any member of the Mission, or any of his family, should die in the Republic of Nicaragua, the Government of the Republic of Nicaragua shall bear the cost of transporting the body to such place in the United States of America as the surviving members of the family may decide, but the cost to the Government of the Republic of Nicaragua shall not exceed the cost of transporting the remains from the place of decease to New York City. United States military authorities shall remove and dispose of the remains in accordance with the regulations of the Department of the Army of the United States of America. Should the deceased be a member of the Mission, his services with the Government of the Republic of Nicaragua shall be considered to have terminated fifteen (15) days after his death. Return transportation to New York City for the family of the deceased member and for their baggage, household goods and automobile shall be provided as prescribed in Article 18. All compensation due the deceased member, including salary for fifteen (15) days subsequent to his death, and reimbursement for expenses and transportation due the deceased member for travel performed of official business of the Government of the Republic of Nicaragua, but excluding compensation for accrued leave and not taken by the deceased, shall be paid direct to such person as may be authorized or prescribed by United States Military Law for appropriate disposition. All compensation due the deceased under the provisions of this Article shall be paid within fifteen (15) days of the decease of the said member.

TITLE VI

Requisites and Conditions

ARTICLE 25. So long as this Agreement is in effect, the Government of the Republic of Nicaragua shall not engage or accept the services of any personnel of any other foreign government nor of any individual who is not a citizen of Nicaragua, for duties of any nature connected with the Nicaraguan National Guard except by prior mutual agreement between the Government of the United States of America and the Government of the Republic of Nicaragua.

ARTICLE 26. Each member of the Mission shall agree not to divulge or in any way disclose any classified information of which he may become cognizant in his capacity as a member of the Mission. This requirement shall continue in force after the termination of service with the Mission and after the cancellation of this Agreement.

ARTICLE 27. Throughout this Agreement, the term "family" is limited to mean wife and dependent children.

ARTICLE 28. Each member of the Mission shall be entitled to one month's annual leave with pay, or to a proportional part thereof with pay for any fractional part of a year. Unused portions of said leave shall be cumulative from year to year during service as a member of the Mission.

ARTICLE 29. The leave specified in the preceding Article may be spent in the Republic of Nicaragua, in the United States of America, or in any other country, but the expense of travel and transportation not otherwise provided for in this Agreement shall be borne by the member of the Mission taking such leave. All travel time shall count as leave and shall not be in addition to the time authorized in the preceding Article.

ARTICLE 30. The Republic of Nicaragua agrees to grant the leave specified in Article 28 upon receipt of written application, approved by the Chief of Mission with due consideration for the convenience of the Government of the Republic of Nicaragua.

ARTICLE 31. Members of the Mission who may be replaced shall terminate their services only upon the arrival of their replacements, except when otherwise mutually agreed upon in advance as provided in Article 5.

ARTICLE 32. The Government of the Republic of Nicaragua shall provide suitable medical and dental care to members of the Mission and their families. In case a member of the Mission becomes ill or suffers injury, he shall be placed in such hospital or receive the attention of such doctors as the Chief of Mission deems suitable. Such doctors and hospitals shall normally be chosen from doctors, hospitals and pharmacies, all acceptable to the Chief of Mission which shall have been designated in advance for regular use by the Ministry of War, Navy and Aviation of the Republic of Nicaragua in consultation with the Chief of Mission. All expenses incurred as the result of such illness or injury while the patient is a member of the Mission and remains in Nicaragua shall be paid by the Government of the Republic of Nicaragua. If the hospitalized member is a commissioned officer, he shall pay his cost of subsistence, but if he is an enlisted man, the cost of subsistence shall be paid by the Government of the Republic of Nicaragua. Families shall enjoy the same privileges agreed upon in this Article for members of the Mission, except that a member of the Mission shall in all cases pay the cost of subsistence incident to hospitalization of a member of his family.

ARTICLE 33. Any member of the Mission unable to perform

his duties with the Mission by reason of long-continued physical disability shall be replaced.

ARTICLE 34. It is understood that the personnel of the United States Army, to be stationed within the territory of the Republic of Nicaragua under this Agreement, do not and will not comprise any combat forces.

IN WITNESS WHEREOF the undersigned, Thomas E. Whelan, Ambassador of the United States of America to Nicaragua, and Oscar Sevilla Sacasa, Minister of Foreign Affairs of the Republic of Nicaragua, duly authorized thereto, have signed this Agreement in duplicate, in the English and Spanish languages, in Managua, this nineteenth day of November, one thousand nine hundred and fifty three.

APPENDIX B

MILITARY ASSISTANCE

Agreement between the UNITED STATES OF AMERICA and HONDURAS
Signed at Tegucigalpa May 20, 1954
Entered into force May 20, 1954

Bilateral Military Assistance Agreement between the Government of the United States of America and the Government of Honduras

The Governments of the United States of America and of Honduras:

Conscious of their pledges under the Inter-American Treaty of Reciprocal Assistance [1] and other international instruments to assist any American State subjected to an armed attack and to act together for the common defense and for the maintenance of the peace and security of the Western Hemisphere;

Desiring to foster international peace and security within the framework of the Charter [2] of the United Nations through measures which will further the ability of nations dedicated to the purposes and principles of the Charter to participate effectively in arrangements for individual and collective self-defense in support of those purposes and principles;

Reaffirming their determination to give their full cooperation to the efforts to provide the United Nations with armed forces as contemplated by the Charter and to obtain agreement on universal regulation and reduction of armaments under adequate guarantee against violation;

Taking into consideration the support that the Government of the United States of America has brought to these princi-

[1] Treaties and other International Acts Series 1838; 62 Stat., pt. 2, p. 1681.

[2] Treaty Series 993; 59 Stat. 1031.

ples by enacting legislation which provides for the furnishing of military assistance to nations which have joined with it in collective security arrangements;

Desiring to set forth the conditions which will govern the furnishing of such assistance by one government to the other;

Have agreed as follows:

ARTICLE I

1. Each Government will make or continue to make available to the other, and to such additional governments as the parties hereto may in each case agree upon, such equipment, materials, services, or other military assistance as the Government furnishing such assistance may authorize and in accordance with such terms and conditions as may be agreed. The furnishing of any such assistance as may be authorized by either party hereto shall be consistent with the Charter of the United Nations. Such assistance shall be so designed as to promote the defense of the Western Hemisphere and be in accordance with defense plans under which both Governments will participate in missions important to the defense of the Western Hemisphere. Assistance made available by the Government of the United States of America pursuant to this Agreement will be furnished under the provisions, and subject to all the terms, conditions and termination provisions of applicable United States legislation. The two Governments will, from time to time, negotiate detailed arrangements necessary to carry out the provisions of this paragraph.

2. The Government of Honduras undertakes to make effective use of assistance received from the Government of the United States of America pursuant to this Agreement for the purpose of implementing defense plans, accepted by the two Governments, under which the two Governments will participate in missions important to the defense of the Western Hemisphere, and will not, without the prior agreement of the Government of the United States of America, devote such assistance to purposes other than those for which it was furnished.

3. Arrangements will be entered into under which equipment and materials furnished pursuant to this Agreement and no longer required for the purposes for which it was originally made available (except equipment and materials furnished

under terms requiring reimbursement) will be returned to the Government which furnished such assistance for appropriate disposition.

4. In the common security interest of both Governments, the Government of Honduras undertakes not to transfer to any person not an officer or agent of such Government, or to any other Government, title to or possession of any equipment, materials, or services furnished to it by the Government of the United States of America under this Agreement, without the prior agreement of the Government of the United States of America.

5. The two Governments will establish procedures whereby the Government of Honduras will so deposit, segregate, or assure title to all funds allocated to or derived from any program of Assistance undertaken by the Government of the United States of America so that such funds shall not be subject to garnishment, attachment, seizure or other legal process by any person, firm, agency, corporation, organization or government, when in the opinion of the Government of the United States of America any such legal process would interfere with the attainment of the objectives of the said program of assistance.

6. Each Government will take such security measures as may be agreed in each case between the two Governments in order to prevent the disclosure or compromise of classified military articles; services or information furnished by the other Government pursuant to this Agreement.

ARTICLE II

Each Government will take appropriate measures consistent with security to keep the public informed of operations under this Agreement.

ARTICLE III

The two Governments will, upon request of either of them, negotiate appropriate arrangements relating to the exchange of patent rights and technical information for defense in order to expedite such exchanges and at the same time to protect private interests and maintain security safeguards.

ARTICLE IV

1. The Government of Honduras will make available to

the Government of the United States of America Lempiras in an amount to be agreed for the use of the latter Government for its administrative and operating expenditures in connection with carrying out the purposes of this Agreement.

The two Governments will forthwith initiate discussions with a view to determining the amount of such Lempiras and to agreeing upon arrangements for the furnishing of such Lempiras.

2. The Government of Honduras will, except as otherwise agreed, grant duty-free treatment and exemption from internal taxation upon importation or exportation to products, property, materials or equipment imported into its territory in connection with this Agreement or any similar agreement between the United States of America and any other country receiving military assistance.

3. The operations and expenditures effected in Honduras by or on behalf of the Government of the United States of America for the common defense effort including those carried out as a consequence of any other foreign aid program will be relieved from all taxation. To this end the Government of Honduras will prescribe pertinent procedures satisfactory to both Governments.

ARTICLE V

1. Each Government agrees to receive personnel of the other Government who will discharge responsibilities of the other Government in connection with the implementation of this Agreement. Such personnel will be accorded facilities to observe the progress of assistance furnished pursuant to this Agreement. Such personnel who are nationals of that other country, including personnel temporarily assigned, will, in their relations with the Government of the country to which they are assigned, operate as a part of the Embassy under the direction and control of the Chief of the Diplomatic Mission of the Government of the sending country, and shall be accorded all privileges and immunities conferred by international custom to Embassy personnel of corresponding rank. Privileges and courtesies incident to diplomatic status, such as diplomatic automobile license plates, inclusion on the "diplomatic list," and social courtesies may be waived by the sending Government for its personnel other than the senior

military member and the senior Army, Navy and Air Force officer and their respective immediate deputies.

2. The two Governments will negotiate arrangements for classification of personnel and for appropriate notification thereof to the host Government.

3. The Government of Honduras will grant exemption from import and export duties on articles imported for the personal use of such personnel and of members of their families and will take adequate administrative measures to facilitate and expedite the importation and exportation of the personal property of such individuals and their families.

ARTICLE VI

Existing arrangements relating to Armed Forces missions of the United States of America established under other instruments are not affected by this Agreement and will remain in full force.

ARTICLE VII

In conformity with the principle of mutual aid, under which the two Governments have agreed as provided in Article I, to furnish assistance to each other, the Government of Honduras agrees to facilitate the production and transfer to the Government of the United States of America for such period of time, in such quantities and upon such terms and conditions as may be agreed upon, of raw and semi-processed materials required by the United States of America as a result of deficiencies or potential deficiencies in its own resources, and which may be available in Honduras and in territories under its sovereignty. Arrangements for such transfers shall give due regard to reasonable requirements for domestic use and commercial export of Honduras.

ARTICLE VIII

In the interest of their mutual security, the Government of Honduras will cooperate with the Government of the United States of America in measures designed to control trade with nations which threaten the security of the Western Hemisphere.

ARTICLE IX

The two Governments reaffirm their determination to join in promoting international understanding and goodwill and maintaining world peace, to proceed as may be mutually agreed upon to eliminate causes of international tension, and to fulfil the military obligations assumed under multilateral or bilateral agreements and treaties to which both are parties. The Government of Honduras will make the full contribution permitted by its manpower, resources, facilities and general economic condition to the development and maintenance of its defensive strength as well as that of the free world, and will take all reasonable measures which may be needed to develop its defense capacities.

ARTICLE X

Whereas this Agreement, having been negotiated and concluded on the basis that the Government of the United States of America will extend to the other party thereto the benefits of any provision in a similar agreement concluded by the Government of the United States of America with any other American Republic, it is understood that the Government of the United States of America will interpose no objection to amending this Agreement in order that its provisions may conform, in whole or in part, to the corresponding provisions of any similar Military Assistance Agreement, or agreements amendatory thereto, concluded with an American Republic.

ARTICLE XI

1. This Agreement shall enter into force on the date of signature, and shall continue in force until one year after the receipt by either party of written notice of the intention of the other party to terminate it, except that the provisions of Article I, paragraphs 2 and 4 and arrangements made pursuant to the provisions of Article I, paragraphs 3, 5 and 6 and of Article III shall remain in force unless otherwise agreed by the two Governments.

2. The two Governments shall, upon the request of either of them, consult regarding any matter relating to the application or amendment of this Agreement.

3. This Agreement shall be registered with the Secretary General of the United Nations.

DONE in duplicate, in the English and Spanish languages, at Tegucigalpa, D.C., on the twentieth day of May, nineteen hundred and fifty four.

BIBLIOGRAPHICAL NOTE

THIS BIBLIOGRAPHY is a highly selective one. Only those items directly pertinent to the general subject and particularly useful in the actual preparation of the book have been included.

I. Latin America's Armed Forces

An introduction to the general problem of militarism is best provided by Alfred Vagts' *History of Militarism* (New York: Norton, 1937) and his more recent *Defense and Diplomacy* (New York: King's Crown Press, 1956). In neither book, however, does he deal specifically with the peculiar Latin American problem. Stanislaw Andrzejewski has done some brilliant theorizing in *Military Organization and Society* (London: Routledge and K. Paul, 1954) on the nature of the extramilitary role of the armed forces in a variety of states, and he makes a number of useful specific references to the Latin American situation. Katharine Chorley's *Armies and the Art of Revolution* (London: Faber, 1943) deals with the European situation. Her chapter on Spain has some applicability to Latin America. *The Soldier and the State* (Cambridge: Harvard University Press, 1957) by Samuel P. Huntington analyzes the universal essence of professionalism.

On the general subject of militarism in Latin America, no important books have yet appeared. Prior to World War I, two Ecuadorians, Leonidas García, *El militarismo en Sud América* (Quito: La Prensa, 1912) and Daniel Hidalgo, *El militarismo, sus causes y remedios* (Quito: R. Racines, 1913), touched upon the subject. Subsequently the general problem of military dictatorship was analyzed in such books as Cecil Jane's *Liberty and Despotism in Latin America* (London: Clarendon Press, 1929), Pedro Juan Navarro's *Dictadores de América* (Bogotá: Mundoaldía, 1936), and Germán Arciniegas' *The State of*

Latin America (New York: Knopf, 1952). Cuban officer Colonel Sosa de Quesada defends armed forces political intervention in his *Militarismo* (Havana: Instituto Civico Militar, 1939) while Chilean Colonel Guillermo Prado Vázquez makes a strong plea for professionalism in *La carrera del oficial* (Santiago: 1952). The legal position of the military is discussed in *El ejército en la constitución y en la política* (Mexico City: 1952) by Javier Bazán Pérez, while the technical assistance role of the armed forces is surveyed in *El ejército en las democracias hispanoamericanas* (Chorillos, Peru: Escuela Militar, 1944) by José Cavero Bendzú. The changing political role of the armed forces is discussed in John J. Johnson's *Political Change in Latin America* (Stanford: Stanford University Press, 1958). An excellent portrayal of the influence of foreign military missions is presented in Fritz T. Epstein's *European Military Influences in Latin America* (unpublished manuscript in possession of the author in the Library of Congress, 1941).

On the general role of the armed forces in Latin America, a large number of articles have appeared. Among many worthy of mention should be included J. Fred Rippy, "Dictatorships in Latin America" in Guy S. Ford, ed., *Dictatorships in the Modern World* (Minneapolis: University of Minnesota Press, 1939); Charles E. Chapman, "Age of the Caudillo," and Kurt Arnada, "The Technique of the Coup d'Etat in Latin America," both of which are reprinted in Asher N. Christensen, ed., *The Evolution of Latin American Governments* (New York: Holt, 1951); William S. Stokes, "Violence as a Power Factor in Latin American Politics," in *Western Political Science Quarterly,* September 1952; Jesús Silva Herzog, "Las juntas militares de gobierno," in *Cuadernos Americanos,* July-August 1949; Eduardo Santos, "Latin American Realities," in *Foreign Affairs,* January 1956; and Robert J. Alexander, "The Army in Politics," in Harold E. Davis, ed., *Government and Politics in Latin America* (New York: Ronald Press, 1958).

ARGENTINA: Much attention has been paid to the role of the armed forces under the Perón regime in such works as Ernesto Sammartino, *La verdad sobre la situación argentina* (Montevideo: 1st ed., 1950), Jorge Abelardo Ramos, *América latina: un país* (Buenos Aires: Ediciones Octubre, 1949), Robert J. Alexander, *The Perón Era* (London: Gollancz, 1952), George I. Blanksten, *Perón's Argentina* (Chicago: University of Chicago

Press, 1953), James Bruce, *Those Perplexing Argentines* (New York: Longmans, Green, 1953), Ruth and Leonard Greenup, *Revolution before Breakfast* (Chapel Hill: University of North Carolina Press, 1947), and Arthur P. Whitaker, *The United States and Argentina* (Cambridge: Harvard University Press, 1954), but little has been done with the earlier period. Isabel F. Rennie touches on the problem in a general way in her *Argentine Republic* (New York: Macmillan, 1945). The evolution of the German and Nazi influence in the army is discussed by Hugo Fernández Artucio, *The Nazi Underground in South America* (New York: Farrar and Rinehart, 1942), Ray Josephs, *Argentine Diary* (New York: Random House, 1944), and Silvano Santander, *Nazismo en Argentina: la conquista del ejército* (Montevideo: Pueblos Unidos, 1945). The benevolent extramilitary contributions of the army to the Argentine nation are discussed by Rafael Bielsa, *Caracteres jurídicos y políticos del ejército: su misión esencial* (Santa Fé: Instituto Social, Universidad Nacional del Litoral, 1937), and General Laureano Orcencio Amaya, *El ejército: factor ponderable en el desenvolvimiento económico, social, y político de la nación* (Buenos Aires: 1949).

BRAZIL: Minister João Pandía Calogeras, noted statesman and historian, ably describes the evolving role of the armed forces generally in the first century of independence in his *History of Brazil* (Percy A. Martin's translation, Chapel Hill: University of North Carolina Press, 1939) and more particularly the 1890-1920 period in his *Problemas de governo* (Rio de Janeiro: Companhia Editora Nacional, 1936). Charles Simmons, "The Rise of the Brazilian Military Class, 1870-1890," in *Mid-America,* October 1957, discusses the origins of Brazilian militarism. Gilberto Freyre in his *Nação e exército* (Rio de Janeiro: J. Olympio, 1949) lauds the army's social responsibility, while Roberto C. Simonsen also praises their extramilitary contributions in *A construcção dos quarteis para o exército* (São Paulo: 1931). A less charitable view of the armed forces nonmilitary activities is taken by Heraclito Sobral Pinto, *Os forcas armadas em face de momento político* (Rio de Janeiro: Editorial Ercilla, 1945), and by Ernest Hambloch, *His Majesty the President* (London: Methuen, 1935). The armed forces during the Vargas regime are described in Karl Lowenstein, *Brazil under Vargas* (New York: Macmillan, 1942), José de

Lima Figueiredo, *Brasil militar* (Rio de Janeiro: 1944), General Eurico Gaspar Dutra, *O exército em dez anos de govêrno do presidente Vargas* (Rio de Janeiro: D.I.P., 1914), and Lourival Coutinho, *O general Góes depõe* (Rio de Janeiro: Coelho Branco, 1956). Social radicalism amongst the officer corps is described by Robert J. Alexander, "Brazilian Tenantismo," in *Hispanic American Historical Review*, May 1956.

CHILE, URUGUAY, AND PARAGUAY: Luís Goldames' *History of Chile* (I. J. Cox translation, Chapel Hill: University of North Carolina Press, 1941) describes how only in the 1924-1932 era did the armed forces intrude in the socio-political arena for any sustained length of time. Good accounts of this period can be found in Alberto Edwards' *La fronda aristocrática: historia política de Chile* (Santiago: Editorial del Pacífico, 1952) and John R. Stevenson's *Chilean Popular Front* (Philadelphia: University of Pennsylvania Press, 1942). Former War Minister General Carlos Saez Morales gives a balanced account of the political activities of the army in the 1890-1932 period in his *Recuerdos de un soldado* (Santiago: Editorial Ercilla, 1933-1934; 3 v.).

The history of Paraguay is a history of militarism. It can be followed in such general works as Harris Gaylord Warren, *Paraguay: An Informal History* (Norman: University of Oklahoma Press, 1949) or Phillip Raine, *Paraguay* (New Brunswick, N. J.: Scarecrow Press, 1956). On the other hand, neighboring Uruguay experienced a flurry of militarism only in the late nineteenth century, which is described in Russell H. Fitzgibbon's *Uruguay: Portrait of a Democracy* (New Brunswick, N. J.: Rutgers University Press, 1956).

THE BOLIVARIAN REPUBLICS: Until the 1952 revolution, Bolivia, like Paraguay, was saddled with the curse of militarism best described in Colonel Julio Diaz Arguedas' *Historia del ejército del Bolivia, 1825-1932* (La Paz: Instituto Central del Ejército, 1940). The attempts of the MNR government to build more responsible armed forces are related in Robert J. Alexander's *Bolivian National Revolution* (New Brunswick, N. J.: Rutgers University Press, 1958). *The Political Organization of Bolivia* (Washington: Carnegie Institution, 1940) by N. A. Cleven describes the role of the armed forces on the eve of World War II. For Peru, the only general work on the armed forces in politics is *El militarismo en el Perú, 1821-*

1930 (Lima: American Express, 1930) by Luís Humberto Delgado. However, the recent socio-political currents operative in the military are ably discussed in José Luís Bustamante's *Tres años de lucha por la democracia en el Perú* (Buenos Aires: Bartolomé U. Chiesino, 1949).

Ecuador: Country of Contrasts (London: Royal Institute of International Affairs, 1955) by Lilo Linke contains a brief chapter on the armed forces. While the latter's political and social responsibility are praised in General Angel I. Chiriboga's *Fuerzas morales en el ejército* (Quito: Imprenta Nacional, 1932), a more critical view of the military's political activities is taken in George I. Blanksten's *Constitutions and Caudillos* (Berkeley: University of California Press, 1951). For an account of the 1944 revolution by Captain Sergio Enrique Girón, one of the leaders of the rebel movement, see *Revolución de mayo* (Quito: Editorial Atahualpa, 1945). A benevolent attitude toward the armed forces of Ecuador is assumed by Galo Plaza Lasso in his *Problems of Democracy in Latin America* (Chapel Hill: University of North Carolina Press, 1955).

The retrogressive role of the Venezuelan army in the twentieth century is discussed in Romulo Betancourt's *Venezuela: política y petróleo* (Mexico City: Fondo de Cultura Económica, 1956). A defense of the armed forces' political intervention in 1948 is made in the volume put out by the Oficina Nacional de Información, *Documentos relativos al movimiento militar de 24 de noviembre de 1948* (Caracas: Imprenta Nacional, 1949). Illustrations of the type of peculation that has occurred under some recent military regimes can be found in the publication of the Venezuelan Ministerio de Relaciones Interiores, *Sentencias del jurado de responsibilidad civil y administrativa* (Caracas: Imprenta Nacional, 1946; 5 v.).

Colombia, in the twentieth century, has experienced only a brief interlude of military rule which is best described by Vernon Lee Fluharty, *Dance of the Millions: Military Rule and the Social Revolutions in Colombia, 1930-1956* (Pittsburgh: University of Pittsburgh Press, 1957). The story of professionalization of the Colombian army is told by former War Minister General Tomás Rueda Vargas in his *El ejército nacional* (Bogotá: Comacho Roldán, 1944).

MEXICO: There is probably more literature on the extramilitary role of the armed forces in Mexico than in any Latin American country. The best items include Lyle N. McAlister's *The "Fuero Militar" in New Spain* (Gainesville: University of Florida Press, 1957), which describes the colonial background contributing to militarism in the national period; Lucas Alamán's *Historia de Méjico* (Mexico City: J. M. Lara, 1849-1852; 5 v.), which deals with the problem during the early nineteenth century; Francisco Bulnes' *Las grandes mentiras de nuestra historia* (Paris: C. Bouret, 1904) which treats, in a general way, the whole of the nineteenth century; Ernest Gruening's *Mexico and Its Heritage* (New York: Century, 1928), which includes an excellent chapter on the army as it existed both before and during the 1910-1920 revolution; Frank Tannenbaum's *Peace by Revolution* (New York: Columbia University Press, 1933), and his *Mexico: The Struggle for Peace and Bread* (New York: Knopf, 1950), both of which deal with the general problem of militarism particularly during and after the 1910 revolution. *La lealtad en el ejército mejicano* (Mexico City: Ediciones Joloco, 1934), by General Juan Manuel Torrea, decries the corruption of the army by their political activities during the nineteenth century, while Carleton Beals in his *Porfirio Díaz* (Philadelphia: Lippincott, 1932), gives a vivid picture of predatory militarism at the turn of the century. Percy F. Martin's *Mexico in the Twentieth Century* (London: E. Arnold, 1907; 2 v.) describes the armed forces on the eve of the great revolution; Charles L. Cumberland's *Mexican Revolution: Genesis under Madero* (Austin: University of Texas Press, 1952) takes up the initial years of the revolution; and Vicente Blasco Ibáñez' *El militarismo mejicano* (Valencia: Prometeo, 1920) presents a literary account of the role of the military in the period 1910-1918. For the critical Cárdenas reforms which began to render the armed forces, on balance, apolitical, see the government-published *Reglamento general de deberes militares* (Mexico City: Imprenta Nacional, 1936); Colonel Luís Alamillo Flores, *Doctrina mejicana de guerra* (Mexico City: Talleres de Costa, 1943); Virginia Prewitt, *Reportage on Mexico* (New York: Dutton, 1941) and, by the same author, "The Mexican Army," in *Foreign Affairs,* April 1941. The role of Mexico's armed forces during World War II is discussed in Howard Cline's *Mexico and the United States* (Cambridge: Harvard University Press, 1943), and their contemporary role in William P. Tucker's *Mexican Government Today* (Minneapolis: University of Minnesota Press, 1957). José M. Mansilla Cortes describes the army's unique mission as that of protector of the revolution in his *Justicia al soldado* (Mexico City: 1952).

CENTRAL AMERICA AND THE CARIBBEAN: Still useful for general observations on the role of the military in Central America is Dana G. Munro's *Five Republics of Central America* (New York: Oxford University Press, 1918). For Guatemala, Amy Elizabeth Jenson's *Guatemala* (New York: Exposition Press, 1955) surveys briefly the history of caudillism and militarism. The critical 1944 revolution is described by Medrado Mejia, a young-officer participant, in *El movimiento obrero en la revolución de octubre* (Guatemala City: Tipografía Nacional, 1949). The post-1944 Communist infiltration of the Guatemalan army is overdrawn in Daniel James, *Red Design for the Americas* (New York: Day, 1954). Guillermo Toriello, foreign minister under the Arbenz regime, describes the attempt and failure to render the armed forces apolitical in *La batalla de Guatemala* (Mexico City: Ediciones Cuadernos Americanos, 1955). The growth of the military organization in El Salvador is depicted in *Historia militar de El Salvador* (San Salvador: Imprenta Nacional, 1951), by Colonel Gregorio Bustamante Maceo, while its socio-political role during, and subsequent to, the 1948 revolution is described by Lt. Colonel José María Lemus, at present the president of the republic, in his *Pueblo, ejército, y doctrina revolucionaria* (San Salvador: Imprenta Nacional, 1952). The place of the military in the politics of Honduras is adequately covered in *Honduras: An Area Study in Government* (Madison: University of Wisconsin Press, 1950), by William S. Stokes. *Historia de Costa Rica* (San José: Talleres Tipográficos Barrasé, 1947), by Carlos Monge and Ernesto J. Wender, accounts for the presence of militarism in late nineteenth-century Costa Rica, while the reasons for its absence in the twentieth century are made clear by Chester L. Jones' *Costa Rica and the Civilization of the Caribbean* (Madison: University of Wisconsin Press, 1941). For an understanding of the role of the police forces in Panama, see John and Marie Biesanz, *The People of Panama* (New York: Columbia University Press, 1955) and John Biesanz and Luke M. Smith, "Panamanian Politics," in *Journal of Politics*, August 1952.

The Batista regime and the Castro revolution in Cuba are described by veteran journalists Jules Dubois, *Fidel Castro* (New York: Bobbs-Merrill, 1959), and Ruby (Hart) Phillips, *Cuba: Island of Paradox* (New York: McDowell, Obolensky, 1959). The role of the military in Nicaragua and the island republics of the Caribbean is best described in studies dealing with United States foreign policy in those countries, which are listed under Part II of this bibliography.

II. Military Aspects of United States Foreign Policy in Latin America

There have appeared a number of studies dealing with United States intervention in the Caribbean area and attempts to build up responsible armed forces there during the first quarter of the twentieth century. General accounts include H. C. Hill, *Roosevelt and the Caribbean* (Chicago: University of Chicago Press, 1927); Wilifred H. Calcott, *The Caribbean Policy of the United States* (Baltimore: Johns Hopkins Press, 1942); Dexter Perkins, *The United States and the Caribbean* (Cambridge: Harvard University Press, 1947); and Dana G. Munro, *The United States and the Caribbean Area* (Cambridge: Harvard University Press, 1934). In addition, a number of good individual country studies have been done, such as Russell H. Fitzgibbon's *Cuba and the United States, 1900-1935* (Menasha, Wis.: George Banta, 1935); David Lockmiller's *Magoon in Cuba: A History of the Second Intervention, 1906-1909* (Chapel Hill: University of North Carolina Press, 1938); Ludwig L. Montague's *Haiti and the United States, 1714-1938* (Durham, N. C.: Duke University Press, 1940); James H. McCrocklin's *Garde d'Haiti: Twenty Years of Organization and Training by the United States Marine Corps, 1913-1934* (Annapolis: U.S. Naval Institute, 1957); W. D. McCain's *The United States and the Republic of Panama* (Durham, N.C.: Duke University Press, 1940); Isaac J. Cox's *Nicaragua and the United States, 1909-1927* (Boston: World Peace Foundation, 1927); and Henry L. Stimson's *American Policy in Nicaragua* (New York: Scribner, 1927).

The origins of present aspects of United States military policy in Latin America are nowhere treated as well as in *The Challenge to Isolation, 1937-1940* (New York: Harper, for the

Council on Foreign Relations, 1952) and *The Undeclared War, 1940-1941* (New York: Harper, for the Council on Foreign Relations, 1953), both by William L. Langer and S. Everett Gleason. Policies during World War II are covered generally in Edward O. Guerrant's *Roosevelt's Good Neighbor Policy* (Albuquerque: University of New Mexico Press, 1950), while individual aspects of that policy are treated in Cordell Hull's *Memoirs* (New York: Macmillan, 1948; 2 v.). General postwar military policy developments can be followed in *The Revolution in American Foreign Policy* (Garden City, N. Y.: Doubleday, 1954) by William G. Carleton; *The Role of the Military in American Foreign Policy* (Garden City, N. Y.: Doubleday, 1954) by Burton M. Sapin and Richard C. Snyder; *American Strategy in the Atomic Age* (Norman: University of Oklahoma Press, 1955) by Colonel George C. Reinhardt; and *American Military Policy* (New Brunswick, N. J.: Rutgers University Press, 1957) edited by Edgar S. Furniss, Jr.

Congressional documents offer the best description of present policies. The most valuable sources are the annual Hearings on the Mutual Security Program by the Senate Foreign Relations Committee and the House Committee on Foreign Affairs, and the yearly Hearings on Department of Defense Appropriations by the Senate and House Appropriations Committees. From the Special Senate Committee to Study the Foreign Aid Program, 85th Congress, 1st session, there emanated a comprehensive review of the military aspects of foreign policy. Particularly useful for information relating to Latin America are this committee's Hearings entitled *The Military Assistance Program of the United States,* Committee print no. 10, (Washington: GPO, 1957), and a special study on *Military Assistance and the Security of the United States, 1947-1956* (Washington: GPO, 1957). Three other particularly useful Congressional documents are U.S. Senate Committee on Interior and Insular Affairs, *Accessibility of Strategic and Critical Material to the United States in Time of War and for our Expanding Economy,* 83rd Congress, 2nd session (Washington: GPO, 1954); U.S. Senate Committee on Foreign Relations, Subcommittee on Disarmament, *Control and Reduction of Armaments: Disarmament and Security in Latin America,* 85th Congress, 1st session, Staff Study no. 7 (Washington: GPO, 1957); and U.S. House Committee on Foreign Affairs,

Subcommittee on Inter-American Affairs, *Report on United States Relations with Latin America,* 86th Congress, 1st session, House Report no. 354 (Washington: GPO, 1959).

Concerning the pros and cons of military aspects of United States policy in Latin America, one can find support for these policies in official sources and publications, such as the State Department's *Press Releases* and its *Bulletin.* Criticism, particularly in the form of articles, has been heavy. For example, see John N. Sayre, "Shall We Arm Our Neighbors?" in *Christian Century,* October 1947; Edgar S. Furniss, Jr., "Our Policy in Latin America," in *Forum,* April 1949; Kurt Arnade, "Should the United States Arm Latin America?" in *United Nations World,* October 1949; Simon Hanson, "The End of the Good Neighbor Policy," in *Inter-American Economic Affairs,* Autumn 1953; Louis J. Halle, "Why We Are Losing Latin America," in *Harper's,* April 1955; and Eduardo Santos, "The Defense of Freedom in Latin America," in Angel del Río, ed., *Responsible Freedom in the Americas,* Columbia University Bicentennial Conference Series (Garden City, N. Y.: Doubleday, 1955). Also useful is Laurence Duggan's *The Americas: The Search for Hemisphere Security* (New York: Holt, 1949).

III. Recent Publications: 1959-1961

Though the recent Cuban upheaval has already given rise to a large quantity of literature, there is still no satisfactory, full-scale, objective analysis of the Castro regime. The pro-Castro, Marxist-oriented treatises of Leo Huberman and Paul M. Sweezy, *Cuba: Anatomy of a Revolution* (New York: Monthly Review Press, 1960), and Charles Wright Mills, *Listen Yankee: The Revolution in Cuba* (New York: McGraw-Hill, 1960) are overly doctrinaire, while Nathaniel Weyl, *Red Star over Cuba* (New York: Devin Adair, 1961), goes beyond the evidence in attempting to represent the Castro revolution as a sinister Communist conspiracy from start to finish. Much more rewarding are the two studies of Theodore Draper: "Castro's Cuba: A Revolution Betrayed?" *The New Leader,* March 27, 1961, and "Cuba and United States Policy," *The New Leader,* June 5, 1961. (These two extended articles by

Mr. Draper also were published in *Encounter* in its March and July 1961 issues respectively.)

High-quality recent publications pertinent to the broad general subject matter of this volume are: U.S. Senate Committee on Foreign Relations, *United States-Latin American Relations,* 86th Cong., 2nd sess. (Washington: GPO, 1960), which is a compilation of seven studies prepared under the direction of the Subcommittee on American Republics Affairs; American Assembly, Columbia University, *The United States and Latin America* (New York: Author, 1959); Robert N. Burr, ed., *Latin America's Nationalistic Revolutions,* the March 1961 issue of *The Annals of the American Academy of Political and Social Science;* and Richard N. Adams and others, *Social Change in Latin America Today* (New York: Harper, for the Council on Foreign Relations, 1960). On the specific problem of militarism see Victor Alba, *El militarismo* (Mexico City: Editorial Cultura, 1960); Tad Szulc, *Twilight of the Tyrants* (New York: Holt, 1959); and Charles O. Porter and Robert J. Alexander, *The Struggle for Democracy in Latin America* (New York: Macmillan, 1961).

INDEX